The Interpretation of Medieval Lyric Poetry

Also by W. T. H. Jackson
The Literature of the Middle Ages
The Anatomy of Love. The *Tristan* of Gottfried von Strassburg
Medieval Literature. A History and a Guide
Essential Works of Erasmus

The Interpretation of Medieval Lyric Poetry

Edited by
W. T. H. Jackson

© Columbia University Press 1980

All rights reserved. No part of this publication may be
reproduced or transmitted, in any form or by any means,
without permission

First published 1980 by
THE MACMILLAN PRESS LTD
London and Basingstoke
Companies and representatives
throughout the world

Typeset in Great Britain by
Vantage Photosetting Co. Ltd, Southampton and London
and printed by
Unwin Bros, The Gresham Press, Old Woking, Surrey

British Library Cataloguing in Publication Data

The interpretation of medieval lyric poetry
   1. Lyric poetry – History and criticism
   2. Poetry, Medieval – History and criticism
   I. Jackson, William Thomas Hobdell
   809.1′4   PN691

   ISBN 0-333-24816-3

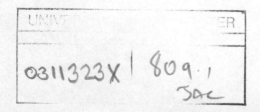

Contents

Preface

There are many books about medieval lyric but very few about its interpretation. Few authors have found it worthwhile to write full interpretative studies of individual poems. It is true that one may find discussions of one or more lyrics in works on particular authors, and these often proffer comments on such matters as metre, imagery, the nature of love, relation to tradition, irony, vocabulary, and social background, but rarely do they attempt to integrate these comments into a study of the poem as a whole. Very seldom is a specific theory of interpretation proposed and examples provided of the application of that theory. This book attempts to remedy this deficiency, at least in part, by presenting examples of detailed interpretation of lyrics in Latin and the principal vernaculars. The authors chose their own poems, and no attempt was made to coordinate their efforts. The result is a demonstration of varied types of interpretation. Some lay stress on verbal and sound patterns, some on verbal meaning, some on lyric tradition and reverberation. Consideration and comparison of all these methods will, I hope, provide a good guide to the study of medieval lyric.

It is a pity that there is no essay representing the neostructuralist approach. Such an essay was written but proved to be too long for inclusion. Professor Joachim Bumke was prevented by illness from making a contribution on the German lyric.

The introductory essay is intended to summarize briefly the chief critical attitudes of the past and to put forward possible considerations for contemporary critical approaches. The essay represents only my own views, and the other contributors are not to be blamed for its deficiencies. The notes to the essay do no more than list books and articles which seem to me significant for the points I make. A bibliography of medieval lyric would be enormous, and the relevant information is easily obtainable in the standard bibliographies.

I would like to express my gratitude to the contributors who so readily undertook the task of contributing to this volume and who – *mirabile dictu* – sent in their contributions on time.

W.T.H.J.

Notes on the Contributors

Charles Camproux
Professor of Modern Philology and French at the Department of Letters, Philosophy and Arts, Montpellier University, France

Glynnis M. Cropp
Lecturer in French at Massey University, Palmerston North, New Zealand

Peter Dronke
Lecturer in Medieval Latin at Clare Hall, Cambridge, England

Joan M. Ferrante
Professor of Comparative Literature, Columbia University, New York, USA

W. T. H. Jackson
Professor of Comparative Literature and German, Columbia University, New York, USA

Mark Musa
Professor at the Center for Italian Studies, Indiana University, USA

Rossell Hope Robbins
Professor of English at the State University of New York, Albany, New York, USA

Peter Wapnewski
Professor of German at Karlsruhe University, West Germany

Bruce W. Wardropper
Professor of Spanish at Duke University, Durham, North Carolina, USA

Paul Zumthor
Professor, Programme de Littérature Comparée, Université de Montréal, Canada

Introduction

W. T. H. JACKSON

Not very many years ago, it would have been perfectly possible to argue that interpretation of medieval lyric poetry, in the sense in which the term is used of post-Renaissance poetry, simply did not exist. There were, of course, books and articles about the lyric, but they were not concerned with the interpretation or evaluation of individual lyrics nor with the question of how good evaluation might be achieved. Still less did they attempt to propose any theory of interpretation or creation which might be of general use in studying lyric poetry. The truth of these remarks is very easily verified by a glance at the pages devoted to lyric poetry in such a basic book as Fisher's *The Medieval Literature of Western Europe*.[1] The sections about lyric poetry in all the national literatures are relatively short and even where they are of reasonable length, for example in the section on Provençal and French poetry, very few of the items listed could be called 'interpretative' in any but the broadest sense. The last ten years have seen remarkable changes, and it was for this reason that I asked the distinguished contributors to this book to write an interpretation of a poem in the field they knew best, so that the sum of the interpretations would provide a wide variety of interpretative methods for those interested in the subject.

In all languages of Western Europe, Latin and the vernaculars, the great task of the nineteenth century was the establishing of texts. It is a task which is still by no means complete. Many of the lyric texts are available only in antiquated editions or have not been edited at all. Nevertheless, the works which are generally regarded as most important are available and in some cases it is permissible to speak rather of overediting than of the reverse.[2] The printed editions of the Latin texts are usually normalized to some degree, but little distortion of the texts is involved. The same cannot be said of the works written in the *langue d'oc* and the *langue d'oil*. In the texts of the former there is confusion caused by the chaotic spelling in the manuscripts, a confusion not in the least resolved by the decisions of various editors to adopt a system of their own. In the works in the latter language, the text is often written in a different dialect in different manuscripts of the same poem, so that the choice of a main manuscript involves the choice of a dialect. Editors of German texts have shown a great deal of arbitrariness in their decisions to normalize and change spelling, often in pursuit of an assumed 'regularity' of metre. Recent editions of such works have tended to keep more closely to the manuscript forms. The editors of Italian, Iberian, and Middle English lyrics have, in general, been fairly conservative in their treatment of the manuscripts.

Several recent critics have laid great stress on the importance of awareness of manuscript variants in making interpretations.[3] They have pointed out the dangers of accepting uncritically emendations which 'make sense' and still more of making emendations in conformity with a pattern of interpretation already determined by the critic.[4] The warning is undoubtedly justified, but the fact remains that in most fields the need is still rather for better critical texts than for a 'back to the manuscripts' movement.

We can be very thankful to the scholars of the nineteenth and twentieth centuries who did so much arduous labour in providing texts. Less credit is due to those who spilled so much ink on the question of 'origins'.[5] For some reason, the question of whether the medieval lyric in the vernacular was the result of the 'influence' of classical and/or medieval Latin or derived from a largely hypothetical folksong became an obsession with several generations of critics.[6] The great *Carmina Burana* dispute is an example of what can happen when a work is used to support a position already firmly fixed in the mind of a critic. Although the majority of the German poems in the manuscript can be proved to be of the late twelfth or early thirteenth century, and are in any case frequently no more than parts of poems found in other manuscripts, numerous attempts were made to show that the Latin poems appearing next to them in this thirteenth-century manuscript were derived from them – or the reverse. It should have been clear from the start that such late works could throw no light on origins. A great deal of the trouble was due to another obsession which still lingers in popular books – that most of the Latin poems were the work of 'wandering scholars'[7] and that the *Carmina Burana* was a 'Goliard's song-book'. There is no evidence for such a supposition. It sprang from the idea that only such persons on the fringe of medieval society could have written poems critical of the church and those dealing with the pleasures of wine, women and gambling.

It will be observed that these critical positions, if they deserve the designation, are the offshoots of ideas about medieval society derived from sources other than literature or from mere fantasy. The high regard for folksong is partly derived from the works of such eighteenth-century figures as Hamann and Herder, but it was reinforced by the desire to show the deep roots of national characteristics in poetry which can be seen in much nineteenth-century criticism. This prejudice cannot be dissociated entirely from the Romantic conception of the unity of the medieval church and of Christendom in general, a corollary of which is that faithful members of either church or laity were unlikely to criticize it. (The work being done on the numerous heresies of the twelfth and thirteenth centuries was not at first widely known to students of literature.) These same people were quite prepared to believe, on the evidence of a few scattered references to *scholares vagantes* or Goliards (it is by no means certain that they were identical) that there were large bands of unfrocked or never-frocked persons, educated as clerics, who were responsible for the non-pious works written in Latin and that they were very influential on the development of vernacular poetry.

Such critical positions impeded the study of the lyrics as poetry, since they set up problems which were incapable of solution and which, even if solved, would add little to our understanding of the works themselves. The early twentieth century saw a new possibility, the influence of Arabic poetry on Western love lyric.[8] The idea was not new and had, indeed, been put forward as early as the sixteenth century, but the evidence adduced by its proponents was concrete. Specific images, figures and genre characteristics found in Western lyrics could be shown to have parallels·in Arabic poetry and it could be shown that it was feasible for the influence to have spread to southern France before the appearance of the first extant lyric poetry in that region. The situation was made even more interesting by the discovery of forms written in Arabic with refrains in Iberian vernacular. The case for Arabic influence appeared quite strong, although by no means proven. Again, however, prejudice stood in the way of an objective evaluation of the evidence.

Since the time of Gaston Paris, critics have been concerned with the nature of 'courtly love'. They had observed, correctly, that in certain narrative works and in lyrics written in Provençal, French and, later, in other languages, the treatment of sexual love and the status of women were totally different from those found in classical works, in the national epics, and in religious and popular works. The phenomenon was given the term 'courtly love', and once the term had been coined, it had to be justified, a superb example of the word's demanding the idea.[9] It was assumed by the vast majority of critics that the courtly love of the lyric was the same as the courtly love of the romance and that the same characteristics could and should be found in both genres. The poems were ransacked to find features which would contribute to the type, its spirituality, its worship of women, its concepts of love-service, its connection with contemporary medieval society, and its connections with religion, especially the cult of the Virgin. One feature accepted almost without discussion was that it was essentially adulterous. The evidence for this view was derived from several sources: the mention of liaisons between troubadours and noble ladies in the *Vidas*, the biographies of troubadours written after their deaths which appear in some manuscripts and which are, in fact, almost certainly based on readings or misreadings of the poems themselves; the references to 'jealous men', assumed to be husbands; the assumption that only married women would have the opportunity to meet troubadours; a statement by Andreas Capellanus in the *De Amore* that true love cannot exist between married couples; and finally the insistent belief that the events of the poem really did happen to the poet. Such reasoning makes no distinction between the *canzo*, where it would be hard indeed to demonstrate adultery from the actual texts, and the *alba*, where there is a strong presumption of an illicit liaison, though not necessarily of adultery.

The constant mistranslation of the title of Andreas's work (*De Amore libri tres* or *De Arte honeste amandi*) as 'The Art of Courtly Love' and the equivalent in other languages is an excellent example of the desire of many scholars to document their conception of the nature of courtly love and to connect it with both lyric and narrative poetry. There is no reason to suppose that Andreas was discussing either genre in his treatise, and there is no evidence that he knew the Provençal lyric at all. It is perfectly possible that he was writing for an audience sophisticated enough to understand the Provençal and Northern French lyrics. Indeed it may have been the same type of audience for which they were written, but that does not prove that he was trying to explain in a Latin treatise a specific type of love with invariable characteristics. The element which connects Andreas's work with vernacular and lyric poetry is not the fact that he was trying to codify courtly love but the strong sense of play which is to be found in both. He shares with the lyric poets especially a feeling of gamesmanship. He sets up rules for the love-game at court. The lyric and narrative poets set up their own game-rules and they are not the same in the two main genres nor even in the sub-genres. Hence it is ridiculous to speak of one courtly love or of features of a work which show that the author 'departed from the rules of courtly love'. There were no such rules, but there were rules of love in genres, a very different matter.

Certain critics were happy to have the help of Andreas, or of their interpretation of his work, to make the point about adultery in courtly love. C. S. Lewis and A. J. Denomy, to name only two, seized on the point and made it central in their consideration of the romance and lyric.[10] Lewis saw Lancelot as the greatest of courtly lovers because he is so totally subservient to the demands of another man's wife and that man his king. Denomy went much further. If courtly love was adulterous, it was clearly contrary to Christian teaching, if not always to Christian practice, and Denomy was therefore strongly inclined to accept the Arabic theory of origins, not on the basis of evidence, stylistic or other, but rather because he regarded courtly love as a heresy. The argument about the nature of courtly love continues, and many critics are still of the opinion that there was a well defined type, known to all contemporary writers, which can be traced with only minor variations in lyric and romance. It is perhaps more profitable to think in terms of a standard love situation for each genre or subgenre, with features which overlap.

We may mention in passing another attempt to show the heretical nature of troubadour love, that which seeks to connect it with the Catharist or Albigensian heresy.[11] This thesis has never been more than a specialized criticism, and its effect on the general study of the Provençal lyric has been slight. No one has ever succeeded in proving that any troubadour was a Catharist or that any patron did more than tolerate the heresy in his territories. The undoubted fact that there was Catharism in southern France in the twelfth century has been enough to convince some critics that the adoration of the lady in the *canzo* was in fact a series of hidden references to the movement.[12] It is hard, too, to reconcile troubadour poetry with the charge of homosexuality so frequently levelled at the Catharists by their opponents.

It must now be clear that the main currents of criticism for the first forty years of the twentieth century were much less with the poems themselves than with broad general questions, particularly the nature of the presumed courtly love. Even as late as 1966 Moshe Lazar published a book using love lyrics as evidence for his concept of a more or less unified courtly love and Jean Frappier remains a convinced believer not only in the concept but in a clearly defined set of characteristics.[13]

The fact that so much attention was devoted to these general questions does not mean that other matters were totally ignored. There were studies of particular genres, of versification, and of such significant terms as *fin amors, joia, minne, liebe, hoher muot, cor gentil, dolce stil novo,* and *jarchas*.

Some of these works, such as the monumental volume by Herbert Kolb, covered many forms and many national literatures.[14] Excellent as these studies were, they tended to treat their subjects as isolated phenomena and not as parts of the poem in which they appeared. They were often happier to find references in other writings, particularly Christian material, which would support a particular point of view than to take careful account of the immediate context, the broader context, and intertextual features. Still less were they prepared to differentiate between the differing usage in different genres and the different conditions under which the poems were written. Everyone knew that the Provençal, French and German poems at least were designed to be performed as songs before an audience and that many Iberian, Italian and Middle English poems may have been so performed. There is some evidence for the performance of some of the Latin lyrics. This 'audience factor' may well have influenced the nature and style of the lyrics.

What was the nature of this audience?[15] Was it all noble? How well trained was it in the nuances of language and metre? Was it the same for all poets? These questions have never been satisfactorily answered and it is unlikely that they ever will be. It is probably fair to speculate that the audience for Provençal lyric was more sophisticated than that for any of the others, simply because it was confined much more to a small number of courts, but the audience for the Italian poems may well have been composed largely of professionals for whom the authors were deliberately writing. What has received a great deal less attention from critics but may well be of greater importance than the composition of the actual audience is the role of the audience in the poet's plan. For the poets, and especially those writing in Provençal, French and Italian, clearly envisage the audience as an integral part of the poem, not merely as a group of persons listening. The audience is addressed, appealed to for help, chided for not helping, sometimes even flattered. But is this the real audience? Or is it rather a theoretical audience, postulated by the poet as part of the song, one which will enable him to pose questions and answer them and will allow him to relieve his spirit of a pressing burden? The latter explanation seems by far the most likely. In recent years critics have become more aware of this possibility, although the subject still awaits thorough exploration.

Faral's book on the medieval arts of poetry[16] should have started critics on studies of the role of rhetoric in the medieval lyric, but curiously enough it did not. Long after the appearance of his work, ideal landscapes and spring topoi were still being discussed as if they were the result of personal observation – or of the influence of folksong.[17] in the

most naïve sense of that term. It was not until the appearance in 1948 of
E. R. Curtius's book *Europäische Literatur und lateinisches Mittelalter* (which,
significantly, was quickly translated into several languages)[18] that students became interested in rhetoric and very many articles were published to demonstrate the existence of topoi in the lyric poetry of the
medieval West, both in Latin and in the vernaculars.[19] Although the
compilation of lists of topoi is hardly a subtle aspect of aesthetic
appreciation, the exercise had the great advantage of concentrating
attention on the actual text of the poem and on the way it was
constructed. The search for figures made the reader notice the way in
which they were organized and ultimately made him ask the question:
Why are they organized like this? Here at least was a partial answer to
Jeanroy's disparaging remark about the nature of troubadour poetry.[20]
Perhaps it was rather in their variety of style, form and treatment that its
excellence should be sought. Critics now began to examine the poems in
relation to contemporary use of rhetoric, particularly of ornament, and
also in relation to the rules laid down in the *Artes Poeticae* already
published by Faral. The remarks made by Dante in the *De vulgari
eloquentia* were particularly important. Such examinations showed that
there might be principles of structure quite different from those used by
earlier critics. For example, the poet might be quite indifferent about
whether his strophe formed a 'logical sequence' but very much concerned about a set of variations on a single poetic image.[21]

Study of rhetoric also called attention to the importance of the genre in
which a poet felt himself to be writing. The word 'felt' should be noted. It
may never be assumed that a conscious theory of genres or even a set of
definitions of genres had been formulated. Literary theory, such as it
was, tended to follow the divisions laid down by the Greeks, even though
they did not fit current poetical practice. Nevertheless, the poets were
aware of certain types of writing, defined or not, and they followed the
conventions of the genre faithfully. The *canzo* (*chanson*, *Minnelied*, *canzone*) treated love in a way very different from that found in the *alba* (*aube*,
Tagelied), which again differed from that in the *pastourelle*, but the
treatment was perfectly consistent within each type. The fact that some
of these genres are hardly represented in the German poetry of the late
twelfth and early thirteenth centuries or in Italian poetry shows that
some authors at least avoided them. More important still is the fact that
certain features of language and style were regarded as appropriate for
one genre and not for another, and the importation of characteristics of
the 'wrong' style immediately indicates ironic intent or even parody.
Latin lyric, although it can show some works which are close to the

vernacular genres in style, for example, the *pastourelle*, does not observe the same genre distinctions, and it thus seems likely that the vernaculars developed their distinguishing genre features independently of the Latin tradition.

The types which developed were very numerous. There can be little doubt that their form was initially determined very largely by the music which accompanied them, and some of the names given to them reflect this fact. It is now very hard to decide what was the original meaning of such terms as *carole*, *virelai*, *rondeau*, and *ballade*, although they later became very strictly defined. The factors which determined the later strict forms appear to have been the metrical form, including the question of the presence or absence of refrain, and the number of stanzas, or the way in which the content was treated. It should be noted that the forms seem to become well defined when music is no longer a very important factor, although virtuosity in the use of metrics and rhyme-schemes appears very early in the lyrics written in Provençal.

In Latin lyric, it is hard to establish genre types. The sequence and the 'ambrosian' hymn form are easy enough to recognize on metrical grounds, but they are not an indicator of either subject matter or treatment. There are secular as well as religious sequences, and the Ambrosian form is so widespread and so simple that it could hardly form the basis of a genre definition. The classical ode forms continued to be written both for secular and religious themes. Latin secular poetry written in stressed verse shows the most extraordinary freedom in length of line and length of strophe and great skill and sophistication in combining lines of a varying length and complicated rhyme-schemes into interesting strophic patterns. Yet in all this it is hard to make distinctions of genre except in the most general terms – love poetry, anticlerical satire, moralizing poetry, didactic poetry – and none of these is necessarily associated with any particular poetic form. It would be interesting to see if any connections between form and type can be made by detailed analysis.

If Latin poems can be distinguished only by differences in metrical and strophic form, the reverse is true of those written in Provençal. Here the same form may very well be used for the *alba* and the *canzo*, even though there is strict differentiation between them in the treatment of the subject matter. The best Provençal poets show extraordinary skill in the use of the basic *fronte/cauda* strophic form, particularly in the *canzo*, and introduce further refinements in the shape of interstrophic correspondences. Studies of the relationships between these refinements and the treatment of the love theme have been very tentative and much remains to be done.

The extreme complexity of strophic form characteristic of much Provençal lyric was not imitated in Northern French and Middle High German, although the basic strophic form was used.[22] Metrical and strophic criteria are even less of a genre-indicator in the poetry of these languages than they are in Provençal, but the use of position in the line and of rhyme for emphasis is interesting and often subtle. Iberian poetry developed metrics of its own, aside from those which it took over from Provençal poetry, and Italian produced variations of the Provençal forms of considerable complexity and subtlety. In no case, however, do the forms determine the genre. The fourteenth and fifteenth centuries saw the perfection of the great forms used in Northern France, the *rondeau*, the *ballade* and the *virelai*. These forms became quite rigid and they were used for poetry of all kinds – love poetry, didactic and satirical poetry, and for any kind of occasional poem. They were imitated in Middle English and took their place side by side with native forms. Again, they are no indication of genre. The study of genre theory must be one of the principal concerns of future criticism of the medieval lyric.

There can be little doubt that for many poets the achievement of technical success with difficult forms was an end in itself and that they were little concerned with the triteness of their subject matter, if the poem they produced showed great technical virtuosity. This provides one very good reason for the detailed study of individual poems. Only by comparing such detailed studies can we hope to find out what it was that they considered to be technical virtuosity. Yet there is a connection between content and expression of content.

Poems both in Latin and the vernacular show great sensitivity in two matters: the reflection in words and phrases of meanings already implanted by literary tradition and even by the tradition of earlier interpretation; the positioning of words within the line and within the strophe (in combination with but also independently of the rhyme-scheme), so that there may be an impact of one word on another without any necessary syntactical connection. The 'meaning' of words, especially of those words which may be regarded almost as technical terms in certain kinds of poetry, thus acquires new significance. There may be a considerable difference between the 'dictionary' meaning of a word like 'heart' in the various languages and the way in which the word should be interpreted in the various contexts, where account must be taken of reverberation with semantic tradition and reverberation with genre tradition. Nor should the possibility be overlooked that the author may wish to set up new meanings which clash with or even defy those which have been customary in earlier poems in the same genre. There has recently been a certain amount of critical activity in this field, particularly in the study of

Provençal and German lyrics, with special reference to the significance of individual words in various contexts, groups of words and word-fields.[23] It is, of course, impossible to determine the precise impact of a word or group of words on a contemporary person or audience. The impact would in any case be different for each listener, but we can come closer to the expectations an author might have of the degree of understanding in his audience – and of what expectations he might cheat in order to produce the shock which is one of the most important features of individual style.

Critics will always differ about the degree of intent which can be ascribed to an author in the positioning of words in line and strophe and about the purpose of such positioning when it can be observed. It can be said, however, that definite aesthetic effects can be produced by juxta-position and from vertical reading within strophes. The positioning may be instinctive, but the result is observable. A very important question is raised by the use of this technique and others which are dependent on the eye rather than on the ear: If the works were performed, how could an audience be expected to notice effects which are dependent on visual observation or on the leisurely study of a text? The problem is not so acute in regard to Latin poetry, where it may be fairly assumed that texts were read more than they were sung, but it must certainly be faced in regard to the Provençal, French and German texts of the late twelfth and early thirteenth centuries. The transmission of Middle High German lyric perhaps throws some light on the matter. Most of the great repositories of this lyric contain no musical notation. Clearly by the time they were written down, very late in the thirteenth century or in the fourteenth, the poems were read, not sung. There is no way of determin-ing when the music ceased to be regarded as important, but it may very well be that there was at a very early stage what might be called a secondary audience which read the works, of which the author was conscious, and for which he put in effects not readily observable to a listener, however sophisticated. The case for the presumption of a 'reading' audience is much stronger in the later poetry of Northern France, in Italian poetry, Middle English poetry, and much that was written in Iberia after the twelfth century. Nevertheless, the problem remains. It may very well be that the audience was trained to listen for effects in a way which would be uncharacteristic of a modern listener.

We have mentioned reverberation in connection with the study of meaning. We should also mention it in a larger cultural sense. The most obvious way in which cultural reverberation is used is in connection with Christianity. The question concerns theology much less than the extensive use of Christian imagery, typology, terminology, and sometimes even exegetical method. A poem which begins 'Propter Sion non tacebo/sed ruinam Romae flebo' cannot be fully understood or appreciated without reference to the *Psalms* and the exegesis of them.[24] There has been no lack of critics who have observed and commented on this fact, sometimes to excess. The use of Christian imagery and references in a secular poem does not necessarily imply that a 'Christian meaning' is to be sought or even that Christian factors such as charity are to be determinants of meaning. There were truly secular poems in plenty. The references to Christian imagery simply enrich their meaning and incorporate them into contemporary intellectual consciousness. The degree and kind of appreciation would depend on the capacity of individuals in the audience – as it does on the abilities and interests of modern critics. These reverberations may be traced in poetry of all types and periods. They are perhaps most common in Latin poetry in whose audience familiarity with works and techniques could be more readily assumed than in the audiences for vernacular poetry and they are more likely to be found in social and church satire than in love poetry, which developed its own set of reverberations, but no genre can be excluded. A *pastourelle* will play with references to wolves in sheep's clothing and a drinking song to a hymn to the Virgin. Parody is, indeed, one of the major reverberations.

These facts are well known to critics and have been used frequently in discussing the vernacular lyric in general terms. Many editions of Latin poems contain extensive notes on the classical and Christian references in them.[25] Yet detailed studies of individual poems which attempt to take full account of the reverberations in the construction of the poem and in its interpretation remain relatively rare. Detailed study is essential because it is not only the actual references which are to be noted but the context in which they originally occurred. This context often gives a clue to meaning which is not obvious or is even obscured by the reference alone.

There is another aspect of criticism of lyric poetry which is hard to reconcile with the idea of oral performance, namely the relationship of numbers to lyric poetry. We are not speaking here of numerology, of the significance of specific numbers in such systems as the Pythagorean but of numerical patterns. Several critics have tried to show that poets preferred certain arithmetical groupings of stress and/or syllables in making up their strophes.[26] This is not a question of patterns of stresses in a line, nor, of course, of musical notes, but a deliberate attempt to produce strophes or parts of strophes of a preferred number of syllables.

Such patterns can certainly be demonstrated, but often the divisions postulated by the critics are arbitrary, and it is impossible to prove that the composer of the poem was thinking in the same terms.

A critic is on safer ground when he observes patterns of sound which provide what may be called a second level of understanding.[27] There may be plays on the sounds of individual words, the dominance of particular groups or types of sound (velars, fricatives etc), or simply the reinforcing of the surface meaning by sound-patterns such as alliteration and assonance. It is quite certain that such patterns may work with or against the formal metrical/musical structure, and tensions may thus be created which are independent of the 'meaning' of the poem.

We have mentioned in passing the earlier debate among the critics about the relationship of the poet to the lady he celebrates and to the audience before which the poem was presented. It was frequently assumed that specific ladies were celebrated by the poets, although the poets never mention a lady's name, and that the poems are to that extent autobiographical. Such an interpretation inevitably leads to the further conclusion that when a poet says that he will cease to celebrate a lady or that she is being turned against him by liars and rumour-mongers, this was again a biographical fact. The writers of the *Vidas* of the troubadours seem to have had the same opinion, but we have little corresponding evidence for poetry in other languages, except of course for the lyrics which Dante addressed to Beatrice. There may have been evidence in a poem, understood by contemporaries, which identified the lady addressed as an actual person, and there would certainly be a temptation on the lady's part to accept the flattery implicit in the poem, if it could be construed as addressed to her, but even if we allow for this, there were many poems which were not really addressed to any lady but were abstract love poems. The lyrics, whether love-poems or poems of social comment, do not necessarily reflect either the personal experience or the personal opinions of the writer. A specific form was developed for a specific purpose and within that form the poet takes up a stance. He is the poet-persona, not the poet, committed to a point of view by the form within which he is operating. Some of these stances are easy to determine and would hardly be disputed – the seer-stance and the poverty-stricken-artist stance, so characteristic of the Archipoeta and Walther von der Vogelweide, come to mind, but there were many others, such as the moral-rectitude-stance of Marcabru, the court-critics-stance of Eustache Deschamps, the death-bed confession 'honesty' of François Villon. In all of these there is a deliberate playing-off of the formal position of the poet-persona against the real views of the writer, with elements both of agreement and contradiction. We have in these confrontations one more example of the power of genre expectations and of the cheating of those expectations.

Love poetry developed an even more elaborate set of confrontations. As we have said, the *canzo* is an 'I' form of poetry in which the poet is apparently speaking of his own experience. In fact, however, he is manipulating not one but two personae, those of the poet and the lover.[28] These two personae may be identical and until very recently most critics assumed that they were. Yet the apparently sudden changes of mood in the *canzo* can be far better explained if we assume that the lover-persona and the poet-persona often speak with different voices, and, if the term may be used, conduct a dialogue with one another. The poet-persona has the obligation to present the sentiments of the lover-persona in the best possible light. On his success or failure depends the progress of the lover-persona's quest for the lady. *Hinc lacrimae rerum!* For to the poet-persona this presentation can be little more than a game, whereas to the lover-persona it is deadly serious.

The German poets and, to a far greater extent, the Italian poets complicate this problem by internalization. The poet-persona no longer sings to an audience but formulates to the lover-persona the ways in which he would present his longings. The result is reflection by the lover-persona on the presentations of the poet-persona and a constant re-evaluation of the lover's position and feelings. In Italian poetry especially this re-evaluation may be compounded by the poet-persona's adoption of a particular ethic or religious stance.

The *alba* and the *pastourelle* have often been described as objective genres, since, in the *alba* always and in the *pastourelle* frequently the poet appears to be describing events rather than participating in them. Yet the mere fact that the poet is aware of the events in the *alba* implies participation, and his sympathy with the lovers rather than with those who seek to thwart their love renders any 'objectivity' dubious. The poet-persona actually presents a picture of a woman in love and, usually, but not always, a man who is a partner rather than an active participant. The result is that the poet-persona is presenting a woman's point of view in the *alba*, in contrast to the presentation of the man's point of view in the *canzo*.

The problem is even more complicated with regard to the *pastourelle*. The poems frequently open with an apparently objective description of a peasant girl and her actions. In other words, we are presented with a picture of a person, not a nature topos or study of emotion. Only later in the poem does it become clear that the observer is to be equated with the poet-persona. In any event, the girl speaks on her own behalf and presents her own point of view. In some cases the poem becomes a dialogue between poet-persona and girl. Thus, even though the *pastourelle* is often a brutal genre in conception and execution, it differs from the *canzo* in the fact that it allows the female to speak for herself, even when poet-persona and protagonist are identified. The objectivity is more apparent than real. The words put into the girl's mouth by the poet are such as might be suggested by the poet-persona to justify his actions by her obvious greed, stupidity, or both.

It should be stressed that this emphasis on the importance of the recognition of the existence of a poet-persona does not mean that medieval lyric never deals with personal experience. It is perfectly easy to demonstrate the opposite. Bertran de Born did participate in wars with the lords whom he praises and blames, Wather von der Vogelweide was given a fief by the Emperor Frederick II, the English did burn the house of Eustache Deschamps. What is important is that these and many other such events are treated through the medium of the poet-persona and are thus endowed with universal significance. The most important such event is Dante's meeting with Beatrice.

Consideration of the poet-persona is closely allied with the question of point of view.[29] As we have seen, all authors take up a stance in writing their poetry, and that stance is frequently determined by the genre in which they are writing and by certain traditional positions which were common to literature and training in rhetoric. Such points of view could be easily combined with irony, since they represent only partially what the poet intends to say. But certain aspects of point of view are more fundamental. The *canzo* is written from the point of view of a man. This is not quite such a naïve statement as might appear, for it postulates, among other things, that the man does not know what the woman's point of view is. A great deal of what is said in the *canzo* is really a search for the woman's point of view and the means to express it. The lover-persona does not know how the lady reacts to his feelings, the poet-persona tries to find a way to produce a response. The point of view of the *canzo* is thus a purely masculine attempt to find the key to a woman's responses, a verbal voyage into the unknown. It is significant that the few extant *canzos* written by women use exactly the same technique.

The point of view is no less fixed in the other genres. The poet-persona in the *alba* is a sympathetic recorder, in the *pastourelle* a cynical observer or participant of a superior class. In the *partimen* and *tenzo* the intention is to claim objectivity by presenting both sides. Political songs and those of social comment present a different problem.[30] By their nature they deal with concrete events, sometimes with events that can be established as historical from non-literary sources. They often purport to present the point of view of the individual poet. In practice, however, the poet rarely dares to set up his own judgement as sufficient reason to criticize either a ruler or a social evil. He calls on other authorities, on the Bible, on natural law to support his point of view. His role is to call attention to the correspondences or discrepancies between what is and what should be. There is always, even when the poet is most independent, a standard beyond the poet himself. His point of view is determined by the selection of criteria which conform with his own views. The poet selects, the poet-persona shows the consonance or opposition between the events he is discussing and the 'universal' values selected by the poet.

Some lyric poetry quite deliberately sets up a fictional or at least pretended point of view. This is obviously the case with parody, but there are other and more subtle examples. Neidhart von Reuenthal used the forms and vocabulary of the *Minnelied* in order to mock at its conventions.[31] His use of these forms is not strictly parody, since in many poems it would be impossible to say of numerous strophes that they were not genuine examples if *Minnesang* – if they were read in isolation. The opening strophes in particular could easily pass for good examples of the type. The shock comes when it is realized that forms and terms of *Minnesang* are being used of the wrong social class, of peasants, not knights, and that vocabulary is being used which is entirely inappropriate to the genre. The most significant point, however, is that Neidhart uses a poet-persona who purports to be entirely in tune with the chivalric ideals of the *Minnesang*, to believe in them, and to be persecuted by peasants because he tries to apply them within peasant society. The peasants also attempt to follow the conventions but succeed only in aping them with grotesque results. So effective is Neidhart's pose that many critics, even some writing comparatively recently, have attempted to construct a biography of the poet Neidhart from the details supplied by the poet-persona he created. This kind of pseudopersona is also to be found in the work of François Villon and the assumption of the identity of poet and poet-persona goes far to explain the trouble critics have had with the violent swings in attitude, deeply religious to scandalously secular, humbly repentent to unabashedly sinful, which are found throughout his work. By presenting similar situations from the point of view of various personae, Villon is able to present a fuller world and an effect of universality denied to poets of less originality of technique.

Point of view is not dependent only on the manipulation of the poet-persona. Much Italian poetry depends for its effect on the assumption of a judicial stance. The poem seems to put before the reader the results of calm cogitation, a well considered opinion which is beyond personal feeling, an abstract notion rather than a sentiment. Critics have often noted the scientific nature of some Italian love poetry and also its frequent use of mystical and theological concepts. These features are derived from the 'learned observer' point of view and they gain in impact by that observer's use of imagery which will not only enhance his presentation but will strengthen the impression that he is indeed the observer he claims to be. In the *Vita Nuova* Dante improves on the technique by moving outside to comment on himself.

If it is possible to make such a generalization about large bodies of poetry, it seems to me that an effort is made, both in Iberian and Middle English lyric, to make the poet-persona represent the poet more closely than he does in the works already discussed. In other words, the poet prefers not to use the opportunities provided by the poet-persona to exploit different points of view. This opinion may well be delusory and based on the fact that lyric in these two literatures, although undoubtedly influenced by Romance models, has more examples of folksong and of lyrics based on folksong.

Time and space are not aspects of the lyric which have elicited much critical comment.[32] There are, of course, lyrics in which both time and place are specifically indicated. This is clear in such poems as those of Bertran de Born, Eustache Deschamps, François Villon, and Walther von der Vogelweide, when they are writing of specific political events, in many crusading songs, and in verifiable references to events in the poet's own life. But in love poems always and in most church satire, time and place are not concrete and even in many poems of social comment where there appears to be allusion to persons or events which set a time and place, closer inspection reveals that such references are misleading.

If we consider love poetry, we soon observe that time indicators are virtually never exact but are designed to show either relationships within the poem or to an ideal time which has literary connotations. Many love poems, both in Latin and the vernaculars, use nothing but the present tense, not because the feelings and events are happening in the present but because general statements are being made. When other tenses appear, they are there to show the development of love, to compare the emotions of the present with those of the past and to speculate on the future. The tenses are in relation to each other, not to any actual point in time. The poet-persona speaks from the point of view of a poetic present which partakes of universality, since it speaks of love in general terms as well as in terms of personal experience. It also allows the poet-persona to take advantage of the seer-stance of the poet to speculate about the future and also about the reactions of the lover-persona, from whom he often maintains some distance. The effect of this manipulation is often to make one love affair appear as all love affairs and to make the various aspects of one love affair, its joy and despair, into a description of all love. Each love poem therefore has its own time.

There is, however, another point to consider. Almost all poems have time-indicators other than tense and some of these have a very definite significance in literary tradition. The most important by far is the spring landscape topos. Its use in Latin lyric, and particularly in love lyric, is to set a time and place which is ideal for the flowering of emotion and love and it is often accompanied by a description of rituals appropriate to spring, especially the image of girls dancing and singing in chorus. There is no description of any particular time. Even the 'spring' may be questioned, since there is little distinction between the features charac-teristic of spring and those of summer. The use of the topos becomes more complicated in the Provençal *canzo*, where it is the clear intention of the authors to move time and locale out of normal time and space. The description, now highly formalized, emphasizes the contrast between the lover's frame of mind and his standing with the beloved with that in an idealized nature, where cold and a hostile environment have vanished and where all is warmth and receptiveness. The stress is on the unnatur-alness of the *canzo* situation, where time and space are determined by the lover's emotions as seen by the poet-persona and the lady's attitude as understood by the lover. This interpretation is borne out by the often mocking use of a winter topos to parody or reverse the situation. Time and space are thus created for the poem by the author.

Some Northern French poets follow this principle, others seem more interested in the integration of the topos with personal experience. Certainly the German poets make less use of it than do their Romance predecessors. Their greater concentration on the internalization of the love experience and their minimal interest in the figure of the beloved mean that time and space indicators are less important for them, since most poems were clearly contemplative and not formally addressed to an audience. The same is true of much Italian poetry, although Dante's *Vita Nuova* calls for a sequence and hence a progression within the time he sets up.

Certain genres call for a completely different approach. The *alba*, by definition, must be set at dawn and by convention it is set in a castle room or even on the battlements. These are not true temporal or spatial definitions, any more than is the death-bed in François Villon's *Testa-*

ment. The time and place are set in order to endow a definite situation with its own conventions. The situation portrayed is no more realistic than that in the *canzo* and it also may be repeated indefinitely. As Jonathan Saville has shown, it is the contrast between the attributes associated in literature with light and darkness that are important, not the fact that the events take place at dawn.[33] The situation in the *pastourelle* is very similar. In spite of its apparent realism, it really depicts a fantasy situation which calls for a definite set of temporal and spatial conventions. The peasant girl is always in a wood or at least in a rustic setting because the situation is thus identified: low class girl and superior class man. We are shown not the idealized landscape of the *canzo* but one designed to recall to the audience the crudity of rustic existence so that the approach to the girl may be justified. The poem almost always takes the form of the narration of an event in the past, which means that the events are seen through the eyes of the narrator, who is frequently the principal participant and interlocutor in the poem. This fact raises serious questions about the 'accuracy' of the account. It is palpably the recall of events and such recall is notoriously inaccurate and prejudiced. How far does the setting of the poem in an indefinite past and in a generalized rustic environment indicate that the poem is really no more than an erotic fantasy? It would seem likely that the time and spatial setting of the *pastourelle* both indicate that it has no relation to personal experience but is designed either as a satire on both peasant and aristocratic mores or as a deliberate erotic counterpart to the situation in the *canzo*, with a different formal time- and space-frame in the past.

It may be said with some confidence that love poetry at all times and in all genres sets up its own time-space frame which is concerned only with the relationships between the poet-persona, the lover-persona, and the beloved. This frame isolates them from normal considerations of time and space. Poetry of social comment has a more clearly defined space element, frequently the court, and a time element which, although often clearly enough indicated is not so restrictive that the events of the poem cannot be of universal application. Time assumes a normal function when the poem refers to a specific event in the life of a named and identifiable person or, more frequently, to his death. Yet even here, as for example in the poem of Eustache Deschamps on the death of Bertrand de Guesclin, there are often profound universal applications.

In recent years there have been attempts to apply to medieval lyric the principles of criticism derived from the Russian structuralists and developed in France and under the influence of French critics, particularly for the interpretation of the modern lyric and modern novel. The degree of success is not easy to estimate, since some of the attempts to use these methods are rather forced and it is difficult to gain a balanced view.[34] The use of a specialized terminology also makes some of the efforts difficult of access for a reader not trained in its use. There can be little doubt that the new methods will be of great value when they have been integrated into the mainstream of criticism. It seems likely that the future study of the medieval lyric will concentrate much more on questions of style, structure, and genre than has been the case in the past. The shape of the poem, in the fullest sense, will be a principal interest, and critics will be more concerned with the ways in which love can be expressed than in attempting to define it with reference to religion or social conditions. In other words, it will be the poem, both as an individual work of art and as an example of genre and craftsmanship, which will interest us most.

NOTES

1. John H. Fisher, ed., *The Medieval Literature of Western Europe. A Review of Research, Mainly 1930–1960* (1966).
2. A good example is offered by the vicissitudes of *Des Minnesangs Frühling* under the editorship successively of Lachmann, Haupt, and Carl von Kraus. Each had a very definite idea of what the language and forms of the poems should be and edited accordingly. The latest edition by Moser and Tervooren (1977) adopts a totally different policy of minimal editing.
3. See, for example, David G. Mowatt, *Frîderich von Hûsen: Introduction, Text, Commentary and Glossary* (1970).
4. See the essay by Peter Wapnewski.
5. If proof is needed, a glance at Fisher, pp. 145–50 and 153f. (Provençal and French), pp. 337–39 (Spanish) will suffice. There is less material about the origins of German and Italian lyric because the direct origins in Provençal and French lyric are not disputed: but see the amount of space devoted to the subject in André Moret, *Les Débuts du lyrisme en Allemagne des origines à 1350* (1951).
6. For a summary see W. T. H. Jackson, 'The German Poems in the *Carmina Burana*', *German Life and Letters* (1953).
7. The standard work is Helen Waddell, *The Wandering Scholars* (1927), which reproduces the appropriate documents. For others, see Fisher, p. 19. It should be emphasized that there were always scholars who stood apart from this attitude. Paul Lehmann and Otto Schumann come to mind.
8. The major works to 1960 are listed in Fisher, pp. 148–50. The most important are: A. R. Nykl, *A Book Containing the Risala Known as the Dove's Neck-Ring* (1931) and *Hispano-Arabic Poetry and its Relations with the Old Provençal Troubadours* (1946); A. J. Denomy, 'Concerning the Accessibility of Arabic Influence to the Earliest Provencal Troubadours', *Medieval Studies* (Toronto, 1953); Ramón Menéndez-Pidal, 'Poesía árabe y poesía europea', reprinted

with other essays in 1946, was originally published in 1918 and is thus the earliest major work on the subject but naturally lacks the documentation of later studies. The works which incorporated Romance refrains in Arabic poems are studied in the collection of essays by Samuel S. Stern, *Hispano-Arabic Strophic Poetry: Studies*, ed. L. P. Harvey (1974)

9. Xavier F. Baron and Judith M. Davis, '*Amour courtois*', the Medieval Ideal of Love: A Bibliography (1973).

10. C. S. Lewis, *The Allegory of Love* (1938); A. J. Denomy, *The Heresy of Courtly Love* (1947) and articles (Fisher, p. 151).

11. Denis de Rougement, *L'Amour et l'Occident* (1939), discusses the problem in general terms.

12. For background, see Walter L. Wakefield and Arthur P. Evans, *Heresies of the High Middle Ages* (1969).

13. L. T. Topsfield, *The Troubadours and Love* (1975); F. X. Newman, *The Meaning of Courtly Love* (1967).

14. Herbert Kolb, *Der Begriff der Minne und das Entstehen der höfischen Lyrik* (1958), an original work and an excellent critique of earlier studies of love concepts. See also L. T. Topsfield, '*Jois, Amors* and *Fin Amors* in the Poetry of Jaufre Rudel', *Neophilologische Mitteilungen* (1970); Wolf Gewehr, 'Der Topos "Augen des Herzens": Versuch einer Deutung durch die scholastische Erkenntnis-theorie', *Deutsche Vierteljahrsschrift für Literaturgeschichte* (1972); Vickie L. Ziegler, *The Leitword in Minnesang: Stylistic Analysis and Textual Criticism* (1975); Glynnis M. Cropp, *Le Vocabulaire courtois des troubadours de l'époque classique* (1975).

15. Stephen G. Nichols, Jr., 'The Medieval Lyric and Its Public', *Medievalia et Humanistica*, NS (1972).

16. Edmond Faral, *Les Arts poétiques du XIIᵉ et XIIIᵉ siècle* (1924).

17. For example, by P. S. Allen, *The Romanesque Lyric* (1928), and Helen Waddell *Medieval Latin Lyric* (1929).

18. Ernst Robert Curtius, *Europäische Literatur und lateinisches Mittelalter* (1948).

19. R. Dragonetti, *La Technique poétique des trouvères dans la chanson courtoise* (1960); Paul Zumthor, 'Rhetorique médiévale et poétique', *Poetics* (1971).

20. Alfred Jeanroy, *La Poésie lyrique des troubadours*, 2 vols. (1934).

21. See the essay by Peter Wapnewski.

22. Karl-Heinz Schirmer, 'Zum Aufbau des hochmittelalterlichen deutschen Strophenliedes', in Siegfried Beyschlag, ed., *Walther von der Vogelweide: 'Wege der Forschung'* (1971); Rocco Vanasco, 'Lingua e tecnica della canzone "Dolce cominciamento" di Giacomo da Lentini', *Lingua e Stile* (Bologna, 1973), and others by the same author; Silvia Ranawake, *Höfische Strophenkunst; Vergleichende Untersuchungen zur Formentypologie an der Wende zum Spätmittelalter* (1976).

23. See the titles in note 14 and the following: P. Schmid, 'Die Entwicklung der Begriffe "Minne" und "Liebe" im deutschen Minnesang bis Walther', *Zeitschrift für deutsche Philologie* (1941); H. Götz, 'Leitwörter des Minnesangs', *Abhandlungen der sächsichen Akademie der Wissenschaften*, Phil-Hist Klasse (1951).

24. D. W. Robertson, 'Some Medieval Literary Terminology', *Studies in Philology* (1951); and 'The Doctrine of Charity in Medieval Literary Gardens: A Topical Approach through Symbolism and Allegory', *Speculum* (1951) set out the basic terms of this approach. See also in this connection P. Mandonnet,

Dante le théologien (1935) and the criticism by E. Gilson, *Dante et la philosophie*; C. S. Singleton, *An Essay on the 'Vita Nuova'* (1949).

25. Notably by H. Watenphul and H. Krefeld (1958) and Max Manitius (1929).
26. For example, J. A. Huisman, *Neue Wege zur dichterischen und musikalischen Technik Walthers von der Vogelweide* (1950); Karl-Heinz Schirmer, *Die Strophik Walthers von der Vogelweide* (1956). See note 22.
27. See the essays by Paul Zumthor and Joan Ferrante.
28. Paul Zumthor and Laura Vaina-Pusca, 'Le *je* de la chanson et le *moi* du poète chez les premiers trouvères 1180–1220', *Canadian Review of Comparative Literature* (1974); Derek Ohlenroth, *Sprechsituation und Sprecheridentität. Eine Untersuchung zum Verhältnis von Sprache und Realität im frühen deutschen Minnesang* (1974); W. T. H. Jackson, 'Persona and Audience in Two Medieval Love Lyrics', *Mosaic* (1975).
29. Norris J. Lacy, 'Villon and His World: The View and Point-of-View of the *Testament*', in Phillip Crant, ed., *Authors and Their Centuries* (1974).
30. Karen W. Klein, *The Partisan Voice: A Study of the Political Lyric in France and Germany 1180–1230* (1971).
31. Michael Titzmann, 'Die Umstruktierung des Minnesang-Sprachsystems zum "offenen" System bei Neidhart', *Deutsche Vierteljahrsschrift für Literaturgeschichte* (1971).
32. Edward D. Blodgett, 'This Other Eden: The Poetics of Space in Horace and Bernart de Ventadorn', *Neohelicon* (1975); Gerald A. Bond, 'M136, 25 and the conceptual Space of Heinrich von Morungen's Poetry', *Euphorion* (1976).
33. Jonathan Saville, *The Medieval Erotic Alba: Structure as Meaning* (1972).
34. For early work, see H. Hatzfeld, *A Critical Bibliography of the New Stylistics Applied to the Romance Literatures 1900–1952* (1953) and *Essai de bibliographie critique de stylistique française et romane, 1955–1960* (1961); Paul Zumthor, *Essai de poétique médiévale* (1972) and *Langue et techniques poétiques à l'époque romane XI–XIII siècles* (1963).

1 The Art of the Archpoet: a Reading of 'Lingua Balbus'

PETER DRONKE

The Archpoet's composition 'Lingua balbus, hebes ingenio'[1] begins with four strophes that are set off sharply against those that follow. They form an overture which can be listened to in diverse ways. It can be enjoyed as a bravura performance, a *captatio benevolentiae* rich in tricks that only a master of rhetoric could devise, rich, too, in adaptations of classical and biblical phrasing. The poet-performer plays with this double language so lightly and, it would seem, so effortlessly, that his audience – the high prelates, judges, diplomats and administrators of Frederick Barbarossa's Empire, and we today – might be forgiven for thinking, all this must be easy, such things could be learnt in the schools, it is no more than well-practised dexterity.

Yet there is another aspect to the overture, which summons another mode of concentration and comprehension. The rhetorical virtuosity, the deftness and subtle grace with which the topoi and allusions are handled, can be recognized by an attentive listener from the start. It is not until the close of the composition, on the other hand, that one can fully perceive that scarcely a note here in the overture was simply what it seemed at first hearing. The phrases are chosen for the reverberations – ironic, or profound, or both – which they will have in the rest of the piece. As in an operatic overture, these introductory strophes sound for the first time all the motifs that will be developed dramatically in the acts of the work that follows; they give hints in advance of all the main themes, though not, of course, of their modulations, or of the harmonies and discords of emotion with which the composer will orchestrate them.

It is not possible to determine, with every allusion that sounds in these lines,[2] how far the poet meant his audience – or his ideal audience – to bear in mind the original context of the allusion and its connotations

there. Yet at times these connotations seem so keenly relevant to the
poem as a whole that it is worth recalling the originals for the light they
help to shed.

1	Lingua balbus, hebes ingenio, viris doctis sermonem facio – sed quod loquor, qui loqui nescio, necessitas est, non presumptio.	With stammering tongue, dull of wit, I make my 'sermon' for men of learning – but that I speak, I who know not how, is a matter of need, not forwardness.
2	Ego iuxta divinum eloquium viris bonis hoc reor congruum,[3] ut subportet magnus exiguum, egrum sanus, et prudens fatuum.	I, in accordance with God's word, think that among men who are good it behoves the great to support the small, the healthy the sick, the wise the foolish.
3	Ne sim reus et dignus odio si lucernam premam sub modio, quod de rebus humanis sentio pia loqui iubet intentio.	Lest I be found guilty and detestable if I hide my light under a bushel, a dutiful intention bids me speak out what I feel about the way of the world.
4	Brevem vero sermonem facio, ne vos gravet longa narracio, ne dormitet lector pre tedio et 'Tu autem' dicat in medio!	The 'sermon' I'll devise will be brief, lest a long story weigh you down, lest the lector drowse with boredom and say 'Tu autem' before the close!

The rhetorical structure of this exordium is, superficially, simple: the
four strophes contain, respectively, a modesty-topos, an *auctoritas,* a
justification-topos: 'the possession of knowledge makes it a duty to
impart it', and a *brevitas*-formula.[4] The opening verse is a doublet, two
variations on the same thought, one ('Lingua balbus') in the language of
Isaiah, the other ('hebes ingenio') in that of Cicero.[5] Such conjunction of
biblical and classical reminiscences, using expressions from the two
traditions as synonyms or alternatives, is characteristic of the Archpoet.[6]
The context in Isaiah is a moment of optimism, which may have stirred,
in the poet's mind, certain ripples that leave widening circles in the
surface of the poem: there will be a king who will reign in justice, and the
chief men of his realm will sit in judgement (cf. 26 and 29 below); their
eyes will not be darkened, and they will listen diligently – and then even
foolish hearts will understand wisdom, and stammering tongues will be
able to speak swiftly and smoothly[7] (as indeed will that of the Archpoet
in what follows!). Isaiah's words, that is, provide the very context in
which the poet hopes to define his relation to his patrons, his audience,
the judges – in both a political and an artistic sense – to whom he will
now address his 'sermo': his discourse, or his homily – the Archpoet
leaves it ambiguous, for it is both.

With the third verse, borrowed from the opening of Jeremiah, the
connotations of the original context are decisively important: they define
the role of the *vates*, the poet-prophet, stammering yet filled with a spirit

that sets him apart from mortal men – the role that, with all his façade of humility, the Archpoet is about to assume:

> et factum est verbum Domini ad me dicens
> priusquam te formarem in utero novi te
> et antequam exires de vulva sanctificavi te
> prophetam gentibus dedi te
> *et dixi a a a Domine Deus ecce nescio loqui quia puer ego sum*
> et dixit Dominus ad me noli dicere puer sum
> quoniam ad omnia quae mittam te ibis
> et universa quaecumque mandavero tibi loqueris
> ne timeas a facie eorum
> quia tecum ego sum ut eruam te dicit Dominus
> et misit Dominus manum suam et tetigit os meum
> et dixit Dominus ad me ecce dedi verba mea in ore tuo
> ecce constitui te hodie super gentes et super regna
> ut evellas et destruas et disperdas et dissipes
>   et aedifices et plantes . . .[8]

Jeremiah too began, we might say, with a modesty-topos, but this was overruled. God summons him to his prophetic task, and he bleats out an excuse, he is too young ('ah, ah, ah . . . I don't know how to speak, for I'm still a boy'). God rejects Jeremiah's excuse – 'don't say "I'm still a boy"' – just as the Archpoet, echoing these words, later rejects it for himself, saying: 'I am not a boy' ('non sum puer', 35). The *vates*, that is, must obey his divine inspiration; to do otherwise would be to betray his role. He must not be afraid to speak even unwelcome, frightening truths: if God is speaking in and through him, the *vates* is in a sense above peoples and kingdoms – he can warn and castigate peoples and kingdoms in God's name, not in his own.

Does the Archpoet truly claim such a role, in the sense that Jeremiah and the other prophets claimed it? That throughout the small surviving corpus of his poetry he styles himself *vates*, even *vates vatum*, is an irony of which the secret, the precise degree of seriousness, the precise mixture of pride ('my art') and humility ('that one talent which is death to hide'), can never be fully ascertained.

But how far we are from a full identification with the prophetic role of a Jeremiah, the role that later Dante was to assume with such passionate seriousness,[9] can be seen from certain witty ambiguities in the lines that follow. That he speaks at all, not knowing how to speak, is 'need, not forwardness'. The prophet's need to proclaim the truth? The poet's compulsion to write? Or the beggar's neediness, that makes him beg? It is, we shall see, all of these, but the last more than the rest.

There is the same ambiguity in the word 'subportet' in the second strophe: the characteristic Pauline phrase 'supporting one another in charity' (*Eph* IV 3 – cf. *Col* III 13) cannot help having a less solemn undertone here – how fitting it is for them (who are great) to 'support' him, who is little! That the poet deliberately introduces this phrase which hints so strongly at his own calculated begging – not just as the words of Paul but as the word of God ('divinum eloquium') is the first prefiguration of that outrageous use of divine *auctoritas* which will bring the composition to its riotous, almost Aristophanic, close. It also links, however, with the only other strophe in the poem that begins with an explicit appeal to divine authority (32, 'Ut divina testatur pagina') – the strophe that represents the turning-point where the homily has moved into the begging-poem.

But this third strophe also sets up a series of antitheses that have reverberations throughout the whole argument: the contrasts between great and little, healthy and sick, anticipate the poet's contrasts signifying the Incarnation – the union of great divinity and little mankind – and the Redemption – it is the saviour, source of health, who heals the sick; but above all the contrast between wise and foolish is at the heart of the poem. In 27, the audience, the 'judges', are told, 'You are not the foolish virgins, your lamps are not empty, your vessels flow constantly with the oil of mutual charity.' The oil that the foolish virgins asked of their wise sisters had been identified in a whole tradition of biblical exegesis as the oil of charity.[10] And yet – this was the bitter message of the parable – the wise virgins had *not* given that vital charity to the foolish ones, but had left them to their fearful doom. The Archpoet prefers not to dwell on this: instead, by stressing that it is the oil of *mutual* charity ('caritatis oleo mutue', 27), he gives an advance hint of that moment of exchange of offerings ('collecta mutua', 42) exploited at the close of his poem, when a widow, deeply charitable, gave oil from her vessel ('caritatis lechitum olei', 44) to a *vates*, Elijah, and the prophet gave her inexhaustible gifts in return.[11] This is the event that the new *vates* longs to re-enact, though in a different way.

The full richness of these allusions will be suggested later; here it is enough to recognize that by means of only two words – 'prudens fatuum' – the poet can sound, in his overture, a motif he will develop with searing variations.

So, too, in the next strophe, one word, 'lucerna', which echoes significantly later (26), sets up a range of resonances for the poem. The biblical allusion in the poet's excuse for composing – he must not hide his light under a bushel[12] – takes us to that moment in the Sermon on the Mount (*Mt* V 13ff.) where the disciples are being addressed – 'you are the salt of the earth . . . you are the light of the world . . . thus may your light shine before mankind that they may see your good works'. Later the Archpoet addresses his patrons in the same style: they are 'the lights of Christendom' ('christiani lucerne populi', 26), he exhorts them to good works ('Insistite piis operibus', 31); but, just as Christ's exalted words to his disciples had also contained a warning and even a threat – if the salt turns out to be savourless, it is worth nothing and men tread it underfoot (*Mt* V 13), the Archpoet's flattery too comes to reveal its moment of menace ('Verumtamen . . . compungendum', 30).

Once more the biblical allusion is not what it seems: it introduces the poet's resolve to speak, not – as might now be expected – of divine matters, but of human: 'de rebus humanis'. It is a premonition that the *sermo* which follows, seemingly full of divinity, will turn out to have an all-too-human message. And yet, with a further flicker of irony, the intention of the discourse is called *pia* – whether the artist's duty and devotion to his audience, or the piety of his subject-matter, be implied, is left open.

In the fourth strophe, the '*brevitas*-formula', the poet shows his audience that he is aware they are an exigent and sophisticated circle, who have to be won over by his skill. He won't bore them by going on too long, he promises; the words of his promise are laden with ambiguities and further associations. The verb *gravari* will gain new shades of meaning when it is echoed, along with the rest of this strophe, in 43. The *lector* is both the reader of the poem and the reader of the last lesson at the evening service, Compline, which concludes formally with the words 'Tu autem, Domine, miserere nobis', and the response 'Deo gratias'. Yet the reader of the poem could well be – and at the first performance almost certainly must have been – the Archpoet himself. Then the comic effect of his proclamation of brevity, lest otherwise he fall asleep in the boredom of reciting his own work, is heightened.

Is it pure coincidence that the last lesson of Compline – the words, that is, immediately preceding 'Tu autem' in the service – are those from Psalm IV 5: 'Quae dicitis in cordibus vestris, in cubilibus vestris compungimini': 'what you say in your hearts, repent it in your chambers', and that this *compunctio*, the stab of conscience leading to a resolve to do good works, is precisely what the Archpoet tries to effect in his audience, using these lines from the Psalm almost verbatim in strophe 30? I suspect that the association of this Psalm-verse with 'Tu autem' was automatic for anyone who attended Compline regularly, and that the innuendo in strophe 4 may well be: 'But there's something important that comes before *Tu autem!*'

In brief, there are many links of thought and language between the four opening strophes – the overture – and those which we might call the entr'acte (26–31). After the overture comes the religious meditation (Act I); after the entr'acte, the poet's importuning of his patrons for gifts of money and clothing, the tone then growing more and more impudent (Act II). Overture and entr'acte are of decisive importance for the whole: potentially, all the riches of the composition lie in these sections that introduce the two acts, and in the links that bind them.[13]

After the overture, the first Act consists of twenty-one strophes of theological reflection, succinct and passionate in their formulations of Christian beliefs. If these strophes had survived alone in manuscripts, no one would have imagined that they were anything but sacred lyric. They combine an objective element, of hymnody, and a subjective one, of contemplation and emotional scrutiny, in a way that distinguishes the high achievements of medieval religious lyric especially in the centuries from Notker Balbulus to Hildegard of Bingen, but which becomes rare from the later twelfth century onwards, when the hymn and the lyrical meditation tend to follow divergent paths in European poetry.

Yet these strophes also have subjective elements of another, still more unusual, kind – for, ultimately, they cannot be considered on their own. The language here has numerous links with the rest of the poem, it shows traces, however unobtrusive during the more solemn moments, of that profane and witty, calculating and subtle artist who chose as his persona the unscrupulous mendicant. The *compunctio* that these strophes on Incarnation, Redemption, and Judgment can bring about – by their terse, lapidary affirmations and impassioned apostrophes and cries – is readily apparent. What needs more underlining, perhaps, is the extent to which a non-religious craft (in both senses of the word) is at work in them as well:

5	Ad eternam beatitudinem lapsum deus revocans hominem, verbum suum, suam imaginem misit ad nos per matrem virginem.	God, calling fallen man back to eternal felicity, sent his Word, his image to us, through the maiden mother.
6	Est unita deitas homini, servo suo persona domini, morti vita, splendor caligini, miseria beatitudini.	Godhead has been joined to man, the person of the master to his slave, life joined to death, splendour to darkness, wretchedness to felicity.
7	Scimus ista potentialiter magis facta quam naturaliter; scrutantibus spiritualiter scire licet quare, non qualiter.	We know this was done through (divine) power rather than by natural means; those who gaze with the spirit's eyes may know the reason, though not the cause.

8   Arte mira, miro consilio
    querens ovem, bonus opilio
    vagantibus in hoc exilio
    locutus est nobis in filio.

With wondrous art, with wondrous plan,
the good shepherd, in search of his sheep,
spoke to us – straying in this our exile –
in his Son.

9   Sanctum sue mentis consilium
    patefecit mundo per filium,
    ut, reiecto cultu sculptilium,
    deum nosset error gentilium.

The holy plan of his mind
he opened to the world through his Son,
so that, rejecting idol-worship,
erring heathendom might know God.

10 Poetarum seductos fabulis
    veritatis instruxit regulis;
    signis multis atque miraculis
    fidem veram dedit incredulis.

He instructed those seduced by poets'
fables, in the rules of truth;
by many signs and miracles
he gave true faith to unbelievers.

11 Obmutescant humana somnia –
    nil occultum, iam patent omnia:
    revelavit fata latentia
    non sapiens, sed Sapientia.

Let human phantasies be still –
nothing's concealed, all is open now:
the hidden fates have been revealed
not by a wise man, but by Wisdom.

12 Conticescat falsa temeritas,
    ubi palam loquitur veritas;
    quod divina probat auctoritas
    non improbet humana falsitas.

Let false temerity hold her peace
where truth speaks openly;
let human falseness not reject
what is shown by divine authority.

13 Huius mundi preterit orbita,
    stricta ducit ad vitam semita:
    qui scrutatur renum abscondita
    trutinabit hominum merita.

The orbit of this world flies past,
the straight path leads to life;
he whose gaze pierces hidden depths
will weigh the worths of men.

14 Iudex iustus, inspector cordium,
    nos ad suum trahit iudicium,
    redditurus ad pondus proprium
    bona bonis, malis contrarium.

The just judge, the searcher of hearts,
brings us to his trial,
to restore the balances –
good to the good, ill to the ill.

15 In hac vita misere vivitur,
    vanitas est omne quod cernitur –
    eri natus hodie moritur,
    finem habet omne quod oritur.

Life here is lived wretchedly,
all that's perceived is vanity –
one born yesterday dies today,
all that arises meets its end.

16 Sed qui dedit ad tempus vivere
    vitam brevem potest producere:
    vitam potest de morte facere
    qui mortuos iubet resurgere.

Yet he who devised timebound life
can extend life's brevity:
he can make life out of death,
the one who bids the dead to rise.

17 Nos ad regna vocat celestia,
    ubi prorsus nulla miseria,
    sed voluptas et vera gaudia,
    que sit deus omnibus omnia.

He calls us to the heavenly realms,
where there's no wretchedness at all,
but voluptuousness and true joys –
that God be all these things in all.

18 Puniamus virtute vicium
    cuius caret fine supplicium:
    terreat nos ignis incendium,
    fetor, fletus, et stridor dentium.

With virtue let us punish that vice
whose torment has no end:
the blazing fire should frighten us,
the stench, the weeping and gnashed teeth.

19 Sciens deus nos esse teneros,
    et Gehenne dolores asperos,
    pia voce revocat miseros,
    ovem suam ponens in humeros.

God, aware that we are tender
and the pains of Gehenna harsh,
devotedly calls us, wretched, back –
setting his sheep upon his shoulders.

20 O pietas inestimabilis: omnipotens incorruptibilis, creature misertus mobilis, est pro nobis factus passibilis!	Oh measureless devotedness: the almighty, incorruptible one, pitying changeable creation, became passible for us!
21 Est alapas passus et verbera, ludicrorum diversa genera, sputa, spinas, et, preter cetera, crucis morte dampnatus aspera.	He endured slaps and scourges, diverse mockeries, spittle, thorns, and, beyond that, the harsh doom of the cross.
22 Cum creator in cruce patitur, ferreus est qui non conpatitur; cum salvator lancea pungitur, saxeus est qui non conpungitur.	When the Creator endures the Passion, a man's of iron who shows no compassion; when with a lance the saviour is pierced, only a heart of stone's not pierced.
23 Conpungamur intus in anima, iram dei placantes lacrima: dies ire, dies novissima cito venit – nimis est proxima.	Let us be pierced, within, in the soul, placating God's wrath by a tear: the day of wrath, the final day, comes quickly – it is very near.
24 Ecce redit districtus arbiter qui passus est misericorditer; redit quidem, sed iam minaciter – coactus est, non potest aliter.	Look how the judge returns, severe, he who, full of mercy, suffered; yes he's returning, but now with menace – he is compelled, he can't do otherwise.
25 Mundus totus conmotus acriter vindicabit auctorem graviter et torquebit reos perhenniter – quamvis iuste, tamen crudeliter.	The World, stirred to ferocity, will avenge the Maker grievously, will forever torment the guilty – justly indeed, yet cruelly.

To overstate the matter momentarily, for greater clarity: the Archpoet relies on an implicit parallel (and ironic contrast) between God saving the world, in a spiritual sense, and the rich patrons saving him, the poet, in a material sense. The divine process of redemption shows 'Ad eternam beatitudinem/lapsum deus revocans hominem'; it is this eternal, spiritual felicity that the poet prays God will grant to his patrons (44) – 'post mortem ad vitam provehi'; but for himself, a 'fallen man' in another sense of the phrase – 'Nobis vero mundo fruentibus . . .' (45) – he prays that God prompt his patrons to grant him felicity of a different kind: an earthly, Bacchic kind.

Such parallels and contrasts can be seen as implicit in the antitheses of strophes 2 ('ut subportet magnus exiguum,/egrum sanus . . .') and 6 ('Est unita . . . servo suo persona domini,/morti vita . . .'): in the material sphere as in the divine, the great can show mercy to the small. And in both spheres (7) mercy and generosity remain, in the last resort, a mystery: they cannot be analysed in terms of nature.

Nor can it be rationally explained why the good shepherd (8) should leave ninety-nine sheep to their fate while concerning himself wholly with the search for a single lost one (*Lc* XV 4ff.; cf. *Mt* XVIII 12ff.). The parable, alluded to swiftly in strophe 8, and recalled in the words of Luke in strophe 19, is evoked a third time in strophe 28, where the poet tells his audience, 'You are the shepherds who pasture the Lord's flock' ('Vos pascitis gregem dominicum'): here, that is, the parallel between the role of the divine shepherd, the redeemer, and that of the patrons, redeemers – or rescuers – of the poor poet, becomes unmistakable.

From strophe 9 onwards, the poet develops a contrast between falsity and truth in which art itself seems to be called in question in an extreme way. The cult of idols and pagan error are set over against the truth of the divine plan revealed in Christ's Incarnation (9), the signs and wonders by which the true God teaches truth against the fables by which poets teach lies (10), the vain imaginings (*somnia*) of mankind against the revelation of the supreme Wisdom (11), the foolhardiness of human speculation, which is false, against divine authority, which is true (12). Hugh Primas had made a similar extravagant outburst against the vanities of poets, and against some of his contemporaries who saw in pagan fables and myths – such as those of Plato's *Timaeus* – images and foreshadowings of the Christian revelation.[14] That there was an element of opportunism in Primas' case – he was addressing masters of a school particularly hostile to the 'Chartrain' humanism of the time – is altogether possible. But the Archpoet's concern is different. He wants to stress that 'the poetry does not matter', because all that truly matters is *compunctio*. And *compunctio* must be true not only in the subjective sense of being emotionally sincere but, more importantly, in the objective one of being grounded in comprehension of the divine truth. The famous passage in Peter of Blois's discussion of penitence, where Peter (developing certain thoughts from Ailred of Rievaulx) tries to define the objectively valid conditions of such *compunctio*, is perhaps the best commentary on the strophes that follow:

If you feel the grace of compunction and a torrent of tears within you, don't imagine at once that you are reconciled with God. . . . You, who are moved to feel pity when a romance is performed, if you hear something devout about God read out to you, which compels you to weep, do you think that because of this weeping you have any conception of what it is to love God? You who feel compassion for God, you feel it for Arthur too! Both kinds of tears are wasteful, if you don't love God . . .[15]

A true, objectively grounded compunction will also show itself objectively, in deeds of mercy. The Archpoet uses all his persuasive powers to induce such a compunction in his patrons. Adapting Aristotle's phrase we might say that, by inspiring pity and terror, he brings about a catharsis of these emotions. He alternates between reminders of the terrors of divine judgement and of the unfathomable extent of divine mercy. Compared with these, transient earthly existence is as nothing. This motif, touched briefly in strophe 13, is developed in 15 in that biblical language of pessimism, deriving especially from Ecclesiastes and Wisdom, which the Archpoet likewise echoes in other poems.[16] Yet there are two very different conclusions which can be drawn from such acute awareness of transience: one is the 'contemptus mundi', that contempt for material riches which the Archpoet claims, or hopes, to find in his patrons, 'contemptores presentis seculi' (26); the other is, to enjoy that fleeting earthly existence itself to the full – 'Nobis vero mundo fruentibus . . .' (Just as in the *Confessio* the life that dies so swiftly can be sweet if the 'dying' is that of love, not of destruction – 'morte bona morior, dulci nece necor').[17] This possibility, made explicit only at the close of 'Lingua Balbus', allows more than one chord to be heard in such lines as (16):

> Sed qui dedit ad tempus vivere
> vitam brevem potest producere:
> vitam potest de morte facere . . .

The primary reference is naturally to the life after death which God can grant; yet it is hardly possible not to overhear the Archpoet's ironic alternative, a whisper behind the solemn proclamations – to make this deathly brief life itself something worth living, through gratification of earthly desires. So, too, 'voluptas et vera gaudia' (17) evidently means the joys of heaven; and yet, if it is literally true that God can be 'omnibus omnia', how can the application (which the poet will indeed go on to make) to earthly voluptuousness be shut out?

Strophe 18 begins with a conceit – punishing vice by virtue – a psychomachia that finds its counterpart in the conceit in 25, where it is the World, the personified Mundus of the Hermetic tradition,[18] who, moved to fierce anger, will avenge the Creator after the Judgement by tormenting the guilty ones. The meditation ends with two strophes (24–5) in which the Judgement is evoked grimly and inexorably, no longer compatible with the thought of divine mercy; yet in the preceding strophes the stress is on pity, not terror. At moments the note is almost playful, with a kind of *faux-naïf* gentleness in 19, where the reason for the divine mercy is given as God's knowing how tender we are and how harsh are the pains of Gehenna. Delicate children should be spared such things! And yet, as the richly suggestive word 'incorruptibilis' (20) indicates, the very contrast between a steadfast God and a fickle, mobile creation implies that as judge too God must be 'incorruptible'. The paradox, that the immutable one can nonetheless undergo suffering, and should choose to do so, leads to the double word-play – 'patitur/conpatitur', 'pungitur/conpungitur' – by which we arrive at what may be seen as the key-concept, the central word, of the poem. It is central even in the formal sense, for the twenty-third strophe – midpoint of the forty-five that form the whole – takes up that last word 'conpungitur' once more, in its incisive opening, 'Conpungamur . . .'

True 'compunction' is, as it were, to be pierced within, even as Christ was pierced physically: if one is not made of stone, one feels a pang at the sight of human *miseria*, and responds mercifully, as Christ did (and as the patrons, imitating Christ by 'com-passion' and 'com-punction', through their generosity, are meant to do, if the Archpoet persuades them successfully).

Some of the verbal richness of the entr'acte that now follows, and some of its links with the overture, have already been indicated. For four strophes it is an unashamed flattery of the patrons, in high-flown biblical terms:

26 Vos iudicis estis discipuli,   You are the disciples of the Judge,
    in scriptura divina seduli,   sedulous in divine scripture,
    christiani lucerne populi,   you are the lights of Christendom,
    contemptores presentis seculi.   despisers of the material world.

27 Vos non estis virgines fatue,   You are not the foolish virgins,
    vestre non sunt lampades vacue,   your lamps are not empty,
    vasa vestra manant assidue   your vessels flow constantly
    caritatis oleo mutue.   with the oil of mutual charity.

28 Vos pascitis gregem dominicum,   You are pasturing the Lord's flock,
    erogantes divinum triticum,   sharing out the divine wheat,
    quibusdam plus, quibusdam modicum,   more to some, to others less,
    prout quemque scitis famelicum.   inasmuch as you know the hunger of each.

29 Decus estis ecclesiasticum.   You are the glory of the Church.
    Cum venerit iudex in publicum,   When the Judge emerges openly
    ut puniat omne maleficum,   to punish every evildoer,
    sedebitis in thronis iudicum.   you will be sitting on judges' thrones.

The praises and reassurance of this audience of exalted prelates and administrators culminate in a phrase that echoes Luke XXII 30, where Christ promises his apostles that they 'shall sit on thrones, judging the twelve tribes of Israel'.

The poet appears to have lulled his listeners into a fine complacency: at that terrifying judgement, that *dies ire*, they will be judges, not victims; it will hold no fears for them, he seems to say, they will be immune.

'Verumtamen' – 'But yet . . .' The very next word, opening strophe 30, brings a change and a shock; dramatically, a peripeteia. ('But yet . . .' 'I do not like "but yet", it does allay/The good precedence; fie upon "but yet"!/"But yet" is as a gaoler to bring forth/Some monstrous malefactor . . .')

Once more the biblical context is imaginatively relevant in the poet's design, and helps us understand that design. Christ's promise to his apostles, that they would sit as judges, had emerged from their quarrel (*contentio*) as to which of them would have the highest places in Christ's kingdom. And directly before that (*Lc* XXII 22–3), Christ's words of reassurance and promise had been preceded by a twofold use of that terrifying 'Verumtamen' – as Christ saw the hand of his betrayer, Judas, on the table ('Verumtamen ecce manus tradentis me mecum est in mensa'); the Son of Man departs, 'but yet, woe to that man by whom he is betrayed!' ('verumtamen vae illi homini per quem traditur').

So, too, when the Archpoet turns upon the 'judges' whom with extravagant, seemingly sycophantic words he has trapped into a sense of security:

30	Verumtamen, in mundi fluctibus,	But yet, in the turmoils of the world,
	ubi nemo mundus a sordibus,	where nobody is free from taint,
	que dicitis in vestris cordibus	what you say within your hearts
	conpungendum est in cubilibus.	must be repented in your chambers.

he startles them into recognizing their true situation: they too are among the guilty, they too will be judged. He has returned to the theme of *compunctio* and brought it home to them, giving new personal import to the hallowed words with which the evening service closed.

Yet here these words are not followed at once by a 'Tu autem': the poet does not relax his hold, but goes on to 'preach' a different kind of sermon. If the judges are guilty, they must atone, they must perform acts of charity, they must give to the poor:

31	Insistite piis operibus,	Devote yourselves to holy works,
	bene vestris utentes opibus;	using your riches well;
	nam deo dat qui dat inopibus:	for, who gives to the needy, gives to God:
	ipse deus est in pauperibus.	God himself is in the poor.
32	Ut divina testatur pagina,	As divine scripture testifies,
	opes multe sunt iusto sarcina;	the just man's burdened by great wealth;
	summa virtus est elemosina –	the supreme virtue is almsgiving –
	dici debet virtutum domina.	it must be called the mistress of the virtues.
33	Hanc conmendo vobis pre ceteris;	This I commend to you above all;
	abscondatur in sinu pauperis.	let the alms be tucked in the poor man's purse.
	Crede mihi, si quid deliqueris,	Believe me, if you've sinned in any way,
	per hanc deum placare poteris.	by this means you can placate God.

34 Hanc conmendo vobis precipue,
   hec est via vite perpetue;
   quod salvator ostendens congrue
   dixit: Omni petenti tribue.

This I commend to you specially,
this is the way of unending life;
the saviour showed it fittingly,
saying: Give to all who ask.

35 Scitis ista, neque vos doceo.
   Sed quod scitis, facere moneo!
   Pro me loqui iam tandem debeo –
   non sum puer, etatem habeo.

You know all this – I'm not teaching you.
Yet I admonish, act on what you know!
Now at last I must speak for myself –
I am no boy, I have years enough.

36 Vitam meam vobis enucleo,
   paupertatem meam non taceo:
   sic sum pauper et sic indigeo,
   quod tam siti quam fame pereo.

I shall unfold my life to you,
I shall not hide my poverty:
I am so poor, I am so needy,
that of thirst and hunger I die.

37 Non sum nequam, nullum decipio:
   uno tantum laboro vitio:
   nam libenter semper accipio
   et plus mihi quam fratri cupio.

I'm not wicked, I don't deceive:
I'm burdened only by one vice:
I'm always happy to receive,
and want more for myself than for my neighbour.

'Ipse deus est in pauperibus. . . .' Overtly it is an expression of Christ's ideal: 'whatever you have given to the least of these my brothers, you have given to me'.[19] But implicitly the poet is already prompting his patrons with the thought, if you are moved by Christ's having been poor and rejected on earth – if you feel that true compunction on which the fate of your souls depends – then you will be moved by my condition too. In 32 the Archpoet goes on to one of his habitual pieces of verbal conjuring with biblical and classical allusions: in the fabric of the language we can perceive at least three distinct threads – Matthew ('it is easier for a camel to pass through the eye of a needle than for a rich man to enter the kingdom of heaven'), Paul ('the greatest of these is charity'), and Cicero ('justice is the mistress of the virtues').[20] Here the problem of Matthew's rich man has become the problem of the just man; at the same time, the mistress of the virtues is no longer Ciceronian justice but Pauline charity.

With 'Give to all who ask', the poet has brought us back to the Sermon on the Mount,[21] but with this difference – he now goes on to say openly, I am the one who is asking. At the opening of 35 (as with 'verumtamen' five strophes earlier) he again in a flash changes his audience's expectation: from a moment of seeming modesty, soothing his patrons – you all know about charity, I can teach you nothing there – he pounces, with the swift arrogance of the *vates*: but I advise you, for the sake of your souls, you'd better put your knowledge into practice! And as he begins unashamedly to speak out on his own behalf, his words 'non sum puer', as was suggested earlier, are a deliberate antithesis to the words of Jeremiah, a deliberate claim to that mantle of the *vates* which the Old Testament prophet was at first too much afraid to make. The phrase 'etatem habeo', which the Archpoet combines with 'non sum puer' as a doublet, is likewise suggestive by its associations: it is a reminiscence of John IX 21, where the parents of the blind lad whom Christ has just given sight say to the Pharisees, who are interrogating them: 'He is old enough, let him speak for himself' ('aetatem habet – ipse de se loquatur'). Thus the miraculously granted sight is here linked implicitly with vatic sight, and the claim to be old enough to speak for oneself is made into a biblical *auctoritas* for the poet's 'pro me loqui', to which he now proceeds.

He begins with his poverty: he is dying, not, as the biblical phrase has it, of hunger and thirst, but of thirst and hunger – even in this small reversal one can see a touch of irony, a hint forward to the Dionysiac dream of limitless wine with which the poem concludes. The irony is deeper in the following strophe: the poet's claim that he is not wicked, he has only a single fault – he cannot love his neighbour as himself. It is both self-mockery and a sardonic look at the second of the two 'great commandments of the law', [22] as if to say, that's quite unattainable.

And yet, by a cunning hyperbole, the Archpoet at once goes on to suggest that one man, a 'prelate, most generous of all who are generous', has more than realized this divine command of charity. It is an allusion to his own Maecenas, Reinald of Dassel, the Chancellor of Barbarossa's Holy Roman Empire. The purpose of this praise of the Chancellor's bounty is plain: to set it before the aristocratic members of the poet's audience as a precedent. The panegyric, though fulsome, is redeemed by humour: the poet's fur coat has too much sentimental value for him to sell it (which is why he needs more money); the Chancellor was twice as generous as Saint Martin, who, after all, gave only half a cloak to the beggar. (That it was half his own cloak, and that the saint had no other to give, is deliberately ignored, to make it sound as if the living patron were holier than the dead saint.)

38	Si vendatur propter denarium indumentum quod porto varium, grande mihi fiet obprobrium – malo diu pati ieiunium.	If I had to sell for money the grey-and-white fur coat I wear, it would be my great dishonour – I'd rather suffer a long fast.
39	Largissimus largorum omnium presul dedit hoc mihi pallium, magis habens in celis premium quam Martinus, qui dedit medium.	The most generous of all generous prelates gave it to me, winning more reward in heaven than Martin, who gave half a coat.
40	Nunc est opus ut vestra copia sublevetur vatis inopia: dent nobiles dona nobilia – aurum, vestes, et his similia.	Now comes the moment when, by your plenty, the prophet's need must be relieved: let the nobles give noble gifts – gold, clothing, and suchlike things.

41 Ne pauperi sit excusacio:	Nor shall the poor be excused from giving
det quadrantem gazofilacio:	their farthing to the treasury:
hec vidue fuit oblacio,	that was the widow's offering,
quam divina conmendat racio.	commended by the Word of God.

The last strophe cited leads over into the four which conclude the poem, four strophes of prayer (in more than one sense of that word), which are as densely textured, compact and consummate in artistry as the four opening ones. The finale is worthy of the overture, and comparable in its techniques and harmonies:

42 Viri digni fama perpetua,	My lords, you who deserve perpetual fame,
prece vestra conplector genua:	with my prayer I embrace your knees:
ne recedam hinc manu vacua,	let me not depart empty-handed,
fiat pro me collecta mutua.	let's have a mutual 'collect' for my sake.
43 Mea vobis patet intencio;	My intention is clear to you;
vos gravari sermone sencio,	I feel you are burdened by what I preach,
unde finem sermonis facio,	so here I make my sermon end,
quem sic finit brevis oracio:	ending thus, with a brief prayer:
44 Prestet vobis creator Eloy	May the Creator, Eloy, grant you
caritatis lechitum olei,	the pitcher of the oil of charity,
spei vinum, frumentum fidei,	the wine of hope, the corn of faith,
et post mortem ad vitam provehi –	and guide you to life after death –
45 Nobis vero mundo fruentibus,[23]	May he grant me, who love the world,
vinum bonum sepe bibentibus,	who often drink delicious wine,
sine vino deficientibus,	who feel like death if there's no wine,
nummos multos pro largis	your wealth to meet my vast debts
sumptibus – amen!	– amen!

These strophes demand, and presuppose, an audience of exceptional imaginative agility and deep familiarity with biblical texts. In 41, the words *quadrans* and *gazofilacium* are inseparable from the Gospel episode of the poor widow (*Mc* XII 41ff.) who, in Christ's words of praise, gave more by offering her two mites, her *quadrans*, to the treasury than all the rich had done – for what she gave was her whole means of subsistence. But here the *gazofilacium* meant is not the Temple treasury – it is a private hoard, the Archpoet's purse. By his phrase 'lechitum olei' (44) the poet links this widow with another, in the Old Testament, the widow who, though on the point of starving, gave Elijah the last of her 'pitcher of oil' (*lecythus olei*: the phrase is used three times in the biblical scene, *III Reg* XVII) – she whom the *vates*, by divine sanction, blessed with a miracle, turning her jug into a magic vessel, inexhaustible, never running dry. The further associations are richer still: the widow's oil becomes (it would seem uniquely in the Archpoet) the 'oil of charity' – that oil which, according to the biblical commentators, the foolish virgins begged from the wise, when they had lost their own. And the choice of the name for God, *Eloy*, in strophe 44 is likewise profound in its reverberations: it is the divine name used by Christ in his moment of anguish (*Mt* XXVII 46–7; *Mc* XV 34–5),[24] when he cried out 'My God, my God, why have you abandoned me?' ('Heloi Heloi lama sabacthani'), and people in the crowd exclaimed 'Look, he is calling Elijah!' As the widows (from the New Testament and the Old) are symbolically identified, so too the *vates*, in their moment of greatest need: Elijah reduced to begging for alms, even Christ begging aid from God (*Eloy* – not, as the crowd thought, Elijah) in his tremor of helplessness. The Archpoet does not assume any explicit symbolic identification for himself at this point: it is left open whether his need is more like that of the foolish virgins, who had wasted their oil imprudently, or more like that of the great *vates*. But the implicit likening to both Christ and Elijah is poetically important. The likeness with Christ is grounded in the earlier claim (31), 'ipse deus est in pauperibus' – if you give to the poor, you are giving to God. But *I* am poor: 'paupertatem meam non taceo' (36); I am one of those who hunger and thirst (or, more precisely, thirst and hunger).

The likeness with Elijah is what the poet is hoping to establish, by way of his audience. As with the widow and Elijah, it is not simply a question of charity, it is an exchange rather than merely a gift. The word-play in 'collecta mutua' brings this out. The Archpoet will offer a 'collect' – that is, a prayer – for his audience;[25] they will offer him a 'collection'. The *collecta mutua* is introduced by another *brevitas*-formula: as at the opening, the rhetorical trick is used to put the audience in the best frame of mind for the startling 'prayer' that follows. Again it is a *captatio benevolentiae* crammed with ambiguities. The reason he'll be brief is because 'vos gravari sermone sencio'. All the connotations of *gravari* are relevant: the *gravity* of his earlier thoughts about Redemption, Judgement, charity; the *boredom* which, he feigns to fear, he has induced by speaking about such things; the *burden* of giving, which he now imposes on them, by his final prayer. The prayer is a double one. For his imperial audience – the nobles and judges, as well as the less wealthy lower clergy – he prays that God grant them spiritual gifts: the allegorical oil, wine and corn – charity, hope and faith; for himself, that, through their charity, God grant him material gifts. He is content to leave the heavenly blessings to his patrons, if the patrons enable him to enjoy the world here and now, to drink his fill.

A new *vates*, a new Elijah, is begging: will they react like the poor widow who gave her farthing, or that other widow who gave Elijah oil, or will their response be that of the stern wise virgins, who denied the oil of charity to their feckless sisters? If they give to the new 'prophet', as the widow gave to the old, then God will grant them the miraculous, spiritual sustenance, the pitcher that never runs dry. But he too wants a pitcher that never runs dry – not of spiritual blessings, but of real earthly wine. Within the parodistic prayer lurks a series of interrelated allusions (the two widows, the wise and the foolish virgins, the two kinds of oil and the two kinds of wine, Elijah, and Christ at the moment of crucifixion) through which the principal motifs of the poem are bound in a strange harmony. Strange, because the finale is in one sense a summation of the whole poem, in another sense an explosion, a completely unexpected irruption into the burlesque, a satyr-play after, if not a tragedy, at least moments of deep seriousness.

It is this paradox which remains to be clarified and explored, and which is crucial to the question of how we are to asses this astonishing poem. In 1927 W. Stapel, in his edition of the Archpoet,[26] called 'Lingua balbus' a 'mock sermon' (*Narrenpredigt, Sermo ridicula* [*sic*]). This characterization has recently been repeated by a British scholar, F. P. Pickering, as if it were self-evident: those who think otherwise are rebuked for 'failure to recognize a mock sermon'.[27] Otto Schumann rightly argued against Stapel's inept and shallow characterization of 'Lingua balbus', 'for . . . the first part of the poem is intended absolutely seriously. The poet is here giving a sample of his art, by versifying the commonplaces of Christian teaching'.[28] Yet this judgement in its turn is not in my view adequate to the poem's complexities.

We know what mock sermons were like in the decades that the Archpoet was composing. The one 'On Loving Wine' ('De diligendo Lieo'[29] – not 'deo') affords an illuminating contrast to 'Lingua balbus':

The first and greatest commandment is: Thou shalt love the Lord thy Wine with all thy mouth and with all thy stomach and with all thy entrails . . .[30] When scripture says 'thou shalt love', it is said not in the imperative mood but in the hortative. 'Thou shalt love' is said not in command but in prophecy, knowing that you will love Wine. For who is there today in Holy Church who does not love Bacchus, and the more mightily the mightier he is? Not without cause, indeed, is Jesus said to have turned water into wine at Cana in Galilee. The Apostle Paul, writing to Timothy, orders him to drink wine – on account of his stomach, he says, and of his frequent infirmities . . .[31]

I baptize you not with water but with wine,[32] and not after many days but at once, upon this day. Twice because of the two

Testaments . . . Eight times because of the eight Beatitudes, nine times
because of the nine choirs of angels, even unto ten times because of the
decalogue of Moses . . .[33]

The mock sermon proceeds by a series of ingenious (though in
principle predictable) misquotations and misapplications of the Christian revelation. The mischievous assumptions – that wine can, and
should, be loved like God, that there is scriptural sanction for doing so,
scriptural authority for a baptism of wine, and the rest – are essentially
playful: for, underlying them, and making them possible as play, is the
recognition of the true God (*Deus*, not *Lieus*) and his true commands, in
the light of which the 'cult' of Wine is revealed as absurd.

The sermon in 'Lingua balbus', by contrast, is moving and magnifi-
cent. That its impassioned moments could be meant frivolously – that
the Archpoet could be mocking the Incarnation, Crucifixion or Judgement in the way the anonymous humourist mocked the 'cult of Bacchus'
– is inconceivable. To this extent Schumann was indeed right. And yet,
in the Archpoet's strophes, Incarnation, Crucifixion and Judgement are
anything but mere 'versified commonplaces of Christian teaching'; for
here they are charged with the hidden anticipation, the subversive *use* to
which this profound and tense homily will, at the end, be put. The poet
uses all his art to cause compunction in his listeners – a compunction that
is no mere sentimental pang but is fixed in the apprehension of a high
truth. And it is this truthfully based and inspired compunction that the
poet, at the close, exploits sardonically, with witty selfishness.

We may say, in the terms of Dr Johnson's famous stricture on Donne,
that the Archpoet has yoked heterogeneous ideas by violence together.
Yet we need not follow Johnson in seeing this as of itself a poetic flaw: on
the contrary, it can be a means of poetic liberation. As Paul Lehmann
suggested perceptively in 1922,[34] the Archpoet's 'uniqueness and individuality, his impulse to make new, may have been too great' for him to
be content with a parodistic imitation of religious prayers or songs, such
as we find in the twelfth century not only in mock sermons but also in
many poems that use similarly conventional techniques.

The Archpoet's techniques are more mercurial: from the rhetorical
display of the opening, where the topoi deliberately conceal the poet's
own feelings, to the religious intensities, that reveal only the faintest
hints of the outrage to come, to the flattery that becomes charged with
meaning, with menace even, or the picture of the poet begging so
humbly, yet with a shock in store for those he begs from, to the violent
and exhilarating burlesque of a prayer at the close, a prayer that

nonetheless still gathers up and contains all the poem's most serious motifs – this gamut of techniques represents a new challenge to a poetic audience. They are kept on edge, frequently disconcerted; they must make swift responses to the changes and complexities. But is it not also a challenge in the sphere of meaning as of technique – a challenge to reflect afresh on the nature of spiritual felicity, the nature of worldly felicity? The persona of the homilist was familiar to the Archpoet's audience, as – in a different context – was the persona of the mendicant. The sophisticated court would know (or would think they know) what homilists say; they would know (or would think they know) what beggars say. Such things, in their places, they had heard before (hence the Archpoet's frequent allusions to possibly wearying his audience with them). But what the Archpoet tells them they had never heard. They had never yet faced this twofold persona, this *vates* who is both ardent homilist and impudent beggar.

Is this new creation 'yoked by violence together' from two incongruous literary contexts, or is it made into an artistic unity? I would suggest that the Archpoet here achieved unity of a rare kind, a unity which, as was hinted at the outset, is perhaps most aptly characterized in musical terms. It is determined by the unique protean relation with his audience that the poet establishes in the poem. In overture, entr'acte and finale the poet's audience become, as it were, the instruments on whom he plays his orchestral passages.

NOTES

1. The text as printed in this essay does not wholly follow any one of the three important editions of the Archpoet: that of Jacob Grimm (*Akad. Wiss. Berlin* 1843, pp. 189–91, = *Kleinere Schriften* III, Berlin, 1866, pp. 49–54), that of Max Manitius (*Die Gedichte des Archipoeta*, München,[2] 1929, pp. 15–22), or that of H. Krefeld and H. Watenphul (*Die Gedichte des Archipoeta*, Heidelberg, 1958, pp. 47–53, 85–93). Of these editions, only the last gives a full *apparatus criticus*; with the help of this, I have restored several readings of the Göttingen MS which Krefeld–Watenphul rejected in their edition (on the most important of these, in strophe 2, 1–2, see note 3 below). Punctuation is my own. The translation is meant only as an aid towards the comprehension of the Latin.

   In preparing the text I have also taken into account the reviews of Krefeld–Watenphul by W. Bulst, *Anzeiger für deutsches Altertum* LXII (1961) 145–59, and by N. Fickermann, *PBB* LXXXII (1960) 173–84. References to other poems of the Archpoet are to the Krefeld–Watenphul edition. The begging-motifs in the Archpoet's work have recently been discussed in a perceptive essay by Anne Betten, 'Lateinische Bettelepik: Literarische Topik oder Ausdruck existentieller Not?', *Mittellateinisches Jahrbuch* XI (1976) 143–50.

2. References to most of the biblical and classical allusions are usefully assembled in Krefeld–Watenphul, pp. 87–93, though the editors do not discuss the functions and contexts of these allusions.

3. For these two lines I believe one must follow the readings of the Göttingen MS as against those of the (later) München and Wrocław ones, adopted by Krefeld–Watenphul. Compare the admirable observations of Walther Bulst (*Anzeiger*, p. 146):

> Mit noch bedenklicherer Eklektik ist der Hsg. an einer Stelle in I verfahren. I 2, 1–2 lauten im G *Ego iuxta diuinum eloquium uiris bonis hoc reor congruum*, in MW *Nulli uestrum reor ambiguum uiris bonis hoc esse congruum*. 2, 1 hat in G eine Silbe zuviel, und 1–2 reimen unrein. Der Hsg. spricht von der 'Fassung' dieser Zeilen in G; da jedoch sie weder als durch Verderbnis entstanden verstehbar, noch es vorstellbar ist, ein anderer hätte diese lectio difficilior durch Umdichtung des in MW überlieferten Textes hergestellt, so bleibt nichts anzunehmen übrig, als dass G die Zeilen in ihrem ursprünglichen Wortlaut erhalten hat. *diuinum* mag aus gekürztem *diuum* durch falsche Auflösung entstanden sein.

4. Cf. E. R. Curtius, *European Literature and the Latin Middle Ages* (English ed., London, 1953) pp. 83ff., 87, 487ff.

5. *Isaiah* XXXII 4; Cicero, *Tusc.* V xv, 45, *Phil.* X viii, 17.

6. Cf. for instance X ('Estuans intrinsecus') 1, 4 (combining Ovid and the Book of Job); 2, 4 (combining Job and Horace); 3, 4 (combining Ovid's *Amores* and the Book of Wisdom). The detailed references are given in Krefeld–Watenphul, p. 140.

7. *Is* XXXII 1ff.:

> ecce in iustitia regnabit rex
> et principes in iudicio praeerunt . . .
> non caligabunt oculi videntium
> et aures audientium diligenter auscultabunt
> et cor stultorum intelleget scientiam
> et lingua balborum velociter loquetur et plane.

Biblical citations, here and below, are from the critical edition of the Vulgate, *Biblia Sacra iuxta Vulgatam Versionem*, ed. R. Weber *et al.*, 2 vols (Stuttgart,[2] 1975).

8. *Ier* I 4–10.

9. Cf. Bruno Nardi, 'Dante profeta', *Dante e la cultura medievale* (Bari,[2] 1949) pp. 336–416.

10. Cf. e.g. Augustine, *Sermo* XCIII 5. Of particular interest, in view of the Archpoet's links with Cologne (see Krefeld–Watenphul, pp. 18ff.), is a passage by his contemporary Wolbero, Abbot of St Pantaleon in Cologne from 1147 until c. 1165, in his commentary on the Song of Songs (P.L. 195, 1032A, with minor corrections):

> In alio quoque loco praecipitur ut *oleum* semper in domo Domini sit *ad concinnandas luцernas* (*Lv* XXIV 2, cf. *Ex* XXXV 14). Per oleum quippe, quod cunctis liquoribus excellit, caritas accipitur, quae cunctis supereminet virtutibus. Per lucernas vero bona opera intelliguntur.

11. *III Reg* XVII 8ff. (see discussion below, p. 36).

12. The expressions *lucernam* and *sub modio* are directly from *Mt* V 15.

13. With this structural scheme goes a certain formal refinement: whilst the Archpoet employs the same rhymes for two strophes running on various occasions both here and in his other poetry (so that it is not a device exclusively for demarcating segments of a poem), I think it can hardly be coincidence that each of the first three segments here – overture, Act I, entr'acte – ends with a group of eight identical rhymes, not merely four. This lends the close of each part a certain weight and sets it off a little more deliberately against the strophes that follow, which in every instance bring new rhymes.

14. *Die Oxforder Gedichte des Primas*, ed. W. Meyer (repr. Darmstadt, 1970), p. 28 (vv. 47ff.):

> non hic vana poetarum,
> sed archana prophetarum;
> non leguntur hic poete,
> sed Iohannes et prophete;
> non est scola vanitatis
> sed doctrina veritatis;
> ibi nomen non Socratis
> sed eterne trinitatis;
> non hic Plato vel Thimeus –
> hic auditur unus deus.

Notwithstanding Meyer's learned explanation of the circumstances of the poem (pp. 30–5), I do not feel there are very good reasons for identifying the nameless 'thief' (*fur*) whom Primas attacks (vv. 97ff.) with Peter Abélard. (Cf. F. J. E. Raby, *Secular Latin Poetry*, Oxford,[2] 1957, II, p. 179.)

15. Cited and discussed by P. Dronke, 'Peter of Blois and Poetry at the Court of Henry II', *Mediaeval Studies* XXXVIII (1976) 185–235 (esp. 198–9).

16. Cf. X 3 ('Feror ego veluti sine nauta navis,/ut per vias aeris vaga fertur avis'), or III 1 ('Omnia tempus habent et ego breve postulo tempus').

17. X 6.

18. I have in mind especially the *deus mundus* of *Asclepius* 10 (*Corpus Hermeticum*, ed. Nock-Festugière, Paris,[2] 1960, II 308), who is the epiphany of the 'lord of eternity' ('aeternitatis dominus deus primus est, secundus est mundus...'). I cannot agree with Fickermann (*PBB*, 177), 'dass mit Vers 3 ein Subjektswechsel eintritt: *auctor torquebit* muss man selbstverständlich interpretieren ... denn es ist nicht Sache des *mundus*, die Verdammten zu bestrafen'. This suggestion would only make the syntax of the strophe poorer, and the thought banal. Nonetheless, Fickermann adduces two valuable hymnic parallels to the notion of the cosmos taking God's part against the wicked: in *Audi tellus* (*AH* XLIX 369ff.) st. 22, and in Peter Damiani's *Iucundantur et laetantur* st. 10 (ed. Lokrantz, p. 86).

19. *Mt* XXV 40.

20. *Mt* XIX 21–4 (note also the phrases 'si vis perfectus esse ... da pauperibus', 21, and 'erat enim habens multas possessiones', 22); *I Cor* XIII 13; *De officiis* III vi, 28.

21. *Lc* VI 30 (cf. *Mt* V 42).

22. *Mt* XXII 36–40, *Mc* XII 28–31.

23. I have left the punctuation open: *vero* can be the adversative particle, or it can

be construed adjectivally, in agreement with *mundo* – 'Nobis, vero mundo fruentibus' ('For us, who enjoy the real world . . .'). However, as the principal caesura in these verses normally comes after the fourth syllable, one should probably read 'Nobis vero, mundo fruentibus . . .'.

24. The divine name *Heloi* occurs nowhere in the Vulgate except at this moment of the Crucifixion in Matthew and Mark; the pair of verses in the two Gospels are almost identical in wording. (Variant MS. spellings in the two passages include *Eli, Eloi, Eloy, Heli*.)
25. Possibly the phrase 'digni fama perpetua' suggests that he, as poet, can immortalize them: cf. e.g. II 74–5 ('poetrias inauditas/scribam tibi'); IV 33 ('Christus tibi tribuat annos et trophea,/et nobis facundiam, ut scribamus ea'); VI 41–2 ('Inde poeta tuus tibi scribam carmen et odas./Sit finis verbi verbum laudabile do, das').
26. *Des Archipoeta erhaltene Gedichte. Metra quaedam Archipoetae* (Hamburg, 1927).
27. *German Life and Letters* XXV (1972) 309. Like Stapel, Pickering could have learnt better from Jacob Grimm's accurate description: 'Das erste gedicht beginnend "lingua balbus, hebes ingenio" leitet aus frommen betrachtungen die mit höchst weltlichem gebet schlieszende bitte um unterstützung des dürftigen dichters' (*Akad. Wiss. Berlin* 1843, p. 163, = *Kleinere Schriften* III 22).
28. *Zeitschrift für romanische Philologie* XLIX (1929) 598.
29. Ed. P. Lehmann, *Die Parodie im Mittelalter* (Stuttgart,² 1963) pp. 231–2.
30. Cf. *Mt* XXII 37, *Mc* XII 30.
31. *I Tim* V 23.
32. Cf. *Io* I 26, 33.
33. Cf. *Tractatus Garsiae*, ed. R. M. Thomson (Leiden, 1973) ll. 54ff., and *Carmina Burana*, ed. Hilka-Schumann-Bischoff (Heidelberg, 1930ff.) no. 196, sts 3–4.
34. *Die Parodie* (München,¹ 1922) p. 139.

2 *Interpretation of* Carmina Burana *62, 'Dum Diane vitrea'*

W. T. H. JACKSON

The poem is extant only in the manuscript of the *Carmina Burana*, and textual questions are therefore confined to possible emendations of the readings of this manuscript.[1] I have accepted Schumann's text, not only in such relatively minor matters as his reading of strophe 3, 4 and 'Morpheus' for the MS. reading 'Orpheus', but also in his decision that the last four strophes of the text in the manuscript are not part of the poem. Peter Dronke has recently made a spirited and persuasive case for the inclusion of these strophes[2] and it must be admitted at once that the decision to include or admit them must in the end be based on subjective feeling rather than on objective criteria. Metrical considerations help us very little. The form of the poem is highly irregular, and there can be no question of a fixed pattern of line-length, whether measured by syllables or stresses, either within the individual strophes or in different strophes. The excluded strophes are, from the metrical point of view, perhaps more 'regular' than the accepted strophes. It is, nevertheless, worth noting that the line-length develops with considerable regularity from the first to the third strophe, reaching its maximum length at the end of that strophe and that the lines remain long in the fourth. There is considerable correlation between length of line and sense, although the number of syllables in the last two strophes is only slightly longer than in the first two (110/101). The rejected strophes show no such correlation. Nor is there any such sense-progression in these strophes as there is in the first four. Rather we find a series of repetitious clichés which seem to be an attempt on the part of the author of these four rejected strophes to restate the material of the first four in different terms. Even though I believe that sense-progression through the strophes of a medieval lyric is not, in general, a criterion to be used either to judge whether a poem is genuine or to determine strophic order, or, indeed, as an important feature of interpretation, I feel that this poem, by the very nature of its theme, moves consciously to a conclusion, and that this conclusion is achieved, as Schumann indicates, by the end of the fourth strophe. The judgement remains subjective.

This poem, perhaps fortunately, defies generic classification. It is not a love-poem, although love is mentioned. Still less is it didactic or concerned with social or political conscience. In interpreting it, therefore, we are deprived of one important tool: we cannot set it against the real or supposed characteristics of a particular genre nor test its reverberations in general or in detail against the sentiments, language, or imagery of that genre. This loss of genre reverberation does not, however, mean that there will be no reverberations at all. Quite the contrary. The poem is highly allusive and clearly dependent for its effects on the fusion of several traditions. The first and most significant is the all-pervasive classical mythology, the second the tradition of associating the night-hours with love, and the third the setting of human activity in a frame of natural phenomena which are themselves significant only as perceived by a human being.

Before examing the effects of these traditions in detail, we should deal with an important and, for this poem, highly significant point. What is the relation between the poet, the poet/persona, and the audience? The word 'I' never appears in the poem, and there are no verbs in the first person. Thus the poet seeks no overt identification of himself as the persona and no 'subjective' or 'personal' experience is related. The poet recounts an experience valid for himself and for all men. He stands aside and purports to describe a series of feelings and sensations brought about in the conscious mind by the impact of light, sound, and touch, and the reaction of these to the active drive of love and the withdrawal of sensation in sleep. Although there is no *statement* that the persona is involved in these feelings and transitions, the implication is that he is so involved, and the use of tenses, as we shall see, strengthens this impression.

Whatever the involvement of the persona, the stress in the poem is on the universality of the experience. This sense of universality is achieved in several ways. We may first examine the question of the audience. Just as there is no mention of an 'I', of a poet-persona, there is no mention of a specific audience. The poet does not seek to enlist the help of any auditor to explain his purpose, he does not appeal to a special group who sympathize with him and support him, nor does he complain of a group within the audience which is opposed to him.[3] By avoiding direct appeals to persons and even the figure of apostrophe, he casts his opinions in the mould of universal truth which is to be accepted as valid by all. To put the matter in another way, the poet never asks or commands but uses the wide-ranging 'third person present tense', which presents both action and state, present and timeless, without any reference to the person thinking or acting. What happens now can happen again and has happened in the past, and everyone is involved, now and forever.

The use of the classics is a different matter. The evidence for their use is entirely positive, unlike the negative evidence for the audience. In three out of the four first lines of strophes, a classical deity appears, and each of these deities is the mythical embodiment of an element fundamental to the theme of the poem. We shall discuss these allusions later. For the present, it is sufficient to note that Diana introduces not only the concept of light at night but also that of borrowed light and that of the threefold goddess of sky, earth, and the underworld, and that of the mirror of love and deception. The same multiple meaning is contained in the second reference to Hesperus. In classical mythology, Hesperus is the son of Eos, the dawn, a fact which may well have been unknown to the author, but in any case the star Hesperus, the evening star, is identical with the morning star, Lucifer or Phosphorus. The identity is of considerable importance for the interpretation of the poem, for the time is indicated by the phase of the moon and the light of the star and in both cases these may indicate an hour late at night or early in the morning. The classical references bring into literature the eternity of repetition, the unending sequence of nights which are always the same and always different, as Diana and Hesperus are the same gods in differing manifestations. They are not merely links with an earlier literature but unchanging literary ikons.

This eternity of symbol lends particular importance to the allusion in the first line of the fourth strophe. The manuscript reading 'Orpheus' would be in complete accord with this view of classical literary connection and may well be intended to show the power of the poet to induce a mood and to demonstrate the power of song to move nature. 'Morpheus' can be little more than a personification of sleep itself.[4] The god has little significance as a deity and none of his associations is with Diana or Hesperus. The emendation, which seems obvious, may well be too facile.

The projection of the reader into the timelessness of the classics has much the same effect as the use of the *paysage idéal* topos. It removes the audience from considerations of time and space and enables it to contemplate pure phenomena. As the lover can think of disembodied love in the *Roman de la Rose* by the intervention of the topos of the dream and that of the ideal landscape, so the participants in this poem, whether they be poet or audience, can yield to the indulgence of sense and withdrawal of sense without reference to any particular occasion. This is the advantage of literary topoi. They are not descriptions of a particular man, woman, or landscape but of the literary representation of the essence of what they portray and of the attitudes of generations of authors towards them. In using these topoi, the author is setting his poem into a literary tradition, recognizable to his audience, and in his variations on them he calls upon his audience to share his personal experience within the timeless and spaceless experience of the topoi. This is not a question of intertextuality but of a relationship between the text and a multifaceted tradition far more significant than any single text. Furthermore, the classical topoi and the mythological figures have a prestige, an air of perfection, which is transmitted by mere reference to them.

Let us examine the time-progression within the poem. The first seven lines of the first strophe are devoted to a time-setting conveyed by the state of the moon, which merges into a sense of night rather than a description of it. Night in nature is succeeded by human activities at night, music and love. The strophe is thus very similar to the spring opening of the *canzo*, except that there is no overt comparison between the state of nature and that of the poet-persona. The second strophe introduces the theme of sleep and the delight it brings to mortals, the third amplifies that theme by talking of sleep as a cure for sadness and as bringing pleasure equal to that of love. The fourth strophe might be called the triumph of sleep, for it describes the gradual drowsiness which overtakes the senses with the onset of slumber.

There are two references to love in the poem. In the first strophe the meaning appears to be that music turns the heart aside from the love it is contemplating; in the third, the pleasure of sleep is compared with that of love. Neither reference is of any great significance except to show that the author thinks of sleep and love as being two important nocturnal activities. Behind him is a long tradition of which an important part is the mutual exclusiveness of the two. Love deprives its devotees of sleep. They cannot close an eye for thinking of the beloved, and the worst thing that can happen to any lover is that he falls asleep in the presence of his mistress. The whole tradition of the *alba* implies that the night has been spent in love-making, not sleeping. Yet in this poem it is love which is conquered and sleep which comes upon the persona. The poem ends in the triumph of sleep. The persona accepts it willingly and without a struggle. Unlike love, which in so many poems is called for and does not come or is unfulfilled, sleep comes and is accepted. The relation between sleep and love is therefore mentioned in the poem only to exalt sleep as superior to love and particularly to show its harmony with nature. A hymn to sleep is, almost by definition, a poem of love unfulfilled and past or it is against love altogether. The poet does not commit himself on the question of love but there can be no doubt of his interest in sleep.

Whatever his intentions are, there can be little doubt that the poet is far more interested in the technical methods of achieving his purpose than he is in that purpose itself. The details of his description show the care with which he operates. The time, as we said, is set by the rising of the moon's orb. *Dum* is used with a present tense, which, in classical grammar, must mean 'while', but here it more probably means 'when at any time', an easy extension of the strict meaning and one common in medieval Latin. It is clear that we are dealing with a sequence of like events. The moon which rises is a 'glassy torch'. The meanings and connotations of the word 'lampas' are important. In its simplest sense it is a light which merely brings illumination to the world at night, an indicator of the time of love and sleep. A connotation of *lampas*, however, is the wedding torch, the glow of passion, a shade of meaning that consorts very ill with Diana and with the clear light demanded by 'vitrea'. The opening lines thus set up an immediate contradiction which is carried further by the word 'sero'. Does the word mean simply 'in the evening', when the moon might be expected to rise or does it mean that part of the moon's phase when it rises very late? At that time the moon is full and illuminates the early morning hours rather than those of the evening, a matter of some importance, as we shall see. Thus we begin with a clear and a confused light, a marriage symbol supplied by a virgin, and a time at the end of the day or the end of the night. The image of reflected light persists in the next to lines with the reference to Diana's brother Apollo and the repetition of the word 'dum'. The brother's light is 'rosea', and here again an ambiguity arises. Neither the sun's nor the moon's light is pink, but the light of the dawn is, both in fact and in literature. Yet Diana's light is inflamed by her brother's light and the image of the torch persists.

One aspect of time and emotional impact has thus been set in an image of light which moves between evening and morning, between true and reflected, between calm and passionate light. The subordinate clause provides the visual parallel to the next sensuous experience, the breath of the wind. The zephyr is frequently part of the spring topos. Its mere

presence indicates the ideal of soft and gentle weather and as early as
Horace it is the indicator of the end of winter.[5] In this sentence, however,
we are not concerned with the coming of spring but with a situation in
the night. The breeze is gentle but the act it performs is one of power –
'tollit'. It acts as a clearing agent to the air and in doing so permits the
clearlight to come through. The phenomenon is well observed, for the
dawn wind frequently clears the sky in this way, and the poet has again
compared nature topos and natural observation. He has also provided
an effective sensory transition. The light imagery of the first four lines is
linked to the sound imagery of the last five by the wind, perceived usually
by sound, clearing the clouds so that light may be joined to music.

The 'sic' which introduces the reference to music is of some significance. It may indicate nothing more than a general parallel between the
action of the 'dulcis aura' and the 'vis chordarum', but it is far more
likely that the poet intends us to understand that music's effect on the
heart parallels that of the breeze on the sky – it reveals the light and turns
to passion, the 'lampas' of the second line. Yet its action is more gentle
than that of the wind ('emollit'), and in working on the heart and
preparing it for love it may produce that same ambivalence we have
already noted. The heart may be inclined to love but uncertain of its way.
The word 'nutat' reinforces this possibility and introduces another. The
basic meaning of *nutat* is 'nod', and for the first time the idea of sleep
appears. The heart may be inclined to love, music may urge it on, but
nature still demands its due. The heart, in contemplating love, thinks of
its *pondera*, not only its burdens but also the demands it makes during the
night hours. Again the author is using expressions from the classical
literature of love, but he is adapting them to his purpose by constant
ambiguity in their use, a situation which must raise the question of irony.
The strophe, which began with light and gentle sound and increasing
clarity ends with a soft decline.

The second strophe also begins with a time indicator, the joyous ray of
Hesperus, which, as we have already noted, is ambiguous. Hesperus is
the evening star, but the word *letum* would normally be more applicable
to its manifestation as the star of the morning, an interpretation borne
out by the references to dew in the following lines. Dew is usually
associated with early morning, rather than with the evening, although in
fact it falls both early and late, but the dew here referred to may not be
natural dew. The word is frequently used of the onset of sleep (*soporiferi*)
and that is almost certainly the meaning here. How do we explain
'gratiorem'? Is it merely 'rather pleasant' or is it a true comparative?
There has been no previous mention of any dampness unless it is implied

in the action of the breeze in sweeping away clouds. The meaning seems to be 'more pleasant than any other'. Now the evening star is, in fact, the planet Venus and the implications are clear: love brings a gentler sleep to the eyelids, whether it be evening or morning. There can, however, be no doubt that it is sleep, not love, which is desirable. The strophe again begins with a light-image ('letum iubar'), but the rest of it is series of sleep-images which indicate its desirability for all mankind. Nor should we neglect the second image implicit in *letum*, the connection with *Lethe*, forgetfulness. Such an allusion greatly increases the relevance and power of the first line of the strophe. The second strophe thus parallels the first, but its stress on light, though equally ambiguous, is much reduced, and the author increases the emphasis on sleep by his introduction of the image of dew as a soporific. Even though the whole strophe is a time-indicator, it does not pretend to indicate a specific point of time but only one of the infinite number of occasions on which a human being has been overcome by sleep. Again, it is time as part of humanity.

Only in the third strophe is there any overt expression of emotion. Although the persona of the poet does not appear, the outburst is enthusiastic praise of sleep on behalf of himself and all mankind. Sleep is described as a cure and once again there is ambiguity. Is the genitive 'soporis' subjective or objective? For if it is objective, then surely love must be intended, the opposite of sleep in this poem, and such a meaning would consort very well with the next line. Love, too, can overcome the storms of sorrow. The weakness of such an interpretation lies in the presence of the phrase 'tempestates curarum'. This expression would apply rather to love itself rather than to the sorrows that love cures. It seems much more likely that 'soporis' is subjective and that sleep is to be regarded as a cure for storms of care, including the cares of love. The apostrophe of sleep is followed by a description of its effects, a description which lays great stress on its gradual onset and on the conquest by cunning rather than force. The resemblance to the stealthy capture of a castle is strengthened by the 'poris/portis' *annominatio* and the reminiscence of the idea of love imperceptibly taking over the heart. The next line provides a natural transition to the core idea of the poem, the equality of love and sleep. In spite of the difficulties which this line seems to have caused the textural critics, the meaning is clear enough. *Ipsum* is, as so often, being used like *illud* to refer to something mentioned earlier and the antidote of sleep is said to be equal in joy to the sweetness of love. The line thus states the poem's motif.

It is not surprising, therefore, that the fourth strophe should tell us at last what the characteristics of the state of joy are. The strophe consists of a series of sensuous impressions, all connected with natural phenomena and all connected with sound. Whether we read 'Morpheus' or 'Orpheus', either sleep or sleep induced by music moves the conscious, intelligent mind into a series of increasingly lengthening sound-patterns which bring drowsiness and, in the last line, the loss of sight to the eye and sleep itself. Once again the stress is on the stealthy onset of sleep and its removal of light, not only the light of the sun and the moon but the light of the mind and its replacement by a series of sense-impressions. The poem culminates in the loss of all sensation through sleep.

The four strophes are thus organized as a study in the pleasures of love and sleep. Together the strophes show more coherence and progression than is usual in medieval lyric poetry. There is movement from the time-setting first strophe, with its open description of major and ambiguous light and sound phenomena, through the second, which links these phenomena with sleep, to the third, in which sleep becomes both the grammatical and the thematic subject. Sleep remains the main theme of the last strophe too, but the concentration is now on the effect on an individual person, so that the poem has closed from heavenly phenomena, through abstraction, to the fate of the persona. The work in this respect shows considerable affinity with the *canzo*, but its general theme is very different. Love, although never described, is imagined as an experience of the senses and is totally internalized. The love-object is not important. The paradox proposed by the poem is that the sensuous appreciation of phenomena, the appreciation of light, sound, and touch which precede sleep can provide pleasures very similar to those of love within the individual.

We may now examine the detailed structure of the poem. Metrically, it is an entirely free-form lyric. There is no trace of a fixed strophic length nor of any grouping of lines according to a particular length. There is no formal reason why a division between strophes should be made at all, except that they are so divided in the manuscript. The structure itself gives no clue. Three of the four strophes end in rhyming couplets, but of these three, one is monorhymed and another is written throughout in pair-rhymes, so that the existence of the pair gives no evidence of finality. The division seems to depend on non-formal considerations. The introduction of a new figure, Hesperus, is used to mark the beginning of the second strophe, the evocative O the third, and a final proper name the fourth. Such criteria for division are imprecise, and there is no real reason for a strophic form, either to attain reflection from a fixed form or to divide the treatment into a series of equal sized sections which, by a tight and repeated structure, would emphasize the parallel or repeated nature of the treatment or a series of different points of view. Regular strophic forms predominate in medieval lyrics and the absence of any such regularity in this poem points to a deliberate search for irregular progression. The pauses between strophes, if indeed they exist, are no more than opportunities for slight hesitations in this progression, pauses for reconsideration.

A study of the strophes as they appear in the edition gives little interesting formal data. The verse is rhythmic. The first six lines of the first strophe have each four stresses on seven syllables. The rhythm is descending ('trochaic'). These six lines are followed by a separate pattern of two four-syllable and one seven-syllable, four-stress line. The seven-syllable line thus predominates, with only two pairs of short 'action' lines to break it. The total number of syllables in the first strophe is seventy-two, of stresses, forty. The form is thus dipartite, with its first section composed of lines of even length, the second of two like parts. The first section is broken by a change of rhyme. We are presented with a curious variant of the type of strophic form which became normal in the *canzo*. The second part corresponds to the *fronte*, with its two parts, the first to the *cauda*. The reverse form may well be a deliberate parody of the *canzo* form, since we are here concerned with the triumph of sleep over love, but it is also likely that the distribution is designed to move from smooth regularity to broken regularity and to provide, even within the regularity, variations and breaks. The strophic form is thus designed with the same shifting ambivalence as we observed in the meaning.

The second strophe again emphasizes the seven-syllable, four-stress line. After the first of these come two four-syllable, two-stress lines, with two more seven-syllable, four-stress lines following. Thus there is a careful connection with the form of the first strophe. The only departure from the form of the first is a reduction in size: the first three lines are an exact half of the *cauda* of strophe 1, the second part is an exact third of the *fronte* of strophe 1. The correspondence is certainly deliberate. The two strophes, as we have seen, are descriptions of natural phenomena which lead to and surround love and sleep and the form used for this description is constant in general form but in flux in detail. Nevertheless, the relation between the number of syllables and the number of stresses is virtually the same in both strophes (1.8:1.8125) and so is the proportion of syllables in the two strophes as compared with the proportion of stresses (2.48:2.5). The length of the strophe has been reduced because the conscious feeling is approaching extinction in sleep.

The third strophe breaks away completely from the metrical pattern of the first two. It consists of four lines alternately of twelve and fourteen syllables. The fourth line has sixteen syllables if two elisions are not recognized. The fourth line shows some textual confusion, but the most important feature of the strophe is the overall increase in the number of syllables and stresses. The fifty-two syllables and twenty-six stresses, an exact balance of stressed and unstressed syllables, represent a greater length and weight than the shorter lines of the second strophe. The proportion of syllables between strophes 3 and 2 or between strophes 3 and 1 shows no obvious relationship to the proportions already mentioned. The even length of the lines produces a lack of tension, even a lack of movement, and the two elisions in the last line give a slight effect of lengthening and closure without disturbing the pattern. All lines end with an unstressed syllable and thus provide a rhythmic continuity lacking in the first two strophes, in which all seven-syllable lines end with a technically stressed syllable and are followed by a stressed syllable at the beginning of the next line. The effect is disjunctive and prevents the unbroken flow of sound which we encounter in the third strophe.

The rhythmical form of the final strophe is highly complex. The number of syllables is not in question: two lines of six syllables are followed by one of ten and three of twelve. The increase in length towards the end of the strophe is precisely in accordance with the general tendency of the strophic form in the poem. It is much less easy to determine the stress pattern. Certainly it is possible to force a regular alternation of stressed and unstressed syllables on each line:

<pre>
/x/x/x
/x/x/x
/x/x/x/x/x
/x/x/x/x/x/x
/x/x/x/x/x/x
/x/x/x/x/x/x
</pre>

But if we mark only those syllables which can be confirmed as bearing stress within the word, we have the following schema:

<pre>
/xxx/x
/xxx/x
/x/x/xxx/x
/xxx/xxx/x/x
xx/x/xxxxx/x
/x/x/x/x/x/x
</pre>

There would then be only two stresses in the two short lines, four in the next two, three in the next (although the first syllable might be regarded as stressed) and no less than six in the last line, where we finally reach a smooth alternation of stressed and unstressed syllables. Even this pattern is dependent on the recognition of the stressed nature of the first syllable of a disyllabic word. If we do not admit this, the pattern is:

```
/xxxxx
xxx/xx
xxxx/xxx/x
/xxx/xxx/xxx
xx/x/xx/xx/x
xx/xxxxxxx/x
```

It will be noted that in this schema there is a slow increase in the number of stresses which reaches its peak in the penultimate line. The last line has a mere two stresses and thus becomes the least regular of the long lines. There is once again a contrast and an ambiguity – by formal standards a progression to ultimate regularity but an underlying disunity and discontinuity which culminates in a broken rhythm with few firmly stressed syllables. There is no mathematical relationship between this strophe and the others except in the sense that, formally, it agrees with the third strophe in having an alternation of stressed and unstressed syllables.

The pattern of the poem shows a clear relationship between the first two strophes, deliberately reminiscent of the *canzo* form but departing from it in many ways. The second two strophes abandon any such resemblance and purport to present regular groups of longer lines with a clear pattern of stress-unstress alternation. On closer examination, this regularity proves to be illusory. The apparent order is in fact superficial and beneath it there is a dissolution of rhythmic form, which corresponds to the dissolution of the ordered processes of the mind as sleep approaches. The rhythmical basis of the poem is organized on the basis of a relationship between the poem's subject and its realization in rhythm and sound rather than on any numerical basis or on that of an established strophic order. The poet rejects such frames in favour of an ambiguous loose rhythm which contains its own patterns and variants.

The rhyme scheme does not correspond to any of the set forms. The interest lies in the distribution of the rhymes. In the first strophe the distribution is: *ababccddeffe*. All are full (two-vowel) rhymes, since there can be no doubt that 'zephyri'/'etheri' and 'pectora'/'pondera' are intended to have corresponding sounds in the penultimate syllable. The rhymes thus conform to formal standards, but their distribution is far from normal. Alternating rhymes are followed by two pairs and then 'embracing' rhymes for the last four lines. The three common patterns are thus displayed, but the interest lies, as so often in the medieval Latin lyric, in the words placed in rhyming position and thus emphasized. In the rhyming pair 'vitrea'/'rosea', the pale, colourless, reflective adjective is contrasted with the warmer, colourful, positive adjective and stresses the opposition between moonlight and sunlight, between night and day. It also achieves a second sense by its association between moonlight and dawn, since *rosea* is associated, in classical tradition, with Aurora and even with Phoebus. The night/dawn ambiguity is thus introduced by the rhyme itself.

The rhyme 'oritur'/'succenditur' is used in similar fashion. The moon may rise but it is not usually set aflame. Only the rosy flush of dawn could be so described and the ambiguity between night and morning continues. The two pairs of rhymes introduce a different technique. Although in the genitive case, the word 'Zephiri' is the true subject of the verb 'tollit' and, if the poem were heard for the first time, might also seem to be the subject of 'emollit', until the grammatical subject, 'vis chordarum', is heard in the next line. The two pair-rhymes thus provide a disjunctive rather than a conjunctive effect and heighten the contrast between 'tollit', the verb of action and clarity and the enervating 'emollit', which brings about a situation of dampened sound on the human level which is quite unlike the situation of clear light in the heavens.

The embracing rhymes at the end of the strophe, as might be expected, perform a closure function. The 'pectora' which are the object of 'emollit' have become 'pondera' under its influence (*pignora*, the alternative reading, would not change this function), and the two rhyming verbs between, 'immutat' and 'nutat', carry out and emphasize respectively the instability of the emotional state of love. The rhyme scheme of this first strophe is clearly designed to reinforce the ambiguities of sense and situation which we have designated as the main characteristic of this strophe. The contrast between the early *a b a b* rhymes and the final *e f f e*, linked by two disjunctive pairs points up very effectively the difference between the cosmic-descriptive and the human-emotional parts of the strophe.

There is no such contrast in the second strophe. It is devoted to the description of the hour of sleep, with the ambiguity evening/morning emphasized. The rhyme 'Hesperi'/'soporiferi' is thus the key rhyme of the strophe and it is made to embrace the producer of sleep, the dew, 'gratiorem humorem'. The final rhyming word 'generi' again links the human with the cosmic.

The emphasis on the parallel but contrasting situation of love and sleep, which is the theme of the third strophe, is well served by the four like rhymes. Three of the four are genitive cases of abstract nouns which are at the centre of the situation. The 'soporis' of the first line turns to the 'amoris' of the last, with 'doloris', a conventional attribute of love and the condition cured by sleep, in between. It is hard to escape the conclusion that 'poris' is a rhyme forced on the author by his own scheme. Clearly he wished to use a word to show that both love and sleep enter through the eyes and 'portis' would have been the obvious word to use. He has to settle for 'poris'. The general scheme, however, is effective enough.

The fourth strophe has three rhyming pairs, a regular form suitable for closing the poem. No effort is made in this, the strophe of finality and the triumph of sleep, to set up any disjunctions or antitheses. None of the rhyming words has any grammatical connection with any other, even though three are adjectives and three nouns. 'Impellentem', which could agree with 'mentem' and make sense, in fact agrees with the following 'ventum'; the next two rhyming adjectives qualify immediately preceding nouns and are words of natural description. The poem ends with two rhyming nouns, one very specifically of non-human phenomena which nevertheless are human artifacts ('molendinorum') and the other that part of the human body most obviously concerned with the sleep, the eyes ('oculorum'). The first and last rhymes in the strophe are concerned with the human condition and they embrace four rhyming words concerned with nature. The author could hardly make it clearer that he is concerned with nature within the human state. There can be no doubt, however, that one of the principal functions of the rhyme words in this last strophe is auditory. The first two contain two nasal consonants in the rhyming part, the second pair a liquid preceded and followed by a long vowel and in the third pair the rhyming words are respectively five and four syllables long, with a majority of the consonants either liquid or nasal. The effect is one of progressive lengthening and extension which result in the drowsiness described in the last two lines. The rhyme-scheme thus concludes with regularity and even sound.

There is, in general, considerable use of sound effects in the poem. In the first strophe they are relatively unimportant – 'chordarum'/'pecto-ra'/'cor'/'quod' – but in the second strophe we find frequent repetition of the or/ro sound, emphasizing the connection between the words for dew, moisture, and sleep ('gratiorem'/'humorem roris'/'soporiferi'/'mortalium'. All other words except 'letum' and 'dat' contain an *r + vowel* combination, so that 'roris', the central word of the strophe, is emphasized. The third strophe is characterized by polysyllabic words and by vowels long either by nature or by position. The result is a slowing of pace within the long lines. There is no obvious preference for any sound group, in sharp contrast to the forms of the fourth strophe, in which *vowel + m* or *n* are common: *M*orpheus, *m*ente*m*; i*m*pellente*m*; ve*n*tu*m*, le*n*e*m*, *m*aturas; *m*ur*m*ura, rivoru*m*, hare*n*as; a*m*bitus, *m*ole*n*di*n*oru*m*; fura*n*tur, so*m*n*o, lu*m*en, oculoru*m*. If we were to add *vowel + r* and *vowel + l*, there would be few words in the strophe which did not conform to the pattern. It is clearly the author's intention to use this sound to represent the increasing drowsiness which finds its ultimate expression in the last two lines of slow polysyllables.

One other sound feature should be noted, the distribution of pure vowels in the four strophes. In the first strophe it is remarkable regular, with *a* appearing sixteen times, *e* sixteen, *i* sixteen, *o* twelve and *u* twelve (if we count the diphthong *au*, the only one to appear in the poem, as *u*). The second strophe shows less regularity: *a* four times, *e* eight, *i* seven, *o* six, *u* four, with a sharp decline in the number of *a* sounds. The smaller number of *a* sounds appears again in the third strophe – seven – whereas the others are about equal, eleven, thirteen, twelve, eleven respectively. But in the last strophe the regularity disappears entirely. The sounds *e* and *u*, very frequently accompanied by a nasal or liquid consonant, dominate the strophe with seventeen and fifteen occurrences respectively, whereas *i* and *o* occur only eight times each and *a* ten. There can be little doubt that this move from regularity to irregularity is indicative of the author's intention to illustrate the break-up of sense impression in sleep.

The vocabulary used by the poet is very large classical and we shall discuss the reverberations of this. It is worth noting, however, that the poet uses a few words which are very rare in medieval Latin lyric. Some are connected with sleep almost as medical terms – 'antidotum', 'sedat', 'poris'. The other group is connected with the grinding of grain, a subject totally alien to lyric. 'Circulares ambitus' is, of course, an almost prosaic expression, especially when combined with 'molendinorum', but it expresses perfectly the contrast between direct line movement ('rivorum') and the repetitive movement of the mill which lulls to sleep. The use of such unusual expressions is not without significance, since the triumph of sleep is a rare subject in medieval poetry and the description of it here culminates in a vivid figure whose presence is designed to call the reader's attention to it with a considerable shock.

A few remarks should be made about individual words. The word *vitreus* is used more often in classical literature of water than of light and is very frequently associated with dew (e.g. Ovid, *Amores*, 1). The association between the moon and dew is possibly made as early as the first line, since, according to Macrobius, *Saturnalia* VII 16 1), Ros was the son of Aer and Luna.[6] There is, of course, no way of determining whether the author knew this passage of Macrobius, but it was available in the Middle Ages.

Lampas is very frequently associated with the sun, e.g. Lucretius, *De rerum natura* V. 610 'rosea sol alte lampade lucens'. It will be noted that our poet also describes the sun's rays as '*rosea*', but associates the word *lampas* with the moon. Such an association is very rare in classical poetry. On the other hand, association with *amor* is very common, and the author is quite deliberately using a word in which heat, whether of the sun or of love, is the normal component, of the cool and glassy moon.

There is considerable evidence that *iubar* originally meant 'the first light of day' and indeed even the morning star itself.[7] *Iubar Hesperi* would thus mean 'the morning light of the morning star' and would be totally redundant if it were not for the ambiguity of the word *Hesperus*, which normally means 'evening star'.

I can find no evidence in classical literature for *antidotum amoris*. The parallel with *remedium amoris* is obvious, but in classical authors the word *antidotum* appears strictly in medical contexts and we must therefore regard it as a genuine antidote for love rather than a mere remedy.

Morpheus is not the god of sleep but of dream shapes. It is possible that he could act as the conductor of the figures which follow mention of him in the poem but such an interpretation would be strained. There does seem to be a reference to Vergil, *Aeneid* V. 845, where Somnus causes Palinurus to nod at the steering oar and fall to his death in the sea, since the word *furor* is used in this poem in exactly the same way as Vergil uses it in the scene. Did the author think that Morpheus was the equivalent of Somnus or did he feel that Orpheus could fulfil the same function?

In poems of this type, it is always well to look for evidence of horizontal and vertical juxtaposition of words as a guide to the author's intentions. Horizontal juxtaposition to produce secondary effects is of less importance here than it is in many classical and medieval lyrics. Occasionally a meaning which complements that produced by normal syntax is produced by such juxtaposition – *sero lampas*, for example, further complicates the problem of the time of the moon's rising and of the arrival of love. But such examples are rare. Much more significant is the use of vertical juxtaposition. As usual in medieval lyric, whether Latin or vernacular, the words at the beginning of the line are weak – 'dum' in line 1, 'et' in line 3, 'sic' in line 8, 'et' in line 10, 'quod' in line 19, 'dum' in line 20, 'ipsum' in line 21, and 'qui' in line 27. The last strophe, significantly, has only one such weak word. In the lines which begin with 'stronger' words, nouns and adjectives preponderate – nine nouns, five adjectives, one adverb, one exclamation, and three verb forms. It is clear that action does not take place at the beginning of lines, but that each starts with a pictorial noun-adjective image.

The vertical readings at the middle and end of the lines are of far more interest. With lines of such varying length, it is not possible, of course, to read with such strict verticality as may be employed in the study of regular strophes. It is, nevertheless, perfectly possible to observe clear shadings of meaning through vertical juxtaposition. 'Diane'–'lampas'–'fratris' is a graphic representation of the light rela- tionship between sun and moon, and the following 'dum'–'aura'–'nubes'–['tollit'] fixes the time relationship more clearly than does the normal syntactical reading. Similarly, the relation be- tween love and music is well depicted by the assonance verticality of 'chordarum'–'cor'–'amoris'.

The more regular third strophe is naturally more productive of verticality:

| 'quam felix' | 'antidotum' |
| 'curarum tempestates' | 'sedat' |

As we have already seen, the storms of care could easily refer to love and hence would be 'felix', and the calming effect in 'antidotum sedat' would thus be negative rather than positive. A vertical reading 'surrepit . . . gaudio' virtually reverses the apparent meaning of the two lines, espe- cially if we note the vertical 'oculorum . . . dulcedini', a clear reference to the mystique of eye and heart. These vertical readings reinforce the ambiguity which we have noted as a major characteristic of the poem. On the other hand, the vertical readings in the last strophe reinforce meaning, as we might expect in this climax to the poem: 'rivorum'–'ambitus'–'furantur'; 'molendinorum'–'somno'.

'Dum Diane vitrea' is a learned exercise in poetic technique and a highly successful poem. It does not seek to tell a story, impart a lesson, or relate a personal or pseudo-personal experience. Its object is to catch a moment common to all men, a moment between heightened sensation and the fading of all sense-perception in sleep. To achieve his effects, the author marshals all his knowledge of the eternal mythology of the classics and the literary presentations of love and sleep. Past, present, and future are merged into a shifting present, and light and sound conspire to move the listener to the poet's promised end.

NOTES

1. I have used the edition of Alfons Hilka and Otto Schumann, *Carmina Burana*, Vol. II (Heidelberg, 1941). The text is as follows:

1. Dum Diane vitrea
sero lampas oritur
et a fratris rosea
luce dum succenditur,
dulcis aura zephyri
spirans omnes etheri
nubes tollit;
sic emollit
vis chordarum pectora
et immutat
cor, quod nutat
ad amoris pondera.

2. Letum iubar Hesperi
gratiorem
dat humorem
roris soporiferi
mortalium generi.

3. O quam felix est antidotum soporis,
quod curarum tempestates sedat et doloris!
dum surrepit clausis oculorum poris,
ipsum gaudio equiperat dulcedini amoris.

4. Morphëus in mentem
trahit impellentem
ventum lenem segetes maturas,
murmura rivorum per harenas puras,
circulares ambitus molendinorum,
qui furantur somno lumen oculorum.

2. Peter Dronke, 'Poetic Meaning in the *Carmina Burana*', *Mittellateinisches Jahrbuch*, X (1974/75), 116–37.
3. In Provençal poetry the group is composed of *lauzengiers* and *trichadors*. See in particular the poems of Marcabru (J.-M. L. Dejeanne, ed., *Poésies complètes du troubadour Marcabru*, Toulouse, 1909) and of Arnaut Daniel, ed. Gianluigi Toja (Florence, 1960).
4. For Morpheus, see Pauly-Wissowa, *Real-Encyclopädie der classischen Altertumswissenschaft*, s.v. He does not appear very often in classical literature and may be an Alexandrian invention.
5. Horace, *Odes* IV 7.
6. In this very interesting passage, Macrobius discusses the relationship between dew and the phases of the moon. He cites Alcman as his authority for the belief that Ros was the son of Aer and Luna.
7. *Iubar* means 'first light of day' in Vergil, *Aeneid* IV 130. See also Seneca, *Medea* 100ff.: 'sic nitidum iubar pastor luce nova roscidus aspicit' and the detailed description of the dawn in Statius, *Thebaid* I 343ff.

3 On the Subject of an Argument between Elias and his Cousin

CHARLES CAMPROUX

The poem I am going to discuss is 'Ara. m digatz vostre semblan', which is No. 14 of the works of the four d'Ussel troubadours in Jean Audiau's edition of the manuscripts. It is called by him the 'tenson de Gui et d'Elias'.[1] What interests me here is the arguments exchanged by the two participants, just as they are presented, as it seems to me, in a straightforward way, but I shall take account of the exact details of the text on the one hand and of the personal life of the protagonists on the other, even if this manner of reading does not perhaps fit in with what is generally believed about the troubadour ethic.

The study included by Jean Audiau in the introduction to his edition gives a reasonable degree of credibility to their statements; it also gives a fairly exact idea of the two troubadours face to face. The information that we have about Gui and Elias seems accurate, and Martin de Riquer has recently spoken of the 'noticias seguras' which the *Vida* seems to give; the archival material adduced by Jean Audiau supports these views.[2] It is therefore possible to consider the statements as accurate historical documentation, to the degree that a literary document may be regarded as a historical document.

Before dealing with the statements in question, it may be well to make clear the relationship between Elias and his cousin in their everyday lives, according to Jean Audiau's evidence. Both belonged to a family of noble *châtelains* who were lords of Ussel, 'which is a fine castle and they have many others too'. Thus they did not belong to the 'marginal' class of which Erich Köhler speaks.[3] They belonged to the class of real lords. Nevertheless, they did not both follow the same career. Gui was a canon. A canon and a troubadour. And, apparently, as good a canon as he was a troubadour. As a troubadour he 'paid court for a long time to Mme

Marguerite d'Aubusson and the Countess of Montferrand, in whose honour he composed many fine songs'. (The text of the *Vidas* says precisely, as in many cases, 'si entendent lonc temps en . . .', an expression which, when used of a troubadour, avoids the ambiguity of the French term *courtiser*, the word normally used [to translate it].) Marguerite d'Aubusson was the wife of the Viscount d'Aubusson, Rainaud VI, who, according to Jean Audiau, may himself have disputed in song with Gui d'Ussel. The Countess of Montferrand was the wife of Robert I, Dauphin of Auvergne. We are thus concerned with two ladies of the highest rank, worthy of attracting the attention of a troubadour, himself of noble birth of course but a canon in everyday society, that is to say, an intellectual rather than anything else and in preference to anything else. (This would not be the case with Elias.) He was a good troubadour but a good canon too, for 'the papal legate made him swear that he would never again compose songs, and, for his sake, he stopped composing and singing'. It is generally agreed that this legate was 'el famoso Peire de Castelnau y que tal prohibicion fuera algo anterior a 1209'.[4] So he was a good canon and a good catholic to the point of giving up an intellectual pursuit in which, according to everything we know about the d'Ussel troubadours, he had excelled for a whole lifetime. Elias, his cousin, is a very different character. He was just as noble in birth as Gui, but he did not become a canon. He probably married and lived in his castle of Charlus. This castle was poor enough, but Elias, who liked high living, managed to be contented with it, and if he was a troubadour the reason apparently was that, because of his literary vocation, he liked to 'receive' friends and acquaintances suitably: knights and highly placed people as well as troubadours, intellectuals by profession like Gaucelm Faidit, who wandered throughout the civilized world, accompanied by his wife, who helped him in his 'productions', or like his cousin the canon, who certainly had less need to 'compose' to gain a livelihood, but who nevertheless was part of the intelligentsia of the time, although probably less of a professional than Gaucelm Faidit.[5]

It would thus appear that we are presented not with any two troubadours but with two troubadours of different types. In opposition to the annoying tendency which only too often talks of troubadours 'wholesale', if I may put it that way, we shall not forget in this essay that our two participants are actually different in details. While Gui appears more like a professional, Elias seems to be a distinguished amateur. The nature of their extant work allows us to reach some firm conclusions. Most of Gui's extant poems are *canzons*, whereas Elias has not left us one. It is, of course, well known that the *canzo* was the genre *par excellence* in troubadour poetry. The manuscript evidence – the *canzo* is to be found in twenty-one manuscripts – shows clearly that Gui had a good reputation as an established troubadour, a fact emphasized by the subjects both of his *canzons* and of his graceful *pastourelles*, which are far removed from, for example, Marcabru's famous *pastourelle*, 'L'autrier jost' una sebissa'. As for Elias, he has left us only *coblas*, *tensons* or *partimens*. These were genres which were practiced by many personalities who had little in common with the professional troubadour, such as the King of Aragon, for example.

Furthermore, if one pays close attention to the words of Elias, it is easy to observe that they imply a tone which does not fit in particularly well with certain so-called courtly conventions. In general this tone reveals a highly idiosyncratic temperament, and, although one must naturally keep a sense of proportion in making the comparison, it cannot fail to recall the well known, even legendary temperament of another Occitanian lord, a temperament, it is said, which he retained even on the throne of France. It is, indeed, the good sense, the gallantry, the unaffected natural behaviour combined with good taste of *noste Enric* which the words of Elias conjure up for us in the few *tensons* and *coblas* which have come down to us. In the two *coblas* to Gaucelm, which Jean Mouzat puts together with the two *coblas* of Gaucelm to Elias, correctly presenting the whole as a true *tenson*,[6] Elias's sarcasms are of a more subtle and piquant quality. His good sense and unaffected behaviour shine out clearly in the *tenson* with Aymeric de Péguilhan. Aymeric asks him what is the right thing to do with his lady: she has told him she would allow him to sleep with her for one night, provided that he swore to her that he would not force her against her will and would be satisfied with embracing and kissing her. When Aymeric declares that he will be satisfied with kisses and embraces, Elias, in order not to break his oath, replies that it is 'vilania gran' and adds these charming lines:

> Car s'ab lieis jatz qu'am mais que me
> Ja als non l'irai demandan:
> Mas bellamen rizen jogan
> L'o farai, puois plorarai m'en
> Tro qe.m perdon lo faillimen;
> Puois irai pelegrins part Sur
> Queren Dieu perdon del parjur.

Elias's good sense and happy temperament emerge just as clearly in the *tenson* with Bernart. Bernart defends the traditional conduct of the bashful lover 'cel qi son joi jauzis celan', who, for fear of making a mistake, lacks the courage to speak and thus withdraws into himself ('apensat' – the word is charming). Elias is opposed to such behaviour. His good sense believes that it is more logical that 'l'amics qe trai sidonz enan' speak of her where it is fitting to do so; and besides, the *apensatz* really seems to be 'rendered speechless', and that is why Elias has a much higher opinion of the man who speaks with elegance of his lady than of a man who constantly dreams of doing so. His good sense and natural gallantry are responsible for the charm of his replies to his cousin Gui in the *tenson* 'N'Elias. de vos voill auzir', a tenson with a double subject. Gui maintains that he would rather see the *amie* to whom he has devoted all his heart and all his mind for so long die than be deceived by her. Gui asks Elias what he thinks of this, 'since he claims to be an expert in love'. Elias has no hesitation in saying 'It is easy for me to decide' on the reply: 'Rather than letting my *amie* die, I allow her a slip or two. I would even allow her a hundred because I would love her with a perfect heart and could get her back very easily. Whereas, if I saw her die, I would not live very long after.' The second subject is not as serious but is just as important, since it deals with a theme thoroughly traditional in the *chanson*: springtime, the little birds and love. Gui declares that he has decided to pay court to his lady in the *coingda sazo*, when he hears 'los auzeletz chantar al clar jorn', in order to double his joy on seeing his lady. To this traditional attitude, to this moment of traditional love, Elias opposes what is certainly the reality of his own love with wit and with no false modesty:

> E voill en chambra o en maiso
> Tota nuoig ab midonz estar
> E leis tener et abrassar;
> E ja no voill chant d'auzello
> Car per ren no. l poria auzir;
> Car cui fin'amors capdella
> No sap d'auzel qui favella.

And we shall note that Elias makes no claim to go against the rules of *fine amour*, since he takes care to emphasize 'that a man guided by *fine amour* does not concern himself with a bird that sings'.

I am emphasizing this feature purposely in relation to what follows, for it would be possible to claim that Elias is not really a troubadour but simply an educated aristocrat, full of wit, and that his example cannot be used as evidence for a particular point of view about problems peculiar to troubadour culture. Certainly I would be the first to emphasize Elias's non-conformism in regard to Gui, for example. It is just as important to emphasize that Elias himself thinks that his non-conformism is the best way of serving *fine amour*. All that we shall be able to maintain under these circumstances is that there were several different attitudes among the troubadours on the subject of their ethic, just as there were differences, often huge differences, among the troubadours themselves both from the point of view of social position and from the point of view of character, and thus, necessarily, from the point of view of their choices and commitments. The humanistic culture of the troubadours was no narrower, no more turned in on itself than humanistic culture in our own day. That is what people tend to forget and what causes the naïve surprise which we know so well, such as that of Jeanroy when he cannot understand how there could be 'such an outpouring of the pagan spirit (his words, of course) in a country and in a century which were so thoroughly christianized'. In any case we must reject the view which consists in accepting as absolute truth a generalization which is basically a lack of perspective and which is not even a generalization of the facts, if they are looked at without prejudice. The generalization I am referring to and which we shall discuss in relation to the *tenson*, 'Ara.m digatz vostre semblan' is that which claims that troubadour love is adulterous and that adultery is a characteristic *par excellence* of *fin'amor*.[7]

The adulterous character of troubadour love is still generally accepted as a truth which is, so to speak, obvious, a truth which there is no need to prove. I have no intention of denying, for example, that the troubadours of the class whom Köhler calls 'marginal men' had to sing about the wife of whoever was their lord at any given time, and we know why. Nevertheless, there can be no question of an absolute characteristic but simply of a character related to the situation of the 'marginal man'. And this adulterous character is not carried to any conclusion at all, certainly no further than the gallantries a guest might offer to the wife of his host, who would be very ill-mannered if he regarded such polite and flattering statements as an indication of an adulterous liaison in the normal modern sense of the term. In a well documented study, John F. Benton had no difficulty in demonstrating that aristocrats in medieval Europe saw nothing out of place in the gallantries of the troubadours towards their wives; he points out that adultery committed with the wife of one's lord was punished not only as adultery but also as the highest form of treason.[8] For those who would agree that Köhler's theory completely explains the birth of courtly love, the question of adultery in troubadour love would be resolved perfectly simply and 'with no problems'. It would, in fact, have no significance.

It is well known that under the influence of a 'catharizing' fashion, there is a tendency to ascribe the adulterous character of *fin'amors* to Catharism. Benton, in the article already mentioned, emphasizes that the influence of Catharism on sexual mores in medieval Europe has been overestimated. Furthermore, it is known that very few troubadours were actually Catharists, although it is true that, in general, the troubadours, like all other social strata in the countries of the *langue d'oc* incidentally, were tolerant of the Catharists with whom they might come into contact. Benton recalls the famous poem of Daude de Prades in which he declares that he divides his love into three: 1. for 'midonz per mais valer'; 2. for a 'piucella per tener', a girl who 'no is mou ni.s vira ni s'esglaia' when he wants to 'baisar la maissella' or squeeze 'un pauc la mamella'; 3. for 'a soudadeira coind' e pro' who 'ne fassa plaig ni tenso/d'ostar camisa ni gonella' to teach him everything she knows, not about *joy d'amor* but about the games of love.[9] From this Benton draws the perfectly logical conclusion that there is absolutely no need to find some connection between Catharism or any other heresy and the various forms of chaste or fleshly love. It will be noted that Daude de Prades is documented between 1214 and 1282; he must therefore have been very well acquainted with the Catharist problem, although he was probably sheltered from its dangerous currents in his native Rouergue and was a good Catholic, since he was named Vicar-General by the Pope.

If the socio-economic theory of Köhler tends to challenge the significance of the adulterous character of troubadour love, and if this same character is not to be explained with any degree of certainty by Catharism, the fact nevertheless remains that it is still brought up as a self-evident fact, which may perhaps be the result of a lingering trace of sentimental romanticism, if it is not a manifestation of modern nastiness, fit only for the gutter. In either case it is done with the guarantee of the Countess of Champagne as a support, at least according to Andreas Capellanus. Claude Buridant, in the introduction to his translation of the *De Amore* of Andreas Capellanus, which appeared recently, has not the slightest hesitation in stating with a supporting quotation from Moshé Lazar, *Amour courtois et Fin'Amor* (1964): 'For the troubadours too, *fin'amors* and married love are irreconcilable. Love (*fin'amors, amor veraia, amor bona* etc) cannot exist between man and wife.'[10] That is indeed a clear and definitive statement.[11]

In fact, this exclusion of married couples from love rests entirely on one passage of Andreas Capellanus which allegedly reproduces a letter from 'the Countess of Champagne', sent to her 'by mutual agreement' by the great lord ('nobilior') and the lady of the lesser nobility ('nobilis') of dialogue G in Chapter VI of Book I of the *De Amore*. This well known text says: 'we say and affirm as totally proven that love cannot exercise its rights over two spouses. It is characteristic of lovers that they freely give one another everything, although they are under no obligation to do so. Spouses, on the other hand, are obliged by duty to obey each others' wishes and cannot deny themselves to each other.'[12] If this text really stems from the Countess of Champagne (it is of little importance for us to know which countess is concerned), it would be perfectly easy to see in the declaration an affirmation of contemporary feminism. But the right thing to do is to put the text back in its context. It is a favourable reply to the proposition of the great lord who is debating with the lady of the lower nobility. The great lord is trying to seduce his interlocutor by maintaining in advance, with force and authority, what the Countess of Champagne will maintain in her reply. The lady of the lesser nobility has rejected the advances of the great lord by a very simple and very natural argument. She has stated in effect: 'In addition there is another and by no means trivial motive which forbids me to love. I have a husband, you see, who is distinguished by nobility, courtesy and virtues; it would be criminal to besmirch his bed or to submit to the embraces of another man. I do know that he loves me with all his heart, and I am deeply attached to him. The law itself orders me to refuse to love anywhere else when I have had the good fortune to be the recipient of such a love.' It will be noted that the lady of the lesser nobility does not reject the great lord because she is afraid of the laws but because she really loves her husband, since she is lucky enough to have a husband who loves her 'avec courtoisie'.

It is in order to make a reply to such arguments that the great lord exclaims: 'I am nevertheless surprised to hear you use the word "love" wrongly for the conjugal feeling that husband and wife are bound to feel for each other once they have been joined in marriage: it is well known that love cannot exist between them.' He develops his thought as follows: 'It is possible that they are attached to each other by a powerful feeling which has no limits, but such a feeling would be quite unable to act as a substitute for love, since it cannot comply with the true definition of it. What is love after all if it is not an overwhelming desire to enjoy with passion furtive and secret embraces?' It will be seen in what context the famous reply of the 'Countess of Champagne' is to be found. Certainly not in any context which could be called 'troubadour'. But certainly in the context of Northern French clerics, who did not like women and for whom love was nothing but a sin, 'for them', says F. Schurr, 'courtliness in the North conflicts with certain "bourgeois" tendencies among the clerics, who oppose it with some degree of pedanticism'.[13] In order to plead his case, the great lord goes further and borrows from the theologians of Andreas's country a doctrine which clearly flies in the face of the good sense of the apostle Paul when he says that a man should render to his wife what is her due and that the wife should do the same for her husband. Alain de Lille sums up that doctrine when he says, 'Vehemens amator uxoris adulter est.' The great lord indeed coolly instructs the lady of the lesser nobility – who is presumably ignorant of the theological extravagances of Northern clerics – 'As the law of the Church teaches us, he who loves his wife with too much passion is regarded as guilty of adultery.' He also teaches her that 'when married couples join mutually in pleasures which, in one way or another, go beyond those brought on by a desire to procreate or to fulfil their conjugal duty, there cannot help but be wrongdoing'. Such is the context of the words of the Countess of Champagne, a context never cited by those who apply the words of the countess to *fin'amors* of the troubadours. In reality, these words should be set in a context which is clerical to the point of naïveté if not triviality and there judged at their true value. The naïve character of Andreas the cleric can be best seen in the fact that he has the doctrine under discussion put forward by a *great* lord seeking to seduce a lady of the *lesser* nobility.

One thing should be noted on the subject of love and marriage. The opinion of the theologians in the country of Andreas, the 'royal chaplain', was basically an opinion well known to Catharism. At least the view passes for catharistic according to which marriage was a 'lupanar privatum'. The opinion has been attributed to Peire Oliu, the master of the occitanian Spirituals, who were far from being Catharists. The opinion was widespread in the Beguine movement in the South, particularly in Languedoc and Catalonia.[14] Three residents in the diocese of Narbonne worked it out, a layman, Guillaume Sacourt de Bize, his brother, Raimon Sacourt, a cleric, and a Franciscan lay-brother Guillaume Martin d'Escueillens (Bize and Escueillens are in the Aude); a man from Arièges maintains the same opinion; two priests are questioned on the same subject by the Inquisition. It has been claimed that the origin of the concept is to be sought in the teaching given in Toulouse by Pierre Garsias 'quod pomum vetitum primis parentibus nil aliud fuit quam delectatio coitus'.[15] It is more accurate to see in this an important aspect of the teaching of clerics which spread from Paris and which naturally reached Toulouse with the doctors of the Sorbonne who were sent to the city in 1229 to instruct its inhabitants. Abélard cites the passage from Sextus to St Jerome: 'uxorem ratione suam vir debet amare/et non ad coitum sicut adultera sit'.[16]

It seems clear enough that marriage did not enjoy a particularly favourable reputation in some quarters in the Middle Ages. It goes without saying that these opinions, disseminated by clerics, taught by a certain number of theologians, shared by 'chaplains' like Andreas, could not help but be comforting to some noble women who were obsessed by a definite sense of their individuality and independence, feminists before the expression was invented. They had a considerable scorn for the institution of marriage and the conception of it which they could arrive at naturally did not correspond to their ideas on true love. We must definitely *not* attribute to the troubadours in general either the opinions of the clerics in Northern France (it is well known that culture in the South was primarily secular) or those of noblewomen who were to a greater or less degree eager to get away from the strict laws of matrimonial dependence. In any case, so far as the troubadours are concerned, there is no evidence that love is impossible between husband and wife. All that can be clearly established is that they address themselves to a *domna*, an expression which is by no means synonymous with 'married woman', but which does preserve the shades of meaning of the Latin *domina*. In fact, *domna* is the exact equivalent of the English 'lady', with its various connotations.[17] Among the troubadours there is no evidence of any *a priori* prejudice against marriage. If Marcabru shows open hostility to *molherats* there is no question of his claiming that love cannot exist between spouses: the *molherats* of whom he is speaking are married men, that is to say, men already established in society, as opposed to *jovent*, men with no wife and no position. Marcabru blames people of position for wishing to get involved in singing of love and consequently doing harm to the representatives of *jovent*. Marcabru is attacking the *rics*, the powerful people who are, so to speak, taking the bread out of the mouths of the *jovent*.

> Tant can bos jovens fon paire
> del segle, e fin'amors maire,
> fon proeza mantenguda
> a celat e a saubuda;
> mas er l'ant avilanada
> duc e rei e emperaire;
> . . .
> per que amors es perduda
> e de joi deseretada.

Furthermore, no attacks on marriage can be found in the work of any troubadour, nor can the idea that marriage would prevent love, still less that there can be no love between husband and wife. It is one thing to sing of the love of a *domna*, quite another not to love one's marriage partner for that reason. There is a well known anecdote about Peire Vidal – whether it is true or false it illustrates none the less the mentality of the period – and the kiss stolen from the wife of the lord of Marseilles, En Barral, a kiss which was finally granted to Vidal as a gift from the lady at the insistence of Barral, the lady's husband. Throughout the story, in all the different versions which have come down to us, Barral's behaviour shows great affection, great tenderness in his love for his wife and no less tenderness and love on her side for him. We find plenty of examples in the *Vidas* of the fact that love could very well exist between husband and wife. Thus we are told that Raimon de Miraval fell in love with Aimengarda de Castres and that he begged for her love for a long time. Aimengarda told him that 'ela no.il faria plaiser d'amor per nom de drudaria mais si el volia laissar soa moiller, ela lo tolria per marit'. Raimon was delighted to know that 'ela lo volia tolre per marit'. It is quite clear that our troubadour did not think that marriage was an obstacle to love, whatever may have been the unfortunate turns of events which happened to Raimon de Miraval on this occasion. Raimon, on the other hand, had to be willing to leave his wife in order to marry Aimengarda; he used the pretext that his wife, like him, was a troubadour, and that there could not be two troubadours under the same roof. Huguet de Mataplana did not agree with Raimon and told him that, since his wife was a troubadour, she had the right to practice *fin'amor* under the conjugal roof and to sing the praises of a lover in her songs; then, he says, the home of the married couple will be 'gauzens' and, if 'sos albercs es soven cortejats', the husband should never doubt his wife or take it [her action] 'a grevanssa'. The same opinion is shared by, for example, Na Castelloza, a noblewoman and troubadour of Auvergne, who certainly does not give the impression that the fact of her singing of her love for a man other than her husband could have disagreeable consequences for her relations with her husband. Quite the contrary, since she writes when addressing the person of whom she is singing:

> Tot lo maltraich e.l dompnatge
> Que per vos m'es escaritz
> Me.l fai grazir mos linhatge
> E sobre totz mos maritz . . .

(All the evil and suffering/which has come to me because of you/my lineage makes me accept willingly/and above all, my husband.)[18] Here is a husband who is happy that his wife sings about another man as an expert in *fin'amor* without its having any apparent effect on his own feelings or those of his wife. Nor does anything prove that those feelings between husband and wife had nothing to do with love, even if that love was of a different nature from the one of which Na Castelloza was the celebrant. We have here the same situation which Huguet de Mataplana described as happening well before his own time in the work of Bernart Marti, for example, who sings in 'Bel m'es lai latz la fontana':

> Dona es vas drut trefana
> des'amor, pos tres n'apana:
>> estra lei
>> n'i son trei.
> Mas ab son marit l'autrei
> un amic cortes prezant.
> E si plus n'i vai sercant,
>> es desleialada
>> e puta provada . . .

(A lady is unfaithful to her ami/in her love if she provides for three/[it is] outside the law/if there are three./As well as her husband I grant her/ one courteous lover of quality./But if she goes looking for more,/she is dishonoured/and a proven whore.) There has been a great deal of discussion of this text, but it seems to me clear and explicit. Marti grants the lady just one courtly lover. If she takes two, she has proved herself a whore. Thus she can give her love to two men: her husband and her courtly lover. And it should be noted that the text leads us to think that the lady does love her husband too, since she *apana* the courtly lover *with* her husband. It would be possible to cite more facts or texts which would equally well show that the idea that love is impossible between husband and wife was never put forward in the works of the troubadours. Even the famous words of the Countess de Die:

> Sapchatz, gran talan n'auria
> que.us tengues en luoc del marit,
> ab so que m'aguessetz plevit
> de far tot so qu'eu volria . . .

(Know that I would have great desire/to hold you in my husband's place/provided that you would undertake/to do all that I would desire.) Even these famous words by no means prove that the Countess de Die did not love her 'husband'. Her attitude is comparable with that of Na Castelloza. It should not be said that the feeling behind these words of the Countess de Die is too passionate [to permit such an interpretation]. Those of Na Castelloza are just as much so when she sings:

> Ric soi, ab que.us sovegna
> com pogues en loc venir
> on eu vos bais e.us estregna . . .

(I am overwhelmed provided you remember/how I could come to a place/where I could kiss and embrace you.)[19] Even if the song in which these lines appear is not by Na Castelloza, the attitudes of the two noblewomen-troubadours have points in common, in particular the fact of speaking of love for their *ami* without being disturbed by the idea of the husband, an idea which they certainly did not denigrate by loving elsewhere. Naturally we should not look at these matters with a kind of modern distortion and think that these noblewomen, in their love for someone other than *the* husband, were looking for 'delectatio coïtus'. This attitude (of not being disturbed) is what the Countess de Die means when she says to her lover that she is ready to take him in place of the husband 'provided that he undertakes to do all that she – not he – would desire', which is quite the opposite of the commonly accepted interpretation. We have to get away from the mentality of Jeanroy, whose judgement is clouded by such 'cries' as

> Ben volria mon cavallier
> tener un ser en mos bratz nut
> qu'el s'en tengra per ereubut
> sol qu'a lui fezes cosseillier . . .

and grasp the full quality of the passionate warmth combined with the chaste restraint, if I may so call it, of the last two lines.

Even if this way of looking at the lines of the Countess de Die is not accepted – a way of looking at them, incidentally, which does not in the least detract from their passionate quality – it nevertheless remains true that the Countess de Die makes no more claim than does Na Castelloza that the love which they sing has the corollary that they do not love their husbands. Quite the contrary. Their attitude, firmly based as it is in the milieu, seems to indicate the opposite. In any case, the fact that they were female troubadours in love with someone other than their husbands does not prove in any way that love was impossible between husband and wife. The only thing of which we can be sure, as Na Catelloza and Huguet de Mataplana expressly state, is that a wife to whom another man pays court or who pays court to another man is a real honour to her husband, a fact which naturally presupposes that husband and wife understand one another perfectly, as did Lord Barral and his wife, and that they definitely love one another or at least love one another to some degree.

We have found nothing in the texts which can properly be ascribed to the troubadours which would allow us to think that the statement attributed to the Countess of Champagne by Andreas Capellanus in the *De Amore*, that love is not possible between husband and wife, should be regarded as applicable to the ethic of *fin'amor*. On the contrary, there are indications which would give us reason to think that there could very well be bonds between man and wife different from those dictated only by contemporary views of marriage, bonds of affection, of good will, of shared sentiment, in sum, bonds very close to what could be called love. This is significant in as much as such an affirmation puts in its right place, a truly secondary and incidental place, the notion so often regarded as basic and of absolute validity, that troubadour love is adulterous. It is true that the sentiments mentioned can be attributed to *agape* rather than *eros*, but it is a fact that it has never been proved that troubadour love is proper to *eros* and not to *agape*, still less that it cannot be a mixture of *agape* and *eros*, as is frequently the case with real love, even in modern times.

We should not talk about *agape* or *eros*, since the troubadours do not talk about them either, but only of *fin'amor*. If we do not find in their writings any text which indicates that *fin'amor* is impossible between man and wife, any text, however minor, which stated explicitly that *fin'amor* can be so shared between man and wife would seem to possess a fundamental significance for the solution of the problem which interests us, a significance of much greater validity than the words of the Countess of Champagne, whether ascribed to her or actually spoken by her. Sound reasoning would give far more weight to an authentic Provençal troubadour than to the words of a Countess of Champagne, especially if their support comes from a northern French cleric, who in all probability reacted very badly to worldly love in the form in which it could be transplanted from the region of the *langue d'oc* to the northern courts.

Now, as it happens, such a text does exist, absolutely to the point, as well, no doubt, as others which are less precise but deserve nevertheless to be better known.

The text is the one containing the argument between Elias and his cousin which we propose to discuss in some detail. Here is the text:[20]

> Ara'm digatz vostre semblan,
> N-Elias, d'un fin amador
> C'ama ses cor galiador
> Et es amatz ses tot engan;
> De cal deu plus aver talan
> Segon dreita razon d'amor:
> Que de sidonz sia drutz o maritz,
> Qan s'esdeven qe il n'es datz lo chausitz?
>
> Cosin, cor ai de fin aman
> E non ges de fals trichador,
> Per q'ieu tenc a major honor
> Aver dompna bella e prezan
> Totz temps, que si l'avia un an;
> E pren marit dompnejador
> Que de sidonz sia totz jorns aizitz;
> C'autres dompneis ai mains vegutz partitz.
>
> La ren per c'om vai meilluran,
> N'Elias, tenc eu per meillor,
> E cella tenc per sordeior,
> Per c'om vai totz jorns sordeian;
> Per dompna vai bos pretz enan
> E per moiller pert hom valor,
> E per dompnei de dompna es hom grazitz
> E per dompnei de moiller escarnitz.
>
> Cosin, s'amassetz tan ni qan,
> Vos hi agratz dich gran follor;
> Que ren non cost'a fengedor,
> Si n'a un plazer e pois n'an;
> Per q'ieu vuoil remaner baisan
> Ab midonz, cui am et ador;
> Que per bon dreich n'iria pois faiditz,
> Si, qan mi vol, eu l'en era falhitz.

N'Elias, s'ieu midonz soan
Per moiler, no il fatz sesoner;
Qu'ieu non la lais mas par paor
E per honor qe il port tan gran,
Que s'ieu la pren e pois la blan,
Non puosc far faillimen major,
E s'ieu li sui vilas ni deschausitz,
Faill vas amor, e l dompneis es delitz.

Cosin, be m tengatz per truan;
S'ieu puosc aver ses gardador
E ses parier e ses seignor
Lieys que pus vuelh, s'alre deman;
Maritz a son joi ses affan
E l drutz l'a mesclat ab dolor;
Perq'ieu am mais, cals qu'en sia lo critz,
Esser maritz gauzens que drutz marritz.

A Na Margarita.m coman,
N'Elias, cum a la meillor,
Que jutge.l plait et eu sia aunitz
S'ieu plus non am midonz que sos maritz.

Cosin, ben sai q'ella val tan
Qu'il sap jutgar un plaich d'amor;
E car sos pretz es tant fis e chausitz,
Sai qu'il dira que vos hi etz faillitz.

I should like to offer the following translation:

[GUI:]   Or dites-moi donc votre avis,
               Seigneur Elias, d'un fin amant
               Qui aime d'un coeur simple et franc
               Et est aimé sans tromperie:
               De quoi doit avoir plus envie
               Selon d'amour droit sentiment:
               Etre amant ou bien ami de sa dame
               S'il lui est donné d'en avoir le choix?

[ELIAS:]   Cousin, coeur ai d'amant parfait
               Et non pas de mauvais tricheur:
               Je tiens donc pour plus grand honneur

D'avoir belle dame estimée
Toujours, que de l'avoir un an;
Je veux être mari galant
Qui pour sa dame est toujours préparé:
Autres amours j'en ai trop vu sombrer.

[GUI:]   Celle qui vous conduit à mieux,
Seigneur Elias, est la meilleure
Et je tiens pour inférieure
Celle qui avilit le preux;
Par Dame augmente votre prix
Mais par Epouse perd-on valeur,
Pour service de Dame on est loué
Pour service d'Epouse vilipendé.

[ELIAS:]   Cousin, si vous aimiez tant soit peu
Vous auriez dit là grande folie
Car rien ne coûte à qui feint,
Il prend son cadeau, puis s'en va;
Mais moi toujours veux caresser
Ma dame que j'aime et chéris;
A bon droit sinon je serais banni,
Si quand me veut, défaut je lui faisais.

[GUI:]   Seigneur Elias, si je refuse ma dame
Pour épouse, point ne lui fais affront:
Je ne la laisse que par crainte
Et pour respect si grand que je lui porte:
Si je la prend et puis la loue
Plus grande faute ne puis faire,
Mais si je lui suis vilain et grossier,
Je manque à l'amour, et périt son service.

[ELIAS:]   Cousin, tenez-moi pour bouffon,
Quand je puis avoir librement
Sans partage, sans souverain
Qui plus je veux, si ailleurs je prétends!
L'époux a son joi sans tourment,
Pour l'ami s'y mêle douleur:
Aussi je préfère, quoi qu'on en crie,
Etre mari heureux qu'ami marri.

[GUI:]   A dame Marguerite m'en remets
Seigneur Elias, qui est la meilleure:

Qu'elle prononce et que je sois déshonoré
Si je n'aime plus ma dame que son mari.

[ELIAS:] Cousin, bien sais qu'elle est capable
De juger un procès d'amour:
Elle est d'un discernement si parfait
Qu'elle dira que vous avez failli, je le sais.

There is a study of this discussion by Sebastian Neumeister in Chapter 3 of his book *Das Spiel mit der höfischen Liebe* with the title 'Höfische Liebe und christliche Ehe' and the subtitle 'Die dialektische Umkehrung im Partimen'. The aim which Neumeister is pursuing in this work is to show that in courtly society the *partimen* is essentially a courtly game ('Das höfische Spiel' is the second and last subtitle of the final chapter of the work), and in accordance with this aim, he concludes from his examination of the *partimen* under discussion that 'the problem of marriage and courtly love is never raised here; when marriage is discussed, it is only within the confines of courtly values'. Neumeister's attitude is the traditional one. At bottom, he is not really asking about the extent to which we can give credence to the ideas put forward by the two protagonists nor about their relative importance. That was not his intention in making a study of this *partimen*. A priori he is not interested in the fundamentals of what is said. What does interest him is merely the genre form and the function of this poem as a genre representative, as well as its place in a society traditionally called courtly. This can be observed, among other things, from the care he takes to raise the question of determining who should be regarded as having won the debate. And since his subject is 'a game of courtly love', it is natural that the winner is the one who defends traditional ideas accepted as being 'courtly' ideas. Neumeister actually writes: 'One might be tempted to grant a certain superiority to the cousin, in the sense that he puts forward arguments of a more fundamental nature ('Argumente mehr grundsätzlicher Natur'), especially in strophe 3, whereas Elias claims for marriage principally such material advantages as security, tranquillity and permanence, merely adding the ethical quality of fidelity rather than giving it priority.'[21]

I am perfectly prepared to recognize the systematic character of the debate in the *partimen*; our troubadours observe the rules of the genre very well. But to go on from there and say that the basic subject of the debate is of little or no importance is a step which I personally cannot take. If I did, I would be doing something which certain people do not hesitate to do. We all admit the undeniable, very great, and from a certain point of view even primary importance of form and genre in the poetry of the troubadours. This is not the place to examine it and the criticism of the last few decades has certainly given it plenty of exposure. But the people I refer to go so far as to maintain that what the troubadours sang *about* is basically of no importance because they all say the same thing. To reason like this is to deny the poet any personality whatsoever, other than one dependent on form. Thus the love-song (*canson*), for example, would always be the same thing, and we would have to reach the conclusion that Bernart de Ventadorn is no different from Folquet de Marseille. It needs only a little acquaintance with the troubadours to become aware that, even if form is of primary importance for them, this by no means deprives any of them of his originality and personality in ideas as well as in sentiments, always provided, naturally, that we are dealing with an individual who possesses originality and personality and not with some epigonos or repetitive imitator of words and sounds.

So we shall take the liberty of reading the *partimen* between Gui and Elias d'Ussel by eliminating at the very start any such prejudiced point of view as giving preference to whichever of the two poets best defends what are conventionally called 'courtly' ideas, such as, for example, those of a Countess of Champagne. Another prejudice would be to think that the subject of the debate has absolutely nothing to do with reality, simply because we are dealing with a *partimen*, a genre with very clearly set rules and a genre which, as Sebastian Neumeister has very well shown, is part of a certain 'courtly game', in the sense that the genre was highly appreciated in society at courts. Here it must be remembered that the epithet 'courtly' is imprecise in the extreme. It means not only 'what pertains to the court', 'what is characteristic of the court', and, by extension, 'what is opposite to the peasant', but also – and this unfortunately, is the sense in which it is most frequently understood nowadays – 'what is proper to a certain concept of rather remarkable feelings of love', a concept which a certain man named Cervantes mocked with nobility and genius. The fact that the *partimen* is part of some courtly game or other because it was fashionable at courts, by no means indicates that the authors of the *partimen* all had to have the same 'courtly' views or that each of them could not have a view of his own, or – and this would be fatal in a genre where the rule was to take the opposing line whatever the right line might be – that the points of view defended by one or the other troubadour were merely interchangeable courtly devices.

Besides this there is the well known distinction which has rightly been established between the *partimen* and the *tenso*. Neumeister calls the work we are discussing a *partimen* ('Die dialektische Umkehrung in Parti-men'). In fact, however, we are dealing with a true *tenso* in which each of the two protagonists is defending a personal point of view. In the poem the position of each of the interlocutors is actually as individualized as, for example, are the positions of the King of Aragon and of Giraut de Bornelh in the well known *tenso*, 'Be me plairia, senh' En reis'. The subject of the debate between the King and Giraut is certainly not of concern to them alone, and the problem of knowing whether *fin'amor* was possible between great lords and any particular lady was treated by, among others, Guilhem de St Leidier, Raimbaut d'Orange and Azalais de Porcairgues. Marcabru had given a negative answer for a very personal reason: the competition of already established men prevented marginal men like himself from making a place for themselves in society. What happened to Marcabru was that he never loved and never was loved ('que anc non amet neguna/ni d'autra no fo amatz'). The King of Aragon naturally took the opposite position and used arguments which are based squarely on personal qualities and not on the social position of the individual. This is an eminently original position when opposed to that of Giraut de Bornelh, which is based on the usual '*on-dit*' of the routine troubadours when discussing noblemen.

Elias's position is just as original. Like the King of Aragon, he is defending from his own side an opinion based on his own case in opposition to his cousin's attitude, which represents the commonly accepted position, since he is a lord who is 'molherat', whereas his cousin has embraced the clerical state and has remained single. The *tenso* 'Ara.m digatz vostre semblan' is not a simple *partimen*, where either one of the protagonists defends a given position, but a true *tenso*, where each defends a point of view peculiar to himself, not by arbitrary choice but as a result of the actual circumstances of their lives. It is this that we observe in a sensible reading of the poem, and it is only this kind of directed reading which can make us grasp the importance of *what* is said, which is not something put there to make a flashy point in the debate but which in all seriousness raises a problem directly affecting the two men con-cerned. By the facts of the case the problem in question is not the result of an artificial choice and the reply given by each of the persons concerned will be conditioned by his own case. Each of the replies will have as much *true validity* as the other and especially the one which will argue in favour of *fin'amor* between married couples, if such is the case. Let us therefore look at the features of this *tenso* which are most expressive.

It is Gui, the cleric, who proposes the debate in strophe I, and this is in conformity with his status as an intellectual. It is important to observe that the question is not put as simply as might be supposed from the way it is formulated by Sebastian Neumeister, for example: 'Soll ein höfischer Liebhaber es vorziehen, der Geliebte oder der Ehemann seiner Dame zu sein?' If I use Audiau's terminology, this becomes: 'Should a faithful lover prefer to be the lover or husband of his lady?' Neither the German nor the French text offers a proper translation of 'fin amador'. We are not concerned with some *Liebhaber* or other, nor with an *amant*, even a faithful one, but with a '*fin amador*', that is, with a man who claims to practice *fin'amor*. The matter is important in its consequences, for we are dealing not only with a love which could be the natural love of a husband but rather – and very precisely – with *fin'amor*. The problem is set out clearly and without ambiguity, since the ordinary translations do no more than ask if a man in love should prefer to be the *ami* or the husband of his lady. The question would be pointless if we were discussing a feeling which was commonplace and which applied only to the man's attitude to the lady. So far as Gui is concerned, it is really a question of the *fin amant*, who not only loves with total honesty, but who is himself loved just as much in all truth. Thus we are concerned with true *fin'amor* combined with 'volontat engan', to use the words of Bernart de Ventadorn. It should also be noted that Gui's question posits the possibility that the *fin amador* may be at one and the same time the *drutz* and the *marit* of the lady. This obviously presupposes that *fin amador* and *drutz* are no more to be confounded than are *marit* and *fin amador*. It can be seen in this way how inexact are the translations which render both *fin amador* and *drutz* by the word *amant*. I would remind the reader[22] that the exact sense of *drut* is 'close friend' (Boethius, in the Occitanian *Boeci*, is the *drut* of Jesus) and it does not imply any particularly erotic idea in the modern sense of the term. From the very moment the problem is posed, therefore, it is implied that the *marit* as well as the *drut* (a young squire, for example, a cleric in a lady's service, a troubadour, professional or not etc) can be the *fin amador* of the lady. And this, from the beginning of the *tenso*, is enough to convince us that *fin'amor* can exist between husband and wife and that the *fin'amor* of the troubadours is not essentially adulterous.

The way in which the poem develops can serve only to reinforce this opinion, since it clearly moves forward from this initial point of departure. In the second strophe, Elias immediately protests that he does indeed possess the heart of a *fin aman*. He then adds – and this is an indirect attack on his cousin Gui's way of doing things – that there is nothing about him of the *fals trichador*, that is, of the behaviour of those troubadours, certainly the most numerous, whose show of activity in *fin'amor* is nothing more than deceit whose object is to win the favour, expressed in material benefits, of a lady they 'love' for a period of time. That is why he, Elias, prefers to have 'dompna bella e prezan/totz temps, que si l'avia un an.' This is definitely the expression of Elias's utterly personal attitude, of a troubadour belonging to the social class of nobles when faced by troubadours looking to improve themselves, or professional troubadours like Gui, who had given up their noble status to become clerics. Another significant expression in this strophe is 'aver dompna bella e prezan'. It is obvious that not all married noblemen were lucky enough to have a wife who was 'bella e prezan'. In view of the utilitarian attitude towards marriage in those days, such qualities were of quite secondary importance in a wife. If a wife was rich and had a good dowry, it was of little significance if she was ugly and bad-tempered. Elias is not speaking in the name of *all* husbands to maintain that it is better to be the husband than the simple *drut* of the person one loves. It could not be made more clear that he is speaking on behalf of an ideal couple, of himself (a husband), a *fin aman* without calculation or subterfuge, of a wife who is 'bella e prezan'. There can be no doubt that if the poem is read with any regard to its circumstances, this theoretical couple, this couple with true *joy d'amor* is at the same time the couple which Elias and his wife are capable of becoming. It is because his wife is 'dompna bella e prezan' that Elias chooses to be a 'marit dompnejador'. He has no fear whatever of making word combinations which are the absolute negation of the declaration attributed to the Countess of Champagne and which, as he well knows, since he is Gui's cousin, express the opposite of what unmarried troubadours go about repeating, from various motives, as well as any troubadours who might be unhappily married. It is in the name of the happiness he knows with his 'bella e prezan' wife that he chooses the role he has already made his own of being 'de sidonz totz jorns aizitz'. For he knows how unreliable are the kind of 'services to ladies' practised, for example, by troubadours of the type 'fals trichadors c'autres dompneis ai mains vegutz partitz'.

The words of Elias reflect a real state of happiness which is truly personal and is no less that of a *dompnejador* for being that of a *marit*, because he is truly following *fin'amor*. Gui replies with the arguments which are commonly put forward by the majority of troubadours. The last four lines of strophe 3 are commonplaces widely disseminated by the generality of troubadours. In these last four lines a tone can be felt with all the marks of the schools. The statement is generalized as it would be in precepts. The repeated antithesis drives it home with ponderous insistence: 'per dompna ... e per moiller ... e per dompnei de dompna ... e per dompnei de moiller'. Gui offers no argument. A magisterial statement is enough. Otherwise these four sententious lines do no more than clarify and generalize the first four, where the reason for the distrust of the *dompnei de moiller* is given, namely the lack of *melhurament* in such a case. It is obvious that 'la ren per c'om vai meilluran' is the *dompna* and that the woman on whose account a man always goes *sordejan* is the *moiller*. Gui's reasoning conforms to the sentiments of the troubadours who acquired property and reputation by celebrating a *dompna*. This is precisely the situation with Gui, that he 'si entendet lonc temps en madona Margarida d'Albusson e en la contessa de Montferran'. Gui certainly improved his status as clerk and professional intellectual in serving these noble ladies. It should be noted at this point that the term which is usually used as the antonym of *melhurar* is *mermar* (*minimare*) and that it is not *mermar* that Gui uses here but *sordejar*, which, by comparison with *mermar* (diminish, lessen, reduce, lower) has a further moral connotation (worsen, cheapen, corrupt). Gui, a lover by profession, a celibate cleric, shows perhaps a little of the scorn with which some people regarded marriage when defined as a 'legal brothel'. Here, as elsewhere, Gui does not present any argument. It is probably true that the husband who practises *dompnei de moiller* gains nothing more, does not *melhura* by loving his *bella e prezan* wife as a *dompnejador*, with *fin'amor*, since he already possesses the lady by his marriage. But how can this husband become worse (*sordejar*) if his wife is precisely that, *bella e prezan*, and not, as Gui purports to say of the wife of the husband, *sordejor* (worse). One simply must recognize that Gui's arguments are weak, even misleading and valueless. They may, in fact, be summed up in the statement of opinion current among the troubadours who saw in love a means of improving their social status.

In strophe 4, Elias appears to reply to his cousin tit for tat. Gui had made use of the sentiment which is the basis of the general and commonplace attitude of the majority of troubadours who, in the tradition of Marcabru, thought that *molherats* ought to be excluded from *joi d'amor* and from *fin'amor*. The love of *molherats* is for them *fals amor*, which can only *pejorar*. It seems right that Elias replies by an argument of the same kind, set in commonplaces which were current in the broad circles in which the troubadours moved and among the troubadours themselves, namely, that these troubadour love-songs are actually only literary fictions, only *feintes*, and that in consequence it costs the composer of the fiction: 'que ren non cost'a fengedor'. This is the reason why we should attribute such importance to the first line of the strophe, which is important just by its position, 'cosin, s'amassetz tan no qan' (cousin, if you were to love, however little). We are dealing with a kind of argument *ad hominem.* When the two of them were alone the celibate cousin, probably already a monk, an itinerant troubadour because, as a younger son, he was not the master of the castle of Ussel, could not seriously maintain to his cousin Elias that he was really in love with the great ladies whom he celebrated as he travelled. As a result, Elias takes *fin'amor* to the region of truth outside the usual conventions. Elias himself, a lord, probably poor but master in his castle, is married and really does love his wife.

Levy gives two meanings for *fengedor,* hypocrite and timid lover, when used as a noun. It is obvious that we have the first sense here, according to the context, 'ren non cost'a fengedor'. But, in addition, the term *fengedor* does indeed designate the lover, but by no means necessarily the bashful lover. It is quite natural that *fengedor* should have been used among the troubadours most frequently in the sense 'lover', precisely because the troubadour lover was putting on an act when he sang of love. In any case it is clear that Elias is here mixing together the two notions of 'lover' and 'pretender', one who acts out the fiction of love (Levy actually gives 'fiction', 'invention', as the primary sense of *fenhemen,* with 'work', probably the *canso* as work, as its second sense and 'pretence', 'dissimulation', as the third). Thus Elias undoubtedly regards the troubadour lover as a *fengedor.* And for this pretender everything in his song is good: 'ren li costa!'. The best proof that this lover is not sincere is that 'si n'a un plazer e pois n'an' from his lady. There is no need to take 'plazer' in the sense of 'sensual enjoyment'. These are the meanings given by Levy: 1. pleasure (in a very general sense); 2. something pleasant (another general sense); 3. act of kindness, service (cf. the expression 'do a kindness', 'be kind enough to help me') and in Old Provençal, *se metre al plaser d'alcun*); 4. gift. If one bears in mind the position of ordinary troubadours, it is this last sense which should be kept and it is more common than is usually supposed. The lady's gift consisted in giving pleasure to the troubadour, who was a *fengedor* of love, by allowing him to stay near her, at her husband's court, where he will obtain food and lodging and the honour of being part of the lord's household.

But this *plazer* does not last all one's life. The troubadours usually 'departed' from one castle to another, so as to be able to enjoy the *plazers* of their ladies. Elias contrasts the situation he is defending, that of the husband, which he is himself probably, with that of the *fengedor.* He actually speaks in the first person: 'I would like to stay with my lady, kissing her' ('ieu vuoil romaner baisan/'ab mi dons'), and he does not just love this lady 'tan ni qan' but loves her absolutely and adores her, 'cui am et ador'. The last line of the strophe 'si qan mi vol eu l'en era falhitz' picks up the penultimate line of the second strophe, 'que de si donz sia totz jorns aisitz', and these two lines define the condition of the permanent availability of the husband in contrast to the troubadour, a migratory bird going from one lady to another. Beside this, these two lines emphasize what happens in the case of a *fengedor* troubadour who, by force of circumstances, is not at his lady's beck and call every moment: he finds himself inevitably and rightly 'banni', one day or other, from the presence of the lady whom he is celebrating. All of which emphasizes, incidentally, the precarious nature of the position of the troubadour, which may be observed virtually always in the lives of the poets that Elias calls *fengedors*, who invent their love.

In strophe 5, Gui proceeds to reply to Elias's direct arguments, which are based on reality, by arguments whose essential foundation consists of the conventions which we are in the habit of calling 'courtly' and which govern love between noble ladies and troubadours of the common sort, or those of lower condition who form Köhler's 'fringe group', or again those who can be closely associated with this group, such as monks or canons, men who, for various reasons, were not married. The first two lines of the strophe certainly have no connection with actuality, since Gui 'si era canorgues de Briuda e de Monferran', as the Vida tells us; and Boutière and Schutz make it clear, as we ourselves think, that 'Gui, who was doubtless the younger brother, appears to have renounced his seignural rights in exchange for these benefices.'[23] When Gui speaks of 'midonz', we may refer to the biography which says: 'si era canorgues de Briuda e de Monferran e si entendet longa saison en Na Malgarita d'Albuison et en la comtessa de Monferran dont fetz maintas bonas cansos', and to Boutière and Schutz, who tell us that Marguerite d'Aubusson was the wife of Viscount Rainaut VI (1204–45), and the Countess of Montferrand the wife of Robert I, Dauphin of Auvergne, who was Count of Clermont and of Montferrand from 1168 to 1234. It is perfectly easy to reach the conclusion that the two ladies celebrated by Gui were two noblewomen of the area, two wives of rulers, one of them close by, the other from the very district where Gui lived as an ecclesiastical vassal of Robert I, Dauphin of Auvergne. It is quite clear from this that Gui's love songs to these ladies, who were both *midonz* of Gui, were nothing more than court songs, a fact which puts the first two lines of the strophe in their right place. The lady who rejects Gui as a husband could never have existed except in the imagination of a *fengedor*. It certainly could never have occurred to Gui, a canon, that he could have refused ('soanar') as a wife the lady he celebrated. He never thought of the possibility of such a marriage – and consequently never of any refusal to marry.

All the rest of the strophe develops this non-reality quite logically according to the actual conditions of sham courtliness. The following lines, 'Qu'ieu non la lais mas per paor/e per honor qe.il port tan gran', (I leave her only because of fear and because of the enormous respect I have for her), use a poetic of pretence to move into the domaine of morality, an impediment which is all too obviously practical and which prevents a troubadour of the ordinary kind from marrying the noblewoman whom he is celebrating. In the last four lines of this strophe, Gui sets out clearly the two principal arguments which make it impossible for the lover to marry his lady. If he takes the lady to wife and then boasts of her qualities, he is committing the greatest possible error ('que s'ieu la pren et pois la blan/non puosc far faillimen major'), for it is unbecoming to praise what one possesses, in the name of the humility which every lover should oppose to pride, the pride which would consist in preening oneself to the detriment of the discretion due to the lady. (For by marriage a man did legally possess his wife and his wife's good brought as a dowry, her honour.) Praise of the lady is normally and necessarily the praise of an inaccessible object from whom one begs for grace. To praise one's own goods, to boast about them, to flaunt them, is to behave in singularly vulgar fashion. But if the lover cannot celebrate his lady's virtues, his conduct towards her will, from then on, be base and coarse ('e s'ieu li sui vilas ni deschausitz'), in so far as it is clear that there is no more love-service: 'dompneis es delitz'. That is what will happen if the lover marries his lady: since he cannot praise her because she is his property, he is inevitably failing in his duty to love. Gui's reasoning is logical and perfectly in conformity with the accepted and repeated premises of the rules of court-troubadour love for a lady of the court. But all this is quite clearly artificial.

In strophe 6, Elias replies once more to the scholastic arguments of his cousin by sharply criticizing conventional troubadour love. 'Cosin, be.m tengatz per truan/s'ieu puosc aver ses gardador e ses parier e ses seignor/lieys que pus vuelh, s'alre deman.' The view that one should go looking elsewhere for something one already has without restriction, that is, the view recommended by Gui, is regarded by Elias as the attitude of a *bouffon*.[24] 'Be.m tengatz per truan' – regard me really as a man of little substance, a trifler, a buffoon. The word *truan* is supposed to apply to Gui personally, since Elias identifies the attitude of a troubadour going about celebrating one lady after another to that of a *truan* (*trutanus*). He himself would be no better than one of these buffoons if he desired anything other than the lady he has close to him and whom he can love 'without anyone watching him, with no rival and no overlord.'[25] These are the three obstacles which are the lot of the routine troubadour celebrating his lady: the spectators at court, rival troubadours, and an overlord who must be reckoned with one way or another. For a husband who loves and is loved they have no importance except when, as it says in the first strophe, it is as a 'fin amador, ses cor galiador' and 'ses tot engan'. This fact must be borne in mind if we are to understand Elias's words properly. For a husband who really loves and is loved, it is worthwhile to love and to be loved in the intimate relationship of marriage, far from the curiosity of the court; to love and to be loved without worrying about another possible suitor who has the same rights as oneself; in short, to be one's own master with the lady 'whom one most desires'. Under such conditions, which are those of the husband who is lover and beloved, it really would be buffoonery to pretend to love elsewhere on the pretext that it is more worthwhile to be the *ami* of one's lady than her husband, in accordance with the precepts of courtly love defended by Gui.

'Maritz a son joi ses afan/e.l drutz l'a mesclat ab dolor.' The husband has his 'joi ses afan', that is to say, literally without annoying labour, with no trouble. The sense of 'afan' tells us that it is here the same as *dolor*. We are not concerned with love-pain in the feelings, but, if it may be put that way, with practical pain. It is the pain which the courtier-troubadour encounters, since he has to bow to all sorts of restrictive and formal demands when he pays court to the lady ('gardador'–'parier'–'seignor' especially). In the last two lines of this strophe Elias finishes by setting fashionable opinion ('cals qu'en sia lo critz') against solid common sense, emphasized by the wordplay 'maritz gauzens'/'drutz marritz'.

In the four lines which constitute Gui's conclusion, he decides to refer back to the judgement of Na Margarida, Marguerite d'Abusson. Gui was no doubt celebrating this lady at her court at the very time that the *tenson* was composed. While living in his cousin's castle, he takes her as the proof of his point of view. If this is, in fact, the case (and it probably is), what Gui says, '. . . et eu sia aunitz/s'ieu plus non am midonz que sos maritz' (and that I may be dishonoured/if I do not love my lady more than her husband does) might seem rather misplaced if we think of how the husband might regard such a statement which basically denies his love for his wife. But it is clear that Gui does not dream for one moment of such a situation. The situation he is speaking of is one far outside the reality of the kind of feeling that Elias is defending. Gui's theoretical position could hardly be more obvious. Elias contents himself by merely responding that he is certain that the good sense of Na Margarida will say that Gui is 'faillitz'.

Once the *tenson* of Elias d'Ussel and his cousin Gui, 'Ara.m digatz vostre semblan', has been put back in its context, its importance can be ascertained. The context is double. First there is the particular context of this poem, the fact that there is a discussion between two troubadours of different types. One, Elias, belongs to the class of troubadours whose profession certainly was not singing and who composed simply because they loved poetry and art, 'for fame'. This is the category of Guillaume IX, of the King of Aragon, of great and minor noblemen, some of whom, like Raimbaut d'Orange, Bertran de Born, and Ghuilhem de Berguedan, for example, are among the most famous poets, and all of whom are characterized by a strong personality. The other, Gui, falls into the category of troubadours for whom singing was a profession, a profession which was, for them, more or less a necessity of life. A distinction should be made between those troubadours who belonged to the social class defined by E. Köhler as 'marginal men' and those who, by their literary vocation, were joined to them in a broader class, corresponding roughly to what we call the intelligentsia. It does seem as though the types in this second category, which could range from *jongleur* or younger brother with no position to rich merchant, or a canon with a settled position, are characterized by a certain uniformity of ideas if not of talents. The ideas are those which start with the *joi d'amor* already celebrated by Guilhem IX, and which were gradually elaborated in an atmosphere of courtiers which has been termed 'courtly'. The troubadours of the first category are distinguished by a great freedom of argument, by a generosity of mind and consequently by a more personal originality of inspiration. This is the case when Elias faces Gui, a lord facing a canon, spontaneity facing scholasticism. This is a distinction of great significance: it allows us to perceive the free thought of the troubadours behind the rigidities of troubadour form. What the troubadours of the former category thought and believed in will be of the utmost significance in finding out what the ideas of the troubadours actually were in face of troubadour conventions. Elias's opinion is thus of primary significance in this regard.

It is of primary significance, too, within the framework of the second context, which is that of our *tenson*: the problem of the possibility or impossibility of love between man and wife. We have seen how this context was presented on a scale broad enough for us to sum up by saying: 1. that there is no place where the troubadours tell us that married couples cannot love one another with *fin'amor*; 2. that we have plenty of examples among the troubadours of love and even *fin'amor* between man and wife; 3. that the only authority in favour of the impossibility of love between man and wife is an alleged quotation of the 'Countess of Champagne', reported by a monk of northern France who understood the civilization of the south – more or less. It thus becomes clear that it is on the basis of this quotation that it is stated as an obvious truth that troubadour love was essentially and in an absolute sense adulterous. Thus it is a whole article of faith which collapses when the text of our *tenson* is set in this context. If a text exists, and one does exist here, which declares explicitly from the actual lips of a troubadour that a *fin amador* can love his wife as his *domna*, it can no longer be claimed that troubadour love is essentially and without exception adulterous. It will be necessary to look elsewhere than in innate necessity and in an essential determinant which belongs to *fin'amor* for the, in practice, mostly adulterous love celebrated by our poets.

This is why, we think, the *tenson*, 'Ara.m digatz vostre semblan' of the two d'Ussel troubadours is one of the most important texts in Old Provençal poetry, a text, furthermore, which is infinitely more reliable than the Latin text of a non-Occitanian monk. It is very hard to understand why so much attention has been paid to Andreas Capellanus while none has been paid to Elias d'Ussel. Perhaps it is because some 'generally accepted ideas' have a long and tough existence!

NOTES

1. Jean Audiau, *Les Poésies des quatre troubadours d'Ussel publiées d'après les manuscrits* (Paris, 1922; rpt Geneva 1973).
2. Martin de Riquer, *Los Trovadores. Historia literaria y textos* (Barcelona, 1975), 2, 1009.
3. See in particular 'Observations historiques et sociologiques sur la poésie des troubadours', *Cahiers de civilisation médiévale*, 7 (1964), 27–51, and 'Sens et fonction du terme "jeunesse" dans la poésie des troubadours' in *Mélanges offerts à René Crozet* (Poitiers, 1966).
4. M. de Riquer, *op. cit.*
5. For Gaucelm Faidit see Audiau, p. 14, and the edition of Jean Mouzat, *Les Poèmes de Gaucelm Faidit* (Paris, 1965). The life of Gaucelm Faidit is on pp. 27–41.
6. Cf. Mouzat, pp. 478–82.
7. For a general survey of this question of adulterous love in the troubadours, see Charles Camproux, *Le Joy d'Amour des troubadours: jeu et joie d'amour* (Montpellier, 1965), Ch. viii, p. 135 ('L'amour adultère').
8. See John F. Benton, 'Clio and Venus: an Historical View of Medieval Love', in F. X. Newman, ed., *The Meaning of Courtly Love* (Albany, 1968), pp. 19–43. See also the review of this work in *RLR*, 79 (1970).
9. Cf. A. H. Schutz, *Poésies de Daude de Prades* (Toulouse, Paris, 1933; rpt New York and London, 1971), p. 68.
10. André le Chapelain, *Traité de l'Amour Courtois*, introduction and notes by Claude Buridant (Paris, 1974), p. 24.

11. On the subject of the credibility of Andreas Capellanus' treatise as reflecting the ideas of the troubadours, see my review of Claude Buridant's book in *RLR*, 81 (1975), 167–82.

12. Andreas Capellanus, ed. Buridant, pp. 111–12. The Latin text runs as follows: 'Dicimus enim et stabilitato tenore firmamus non posse suas inter duos jugales extendere vires. Nam amantes sibi invicem gratis omnia largiuntur nullius necessitatis ratione cogente. Jugales vero mutuis tenentur ex debito voluntatibus obedire et in nullo se ipsos sibi invicem denegare.'

13. F. Schürr, *Das altfranzösische Epos; zur Stilgeschichte und inneren Form der Gotik*.

14. Cf. Manselli, *Spirituali e beghini in Provenza* (Rome, 1959).

15. Cf. Richard Wilder Emery, *Heresy and Inquisition in Narbonne* (New York, 1941).

16. Cf. Andreas Capellanus, ed. Buridant, note 76.

17. Cf. William D. Paden, Jr, 'The Troubadour's Lady: her Marital Status and Social Rank', *SP*, 72 (1975), 28–50.

18. Text and translation are taken from R. Lavaud, *Les Troubadours Cantaliens* (Aurillac, 1910), p. 515.

19. Ibid., p. 520. A. Jeanroy, *La Poésie lyrique des troubadours*, 2 vols (Paris, 1934), I, 356, contests the attribution of the song 'Per joi que d'amor m'avegna' to Na Castelloza, a fact which deprives them of none of their meaning.

20. According to Audiau, *Les Poésies des quatre troubadours d'Ussel*, Poem 14.

21. Sebastian Neumeister, *Das Spiel mit der höfischen Liebe* (Munich, 1969).

22. Cf., for example, the revue of Glynnis M. Cropp, *Le Vocabulaire courtois des troubadours de l'époque classique* in *Revue des Langues Romanes*, 81 (1975), 581f.

23. J. Boutière and A. H. Schutz, *Les Biographies des Troubadours*, new ed. (Paris, 1964), p. 204.

24. In his *Petit Dictionnaire Provençal-Français*, Levy gives: *truan*: s.m *truand*; adj. vil, *fripon*. It seems clear that these meanings are due to the influence of the French *truand*. In his *Provenzalisches Supplement-Wörterbuch*, Levy gives:

1. *Landstreicher* (vagabond), with a quotation from Guillem Augier;

2. *Vagant* (wandering scholar), with a quotation from Bernart de Ventadorn and adds the comment: 'See the note to this line which points out the equivalence of meaning of the Latin *trutannos* with 'alios vagos scholares aut goliardos';

3. 'die *Trossleute* usw welche ein Heer begleiten' (the camp-followers etc who accompany an army), with a quotation from *La Chanson de la Croisade contre les Albigeois*;

4. *Betrüger* (cheats), with a quotation from Lanfranc Cigala and from *Flamenca*, 2.6.

As an adjective: *betrügerisch* (cheating) and *lügnerisch* (lying). Finally he notes the sense *fripon*, 'von den Augen der Geliebten'.

He next quotes from Ducange the definition of *trutanus*: 'hace appellatione donantur vulgo ignavi illi qui per provincias passim vagantur et mendaciis ac strophis suis omnibus illudunt, dum alios se fingunt quam re vera sint, unde passim vox haec usurpatur pro mendaciorum conflictoribus'.

In his lexicon of rhymes, Uc Faidit gives th̶e̶ ̶w̶o̶r̶d̶ ̶t̶r̶u̶a̶n̶s̶ ̶a̶n̶d̶ ̶d̶o̶e̶s̶ ̶i̶n̶d̶e̶e̶d̶ derive it from *trutanus*. (Cf. *The Donatz Proensals of Uc Faidit*, ed. J. H. Marshall, Oxford, 1969.) In his glossary, Marshall says, in agreement with Uc Faidit and Ducange: *truans* – 'vagrant'. It seems, however, that the central seme of the word *truan*, which can be present in any of the words proposed as a translation of it, is 'a man who talks rubbish', and in that case the translation I have adopted, *bouffon*, appears to me to be acceptable. Furthermore, the sense that has been preserved in modern Occitanian is precisely 'bouffon', 'farceur'. (See Louis Alibert, *Dictionnaire Occitan-Français*.)

It so happens that it is this sense which seems to be exactly right in this passage.

25. 'Gardador parier seignor'. I understand *gardador* here not in the sense of 'guardian', 'watchman', which is right only when a jealous husband is involved, but in the sense which is normal on other occasions (see Levy), 'a person who looks on, a spectator'. Elias is talking to Gui and Gui has not been in love with ladies whose husbands were some kind of Archambaut. Gui's situation was the same as that of most troubadours at courts, who exercised their talents as lovers under the gaze of all the courtier-spectators. *Perier* means literally 'co-owner, equal, like, participant'. The term designates any rival troubadour who could also try his luck at a lady's court, and it likely that Gui was not the only one at the court of the lady d'Aubusson or at that of the Countess of Montferrant. *Seignor* designates the lord, the husband of the lady who is being celebrated.

4 The Partimen *between Folquet de Marseille and Tostemps*

GLYNNIS M. CROPP

This essay is an attempt to study the *partimen* of Folquet de Marseille and Tostemps as an example of its genre and to situate the poem and genre within Old Provençal lyric poetry. The manuscripts, the poets, the genre and the versification are therefore all described as a preamble to the analysis of the poem itself. The argument of the whole poem is surveyed and then the poem is studied in parts, so that it is possible to draw some conclusions about language, style and ideas. Finally, parallels for some of the main themes are sought in the work of Raimon de Miraval and Folquet de Marseille.

The poem is found in two manuscripts, the *chansonniers R* – Paris, Bibl. nat., fr. 22543, f. 75 col. b – 75v° col. a, known as the La Vallière *chansonnier* because it formerly belonged to the duc de La Vallière (1708–80) – and a¹ – Modena, Bibl. Estense universitario, Campori γ.N.8.4., ff. 578–9, which is really the second part of a copy made in 1589 by Jacques Tessier of Tarascon of the Bernart Amoros *chansonnier* which has since been lost.[1] The first of these two *chansonniers* is a fourteenth-century parchment manuscript, 148 folios measuring 430 by 300 millimetres and copied in Languedoc. It opens with twenty-seven biographies of troubadours (*vidas*), followed by some 1,090 odd *cansos* and *coblas*, grouped according to individual troubadours (Marcabru, Peire d'Auvergne, Raimbaut d'Orange and so on), and then a selection headed *tensos*, and finally other isolated pieces of prose and verse. The *tensos*, poems of debate between two or, occasionally, more troubadours and the work of two different poets, form a separate class. Although the *chansonnier R* includes the music of a number of poems, the music of the Folquet de Marseille-Tostemps *partimen* was not transcribed – the four lines were ruled in red in preparation. A decorated initial T marks the beginning of the poem – a blue letter on a red background with a few worn traces of gilt. It is this manuscript which S. Stroński used as the base for his edition of the text[2] and which has been reproduced here, with only a few slight changes in spelling to make the text more faithful to the manuscript.

Folquet de Marseille was the son of a wealthy Genoese merchant and himself a wealthy, respected merchant, married, with two sons, and living in Marseille at least after 1178. Worldly success and material wealth did not content Folquet: some of his lyrics, which must have been written between about 1185 and 1195, reveal his longing for a deeper spiritual happiness which lay beyond the limits of striving for courtly love.[3] About 1200, together with his wife and sons, he entered the Cistercian abbey of Le Thoronet, of which he became abbot before being made Bishop of Toulouse in 1206, in the middle of the Albigensian crisis. Here he worked in close association with his friend Saint Dominic to found the Order of Preachers; he was a leader in the Crusade, supporting Simon de Montfort in the fight to eradicate heresy in the south of France, and accomplished three diplomatic missions in the north on behalf of the Crusade. During one of these missions, he met, at Liège, Marie d'Oignies (d. 1213), a mystic and saint, leader of the strong feminine spiritual movement of the Béguines, which must have seemed to Folquet like an antidote to the religion of the Catharists and a useful example for his preaching against heresy.[4]

More is known about Folquet de Marseille than about many troubadours, just because he was a public figure: a wealthy citizen involved in trade in an important Mediterranean port, when Raimon Barral was Viscount of Marseilles, and then Bishop of Toulouse opposing the excommunicated Count Raimon VI of Toulouse – distinguished therefore, in turn, in the secular and religious life of his time. Like Guillaume IX of Poitiers, he was not a professional poet, as were Cercamon and Peire Vidal, for example, but a troubadour who wrote poetry in his leisure, exchanging thoughts and ideas with fellow poets and nobles as though the lyric, carried by a jongleur in his services,[5] replaced a conversation or letter, in a society where subtle thoughts on love and compliments were as much a part of the social life as feasts and present-giving. Folquet, by right of his education, intelligence and wealth, participated in an aristocratic pastime.

His opponent in the *partimen* is called Tostemps. This *senhal* is one of three in Folquet de Marseille's poetry, all applying to fellow poets: of the others, *Aziman*, 'Magnet', is Bertran de Born, *Plus-leial*, 'More-loyal' is Pons de Capdueil, who are described in the *Vidas* as 'castellans' and 'gentils bars' respectively.[6] Except in the *partimen*, Folquet uses the *senhals* preceded by the honorific particle *N'*, *En* (derived from Lat. *dominus*), thus expressing deference to these noble seigneurs who, however, use the same *senhals* preceded by *Mon*, thus assuming closer familiarity. The order in which the *senhals* are placed is fixed: *N'Aziman*, followed by *En Tostemps*[7] and in one poem (XI) *En Plus-Leial* is mentioned in third place. *Tornadas* addressed to fellow poets serve as a kind of signature and situate the poems in a particular milieu or *cénacle*. Provençal poetry was not originally composed for as large a public as we might at first imagine when we consider the wide area which made up the region of the troubadours in the twelfth and thirteenth centuries. It depended upon the animated social life of a few related courts or of just one court with which a troubadour was associated, for its public and sponsorship, for some of its allusions and their meaning. Poets knew one another, rivalled one another in composing verses and debated interpretations of love and the art of poetry.

Who then was Tostemps? We do not know for sure, but the only known contender is Raimon de Miraval, who was born c. 1160–65, was writing poetry until 1213, and whose great friend and patron was Raimon VI, Count of Toulouse. Raimon de Miraval was reputedly a poor seigneur, but his wife, Gaudaierenca, attracted to the castle of Miraval a number of aspirants to courtly love and formed a court well known in the Carcassonne region. There are certain parallels between the strict interpretation of courtly love which Tostemps defends and the ideas expressed by Raimon de Miraval, particularly in the early part of his career. We shall return to these later. It is not sufficient to suggest that Raimon acquired the *senhal* because he frequently used the term *tostemps*, 'always', or that having been called Tostemps by other poets he then began to over-use the term. He uses it some fourteen times in eleven out of his forty-four poems.[8] Raimbaut d'Orange uses the word fifteen times in eleven out of his thirty-nine poems.[9] But by both poets *tostemps* is used generally in a statement of the first person: 'eu . . . tostemps . . .', expressing particularly loyalty or a pledge of service and submission; it is therefore an important verbal element reinforcing other terms of constancy and fidelity and underlining the poet-lover's implicit wish that love be eternal. It therefore complements the *senhal Plus-leial* (VIII, 49) which in Raimon's poetry probably refers to the same person as the shortened form *Leial* which he seems to favour (VI, 64, IX, 59, XI, 53,

XV, 55). He uses the word *tostemps* at the beginning of the *cobla* he addresses to another poet (XLIII, 1) and Uc de Mataplana associates it closely with Raimon's name in a *sirventès* addressed to Gaudairenca.[10] These are the only two examples in which *tostemps* might carry some personal significance relating to Raimon, and even then the evidence is slight.

The *partimen* (N.Fr. *jeu-parti*) is the genre in which the paradoxical nature of courtly love is expressed by means of a dialogue between two poets. The term is derived from the expression *joc partir*, 'to choose, or to let some one choose, an alternative'. The first poet sets a problem with two alternatives, the second poet chooses what seems to him the better alternative and replies in the second stanza. Then, in alternating stanzas, the two poets defend their case, usually until there are six stanzas, when in the final two half-stanzas, *tornadas*, they appeal to a judge or sum up their own point of view. In many cases, melody and stanza form were borrowed from other well-known lyrics, which has lent weight to the theory that the *partimen* was, on the first occasion, improvised, although we should not, even if this is so, discount the possibility of poets conferring in advance, preparing their performance, and we must concede that the poems became thereafter part of the courtly repertoire, until they were eventually written down in the *chansonniers*. Various modifications might occur, although, for most of the *partimens*, the manuscripts transmit a single version. This is one of the most structured and most clearly defined genres, with no substantial difference between the southern and northern forms which seem both to have evolved c. 1170–80. The northern poets abuse one another vigorously at times, a practice which the troubadours tend to reserve for the *coblas* and *tensos*. The problems discussed pertain almost exclusively to courtly love or the courtly life-style, which further distinguishes the *partimen* from the *tenso*, an older genre more closely related to the Latin *altercatio* and in which poets are free to develop their arguments as they please. *Partimen* and *tenso* have frequently been confused: in the rubrics of manuscripts, *tensos* indicates the general category of poems of debate as in the *chansonnier R*; within the *partimen*, the word *tenso* is used with the general meaning of discussion, dispute; and in the thirteenth-century poetic treatises, such as the *Doctrina de compondre dictats*, there is a definition of a single form of poem of debate called a *tenso*,[11] but the *Leys d'amor* (c. 1356) distinguishes the two genres.[12]

The *partimen* reflects the twelfth-century interest in dialectic which, renewed and reformed, came to dominate the *trivium* in education of the high Middle Ages. It had the special task of being used to distinguish true from false, in contrast with rhetoric, which could be used on behalf of both. The definitions of Saint Augustine and Cassiodorus[13] are echoed in the *Leys d'amor*:

> Dialecta ensenha tensonar, contendre e disputa e far questios, respostas e defensas la us contra l'autre e mostrar per dreyta razo e per vertadiers argumens la vertat e la veraya oppinio de la questio moguda.[14]

The definition given by Peire de Corbiac in the encyclopaedia he compiled in the thirteenth century applies even more closely to the use of dialectic in the *partimen*:

> Per Dialectica sai arrazonablemens
> a pauzar e respondre e falsar argumens,
> sofismar e conduire, e tot gignozamens
> menar mon aversaire ad inconveniens.[15]

The form of the *disputatio*, the exercise based on dialectic, was of considerable influence from c. 1150 onwards.[16] Consisting of question, proposition in reply, objections to propositions, determination of correct and approved answer, the process was easily remembered and used in various ways outside of the schools as a verbal contest on the truth or falsity of some subject, entertaining both competitors and audience.[17] So in the *partimen* two poets, rivals in the craft of the lyric, engaged in verbal conflict, aiming to distinguish the truth and falsity in courtly matters. This is not an entirely new role for the troubadour: Guillaume IX had initially offered the alternative of the love of a knight or that of a monk or clerk[18] and Marcabru attributed to the troubadour the legal role of 'investigator, defender and inquisitor' in the enquiry into the truth about love.[19] In the *partimen*, a poet is therefore invited to discriminate between right and wrong (*lo dreit* and *lo tort*), to choose the better alternative. Whereas in the *canso* the poet-lover expresses his inner conflict, his difficulty in maintaining his balance between the opposite poles of love,[20] in the *partimen* this conflict has been translated into a problem concerning three or four persons and which is presented as a test of the poet's virtuosity and professional competence. Two poets are thus involved in a controversy about the interpretation of love and the conflicting choices it offers.

The Folquet de Marseille–Tostemps *partimen* has six stanzas of ten lines each and two *tornadas* of six lines each. The rhyme scheme is:

$$a \quad b \quad b \quad a \quad c, \quad d \quad e \quad \alpha \quad \alpha \quad \alpha,$$
$$8 \quad 8 \quad 8 \quad 8 \quad 7 \quad 8 \quad 8 \quad 8 \quad 8 \quad 7$$

The stanzas are *unissonans*, the five rhymes -*or*, -*ais*, -*aire*, -*os*, -*an* recurring in the same position in each stanza. The *tornadas* repeat the scheme of the last six lines of the stanza. The identical scheme is found in a *chanson de croisade* by Raimbaut de Vaqueiras, *Conselh don a l'emperador* (P.-C. 392, 9a).[21]

FOLQUET DE MARSEILLE AND TOSTEMPS, *Tostemps, si vos sabetz d'amor*

Tostemps, si vos sabetz d'amor,
triatz de doas cal val mays:
s'es drutz de tal que no.s biays
vas vos ni sofr' autr' amador,
empero no.us fay veiayre   5
que.us am ni que s'azaut de vos,
o d'autra que.us am atrestan,
et a d'autres drutz un o dos,
e que.us fassa de plazers tan
com fin' amia deu fayre.   10

Folquetz, mes m'avetz en error,
que trop m'avetz partit greus plays,
qu'en cascun a trebalh e fays;
pero si.n penray la melhor:
be.us dic qu'ieu no pretz gaire   15
dona pos hi ay companhos,
sitot m'i fay d'amor semblan;
mays vuelh que m'o tenh ' a rescos
leys que non aya cor truan
c'ab bels plazers me cug trayre.   20

Tostemps, pauc avetz de valor
si per aital amor es gays
que, pus dona.us fay col e cais,

par qe so tengu' a deshonor:
be.us dic, s'era.l reys sos paire,   25
no.us es sos plaitz onratz ni bos;
mays val sela que.us tem e.us blan
e.us mostra semblan amoros,
sitot se vay pueys percassan,
cant vos non es e.l repayre.   30

Folquetz, vos razonatz folor,
que*z* anc dona pus son drut trays
sos pretz no fon fis ni verays,
ni.l sieu semblan gualiador
no.l podon per ren refayre   35
l'anta qu'ilh fay totas sazos;
mas de bona prezan
say qu'en es pus ondratz sos dos:
sitot no.m fay d'amar semblan
no.m cal, sol m'am ses cor vaire.   40

Tostemps, li nessi donador
fan tornar los bos dos savays,
e par a lor semblan malvays
que.l dar non lor aia sabor;
doncx, com pot dona ben fayre   45
que.m mostre semblan ergulhos?
mielhs es c'om suefra.l bel enjan,
c'aisso ja es bes trassios
qu' aven a motz *e* sofrir l'an:
yeu cug que vos n'es cofraire.   50

Folquetz, tals m'ac a servidor
qes anc companhon no m'atrais,
ara.m par qu'ad autre s'*es*lays,
per qu'ieu m'en part e.m vir alhor;
mas vos qi es fis amayre   55
cug que, si a*b* esta razos
cujatz aisi cobrir lo dan
e s'aisi perdes las chansos

quez autre vos parta l'afan,
no say per que.us es chantayre.   60

Tostemps, de tort say dreg fayre,
per c'a mi platz esta razos;
e s'ie.us en vens, joi n'ayatz gran,
car vos sofretz los companhos,
mas eu n'am tal que.m fay semblan   65
d'amor, e no.y ay cofraire.
Folquetz, tostemps fos gabayre!
jutjada si' esta razos:
a Na Gaucelma vuelh que.s n'an,
e si ieu am ab companhos,   70
ja per so no.y ira duptan,
que be crey n'er fis jutjaire.

TRANSLATION

Tostemps, if you have knowledge of love, choose which of the two
alternatives is better: to be the lover either of such a lady who is not
unfaithful to you and does not permit any other lover, but who does
not show you that she loves you and finds pleasure with you, or of
another lady who loves you as much and has one or two other lovers
and grants you as many pleasures as a true lady-love should.

Folquet you have embarrassed me for you have set me for debate
questions which are too hard as they both contain difficulty and
problems; nevertheless, I shall select the better alternative: I tell you
this that I set little value on a lady when I have company (in courting
her) even though she gives me signs of her love; I prefer that a lady
keeps our love secret, in order that she may not feel demeaned, than
that she contemplates duping me with lovely favours.

Tostemps, you are of little worth if you are happy with such a love
that, when the lady embraces and kisses you, it seems that she
considers this dishonourable: I can tell you that, even if her father
were the king, it would not be honourable or good for you to take her
side in the debate; the lady who treats you with respect and appreciation and gives you signs of her love is better, even if she goes chasing
after some one else, when you are not at home.

Folquet, your argument is absurd, for once a lady has betrayed her lover, her merit is not true and perfect and her deceitful looks cannot in the least make up for the shame she constantly incurs; but I know that what is given by a good lady of merit is more honourable: it does not matter if she fails to show me her love, provided that she loves me without a change of heart.

Tostemps, ignorant benefactors turn good gifts into bad and it seems from their nasty appearance that they derive no pleasure from giving; therefore, how can a lady grant me some good when she looks haughty? It is better to endure a nice piece of deceit, for thus is a reward really a betrayal, as happens to many, and they bear it: I think that you are a party to this.

Folquet, I was the suitor of such a lady who did not attract any other companions for me; now it seems to me that she is running after someone else so that I am taking my leave and turning in another direction; but you who are a true lover, I think that if you imagine that with this subject you are covering up your suffering and if you are thus vainly composing songs so that someone else may share your torment, I do not know why you are a poet.

Tostemps, I know how to turn wrong into right, therefore this subject gives me pleasure; and if I defeat you in this way, be very glad, as you put up with companions whereas I love a lady who shows me her love and I do not have any fellow-lovers.

Folquet, you always liked to joke! let this subject be judged: I wish it to be sent to Lady Gaucelma, and if I have rival companions in loving, she will not be fearful because of this, as I believe that she will be an excellent judge.

Written about 1190, this is one of the earliest *partimens* we have. It conforms to the general definition of the genre and illustrates very clearly the way in which two poets combined to compose a poetic debate. Let us firstly sum up the argument of the poem and then study it in detail.

Folquet de Marseille poses the problem: is it preferable to be the sole lover of a lady who is not unfaithful, but who fails to show her love or her pleasure in love, or to be the lover of a lady who shares your love and accords all the appropriate signs of her pleasure, but who has one or two other lovers? As is usual in the *partimen*, there are dual alternatives:

absence or presence of signs of the lady's love, absence or presence of rivals. Is it better to love without rivals and without recognition or to love despite rivals and with the proof that one's love is requited?

Tostemps prefers to love without rivals and without the signs of love which might be fallacious or dishonourable. Folquet attacks him first for proposing that a lady who grants him pleasure might in fact despise this action and then states his preference for evidence of the lady's love even if, in his absence, she seeks the company of other lovers. Tostemps condemns Folquet's argument on the grounds that a lady who deceives her lover ruins her own merit and incurs permanent shame; he appreciates the loyal sentiments of an honourable lady, even if he receives no reward. Folquet questions the value of gifts bestowed reluctantly, of the favours granted by haughty ladies. It is better to enjoy deceiving one another. And he suggests that Tostemps knows something about this. Tostemps confesses that after being the sole lover of a lady, he has been jilted and so he is now going to love another lady. In retaliation, he questions Folquet's motives in discussing such a problem, unless it is that Folquet who is reputed to be a true lover, hopes to share some of his suffering with others by means of his composition. Folquet suddenly plays his trump card, revealing that he has been defending the false as though it were true. He loves without rival, his is a love which is visibly reciprocated. Tostemps exclaims! (he has, after all, had his leg pulled). He requests that the dispute be submitted to the lady Gaucelma for a fair judgement, even if he does have rivals.

The poem concludes as a joke initiated by Folquet de Marseille, who wanted to discomfit his opponent by the argument and by the choice of subject. But the important notions of loyalty, reciprocity and jealousy have all entered the discussion. There is no doubt that for these two poets courtly love has principles and depends on knowledge of what is right and what is wrong in the eyes of others. The behaviour which courtly love prompts in the lover should be conscious and disciplined.

Let us now consider in detail the development of the poem, strophe by strophe. All of the strophes can be divided into two or three parts.

I, vv. 1–2. Folquet challenges Tostemps to a debate, in terms similar to those which open other *partimen*:[22] the opponent is invited to choose the better alternative ('triatz de doas'; cf. v. 14 'la melhor') according to his knowledge of love ('si vos sabetz d'amor').

vv. 3–6. Folquet defines the situation of the lover (and he uses the term *drut* which allows for the enjoyment of sensual pleasure on the lover's part, even though this lover seems deprived of such fulfilment and remains a suitor or aspirant) *vis-à-vis* a lady who is faithful, whose friendship is undivided but who fails to show her love or the delight she should feel. In such an impasse, even the most patient lover feels frustrated, and yet this is the situation very commonly and often poignantly evoked in the *canso*,[23] where the poet-lover strives to persuade his lady to recognize his love, to ease the tension and show him signs of her grace and favour. At least here Folquet does not doubt whether the lady loves.

vv. 7–10. Folquet now sketches the alternative: one lady, several lovers upon whom she bestows her favours equally and who might therefore all be happy, were it not that the courtly lover aspires to the exclusive love of a lady. There is no reproach directed at the lady for her behaviour: she loves truly and is loved in return (v. 7). In keeping with the troubadours' regard for discretion, the kind of pleasure to be experienced is left undefined (vv. 6, 9); there is only the word 'drut' and the vague expression 'de plazers *tan* com fin' amia *deu* fayre' – as many pleasures as are expected of a faithful lady-love – which might be interpreted as fully as one likes.

Notice the way in which the alternatives are presented: Tostemps is to choose which lover he would prefer to be; there is on the one hand 'vos', Tostemps, and on the other the ladies who are at first just 'tal que' and 'autra que' and whose love is then more clearly defined by the verbs of the following relative clauses ('no.s biays vas vos', 'is not inconstant to you', 'us am atrestan', 'loves you as much'. In the final line, the second lady is called 'fin' amia', by which Folquet expresses approval. The epithet *fin* vouches for the courtliness of her behaviour. In general, the troubadours judge a lady on the one hand by her beauty and noble character, and on the other by her behaviour in love. It seems therefore that the unswerving loyalty of the first lady is diminished in Folquet's opinion by her refusal to give of herself, to be generous or even gracious towards her lover.

II, vv. 11–14. Tostemps complains about the difficulty of the choice, both alternatives are perplexing, but he has chosen the better.[24] The terms *partir plai*, 'to give the choice of alternatives (in a dilemma-type of question)', and *la melhor (razo)*, 'the better (alternative)' are some of the technical vocabulary of the genre.

vv. 15–17. Tostemps rejects the approval Folquet has bestowed on the second lady ('qu'ieu no *pretz* gaire'), insisting on his right to be the sole lover: the pleasure he would receive is inadmissible if he has rivals, if there are others who enjoy the same delights. The use of the word *companhos* in this context seems unusual, for the companions in question are in fact rivals for the lady's favours. Is it perhaps Tostemps' sense of affiliation to a fraternity of poet-lovers which has determined the use of the word? Its use is not coincidental, as it recurs (v. 52) and Folquet uses an almost synonymous term *cofraire* (v. 66) with the same meaning.[25]

vv. 18–20. Tostemps next states his preference for a love which remains secret, in order that the lady's conscience be not troubled, than for one manifested by deceitful gratification of pleasure. Not only are vv. 18–20 set in contrast to vv. 15–17 (the clauses 'ieu no pretz gaire . . .', 'mays vuelh . . .' introducing negative and positive statements respectively) but also v. 20 contains a reinterpretation of vv. 9–10 in a derogatory sense: pleasure is now allied with deceit and treachery, not with honourable, reciprocal love. Tostemps forestalls the antithesis by using the negative expression 'non . . . truan', 'not knavish', linked semantically to *traire*, instead of a simple, positive adjective such as *fin* or *verai* to describe the sentiments of the lady. He then makes a positive statement about the insidious motive which can, paradoxically, lie behind 'bels plazers'.

III, vv. 21–6. Folquet immediately rebukes him ('pauc avetz de valor'), taking his allusion to secret love ('m'o tenh' a rescos') to mean the sensual pleasure of love which contents the lover but which is despicable when given by a prudish woman who feels dishonoured by the experience. Although the expression 'faire col et cays' might suggest to Tostemps that the lady is trying her wiles, Folquet claims not to disapprove of such signs of pleasure between lovers.[26] The lady may be of high birth (v. 25) but it is not in Tostemps' interest to become involved in a love of this kind: his worth and honour are to be maintained and increased by loving (vv. 21, 26) – this is the main point of Folquet's argument, with which he begins and ends.

vv. 27–30. Folquet then defends his own alternative in the debate: the behaviour of a 'fin' amia', which is sketched by the terms '.us tem e.us blan' (verbs which usually denote essential aspects of the lover's role, and only occasionally have the lady as their subject)[27] and '.us mostra semblan amoros'. The lady should treat her lover with respect, compliment him and show her inclination towards him, although, as Folquet concedes, she may adopt a double standard and shift her attention to another once he is out of sight. In the courtly lyric of the twelfth century, the loyalty of ladies tends to be less absolute than that avowed by poet-lovers.

IV, vv. 31–6. Tostemps protests about the absurdity of Folquet's argument: a lady would, in behaving as Folquet has just outlined, destroy her merit and incur undying shame. The consequences of her conduct would revert upon her ('*sos pretz* no fon fis ni verays', '*l'anta* qu'*ilh* fay'). The object of the lady's love is no longer Tostemps (v. 20 *me*) but 'son drut', the argument having shifted briefly from the personal to the general.

vv. 37–40. He defends his own choice: the love of a lady of merit, 'bona dona prezan', who loves him truly although she does not reveal it (v. 39). Again he has chosen a negative form of expression to describe the loyàlty expected in love ('*ses* cor vaire'). What she gives will be more honourable than favours granted by a lady who has sullied her reputation by having several lovers – by being faithful to no single one, she betrays one and all.

V, vv. 41–4. Folquet steers the argument back to the general: ladies may be reluctant to grant favours to lovers, but also the wealthy are not always as spontaneously generous as their dependents desire. Folquet seems to be criticizing his rich contemporaries for their avarice and meanness, qualities which Marcabru had found all too prevalent. The choice of words is significant: three pejorative epithets 'nessi', 'savays', 'malvays' emphasise that these 'benefactors' dislike giving away what they have.

vv. 45–6. The poet returns to the proud, disdainful lady: how does she derive pleasure or advantage ('ben') from her ungracious behaviour? The question is rhetorical, and the first instance of Folquet's bringing himself into the argument ('que.*m* mostre . . .').

vv. 47–50. With an easy transition, Folquet resumes the defence of his side of the debate: it is better for both parties to engage in 'bel enjan', pleasurable deceit which amounts to a strategy of love, with which Tostemps is perhaps conversant.[28]

VI, vv. 51–4. Tostemps does not evade the issue: he confesses the truth, his attitude is realistic. He has been the only suitor of a lady who has now abandoned him for another, so he has turned his attention elsewhere. The three terms 's'eslays', 'rushes, hurries', 'm'en part', 'separate', '.m vir alhor', 'go in another direction', are all used to express the rupture of a love-affair. Note the nuance of speed, on the lady's part, conveyed by 's'eslais'. Tostemps does not declare that he has been 'drut' but 'servidor', one who serves or courts a lady, a term which came into more general use to denote the courtly lover in poetry of the late twelfth and thirteenth centuries.

vv. 55–60. Tostemps quickly turns the focus from himself on to Folquet, reproaching him that if the only reason for proposing this subject or theme ('razo') is to camouflage the suffering he, a 'fis amaire', 'true, faithful lover', endures, to share his torment, this is a pointless exercise, contrary to the function of the lyric and to the role of the courtly poet, the *chantayre*. Tostemps is here implying surely that the lyric should faithfully present courtly love and interpret it in the highest sense.

VII, vv. 61–2. Folquet reveals his ruse or strategy: he confidently claims to be the defender of what is right ('de tort say dreg fayre') and the one who has derived pleasure from the subject. He had of course no choice in the argument but might have guessed at the outset the option his partner would select.

vv. 63–6. Hence he is likely to be the winner (v. 63), *venzer*, 'to win, to conquer', appearing frequently in the *partimen* to denote the successful conclusion of a dispute. Folquet sums up the real positions of the two contestants: Tostemps endures the existence of rivals, Folquet has the undisputed privilege of reciprocal love.

VIII, v. 67. Tostemps' exclamation shows that he and Folquet are old friends who have previously joked together.

vv. 68–72. It is left to Tostemps to submit the case to a judge, Na Gaucelma, whose identity has not been established with any certainty. She will be a 'fis jutgaire', that is, one hopes, impartial, and will not be deterred by the question of whether or not Tostemps has rivals – which, after all, has been central to the whole debate.

The division of the strophes shows quite clearly the way in which the *partimen* is constructed; once the subject has been set and accepted, one alternative is taken up and then refuted, the second alternative becoming a counter-argument to the first – an alternation between *pro* and *con, oc* and *non*. Deliberately the poets oppose and contradict one another, the replying poet having three stanzas in which to argue, the initiator of the challenge only two, but it is the latter who has the prerogative of calling a halt to the debate and, perhaps prematurely, declaring himself the winner. There is a marked parallelism in the beginning of some lines: 'be.us dic' (vv. 15, 25), 'sitot' (vv. 17, 29, 39), 'mays vuelh', 'mays val' (vv. 18, 27), 'mas de' (v. 37), 'mas vos' (v. 55), 'mas eu' (v. 65); with the exception of 'sitot', these expressions coincide with a new development in the argument, a point to be emphasised in opposition to the adversary's contention. There are also several statements of personal affirmation introduced by: 'be.us dic (qu')' (vv. 15, 25), 'say qu'en' (v. 38), 'yeu cug que' (v. 50), 'cug que' (v. 56), 'no say per que' (v. 60), 'say' (v. 61), 'be crey' (v. 72). Tostemps, to whom it was said at the outset 'si vos savetz d'amor', uses this form of expression more frequently than Folquet; it is a rhetorical device reinforcing points of the argument and enabling the subject to assert his ideas more vigorously. Tostemps has, after all, been invited to choose a standpoint, to defend a case according to his own knowledge and interpretation of the law of love. The legal overtones are strong in the 'technical' vocabulary of the *partimen*: *plai partir; triar, cauzir lo mielhs, la melhor (razo); dreg, tort; venzer; jutjar razo, fis jutjaire.* In the *partimen* courtly love, courtly principles, are on trial; the poets are more or less eloquent advocates of their cause in an enquiry into the truth about love.

The terms used to refer to courtly love are those found elsewhere in the Provençal courtly lyric and notably in the *canso.* The lover is called *drut, amador, servidor, fis amaire,* the poet *chantayre* and other lovers, the rivals *companhos, cofraire,* terms which seem almost euphemistic given the force of jealousy among courtly lovers, except that here this feeling is second to that of solidarity among troubadours. The lady is denoted by *fin'amia, dona* or an indefinite pronoun completed by a verb describing her fidelity in love. Despite the importance of the theme of loyalty, it is deceit which is here denoted by a larger, more varied range of words: *trayre, gualiador, enjan, trassios,* with which should be associated the derogatory terms: *truan, deshonor, anta, ergulhos.* The higher qualities which make up an ideal of personal attainment for lover and lady respectively are summed up by *valor* and *pretz. Dan* and *afan* denote the lover's suffering.

One further term requires comment: *semblan,* which occurs seven times, always accompanied by an epithet or a noun or verb complement; in fact, in four of these examples it is a question of the outward evidence of love: 'mi fai d'amor semblan' (v. 17), 'us mostra semblan amoros' (v. 28), 'no.m fay d'amar semblan' (v. 39), '.m fay semblan/d'amor' (vv. 65–6). The subject of the verb is in each example the lady who, by certain glances or facial expressions, by certain movements, gives the poet-lover to understand that his love has been recognized and is shared, that is, that he has become an accepted, successful lover. There is pleasure in this intimate communication for both lady and lover,[29] but what is essential for the lover is the *sign* that his love is acknowledged (v. 5). Beyond this lies further pleasure (vv. 9, 20, 23). Appearances betray true feelings; therefore the poet-lover must know how to perceive and interpret looks which are deceitful (v. 34) or wicked (v. 43) or arrogant (v. 46), for these are just some of the inevitable obstacles to be overcome.

The poetic technique of the troubadours relies heavily upon semantic repetition to stress and reinforce capital ideas. All of the binomial expressions found here are of reasonably frequent use, some more so than others: *trebalh e fays, fay col e cays, onratz ni bos, em e blan, fis ni verays, m'en part e.m vir alhor.* The terms came to be linked by more or less spontaneous association of ideas: one term immediately recalls the other and, as is often the case, all six expressions are used here in the second part of the line, the second term serving metrically to complete the line and to supply the rhyme.

Finally, let us look for analogies with the arguments of the *partimen* in the work of Raimon de Miraval and Folquet de Marseille, even though in the case of the former poet these can only be suggested most tentatively. For Raimon de Miraval, love consists of precepts, a *sciensa*, with which the lover must be fully conversant in order to court or to compose:

> Ben aia-l cortes essiens,
> Que tostemps m'aond' enaissi
> Qu'iratz chan e-m deport e-m ri
> E atressi quan sui jauzens   (VII, 1–4)

> (Blessed be the courtly knowledge
> which always comes so freely to me
> that when I am sad, I sing, enjoy myself and laugh
> as I do when I am happy).

It is like a body of secret rites, independent of other education, knowledge gradually acquired and then permanently possessed.[30] His fellow poet-lovers are 'autres conoisedors' (IX, 32).

Raimon regularly states his loyalty and submission, for example:

> Q'ieu non cossir de ren al
> Mas de servir a plazer
> Lieis de cui teing Miraval   (VI, 61–63)[31]

> (For I do not think of anything except
> of being able to serve and give pleasure
> to the lady from whom I hold Miraval).

He expects loyalty to be mutual and to lead to the highest joy (XXIII, 25–40). In praising his lady he includes the details that she is 'Fin' et ab pauc de preyadors' (IX, 50) and says of another 'Q'anc no faillic ni mespres/Ni non amet dos ni tres (XVII, 29–30).[32] He sides with loyal lovers, 'nos leial', even if there must be quarrels and disputes, even if they are the losers (XXI, 9–16), and declares his devotion to one lady (vv. 49–52). In this same poem he makes the clearest allusion to separation from a lady and protests innocence in the matter:

> Sabetz per qe-m torn esquius
> Contra las enguanairitz?
> Quar de midons soi faidtz
> E non sai tort mas lo seu   (vv. 17–20)[33]

(Do you know why I have become hostile
to deceitful women?
because I am exiled from my lady
and, to my knowledge, it is she alone who has done wrong).

One of the dominant themes of Folquet de Marseille's poetry is his
unhappiness in love felt as though it were intense physical suffering:

> Amors, merce!...
> quar viure.m faitz e morir mesclamen
> et enaissi doblatz mi mo martire (IX, 1, 3-4)

(Love, have pity!...
for you make me both live and die at one and the same time,
and thus double my torment).

He wishes to reveal his anguish to his lady, but to conceal it from others:

> A vos volgra mostar lo mal qu'ieu sen
> et als autres celar et escondire;
> qu'anc no.us puec dir mon cor celadamen;
> donc, s'ieu no.m sai cobrir, qui m'er cubrire?
> ni qui m'er fis, s' ieu eis mi sui traire? (vv.29-33)

(I should like to show you the pain I feel
and hide it and camouflage it from others;
for I have never been able in secret to disclose my feelings to you;
therefore if I cannot conceal my own feelings, who will do this for me?
and who will be faithful to me if I betray even myself?)[34]

The poem ends with a *tornada* addressed as a reply to Aziman and
Tostemps, his fellow poets, who have reproached him with his discretion:

> Mas N'Azimans ditz qu'ieu li sui traire,
> el e.N Tostemps dizon qu'ieu sui ginhos,
> car tot cor non retrac ad els dos (vv.39-41)

(But Lord Aziman says that I have betrayed him
and he and Lord Tostemps say that I am cunning[35]
as I do not reveal all my feelings to them.)

More than once he refers to his lady's *orgolh* (IX, 22, XII, str. 1), an
obstacle to his improvement by love. His love is unrequited, his striving
unrewarded.

Although he stresses it less than Raimon de Miraval, love depends for
Folquet de Marseille on knowledge and skill (IV, str. 5, XIII, 12–13),
and he contemplates having recourse to the ruse of pretending not to love
his lady (XIV, str. 2), but rejects this desperate strategy as one contrary
to love. The *partimen* gave this poet-lover, who is elsewhere highly serious
and at times profound in his thinking about love, an opportunity to
amuse himself with the ideas of courtly love at the expense of another
poet who is friend and rival, and to live up to the reputation he has for
Tostemps of being a *gabaire*.

What are the results of the debate between Folquet de Marseille and
Tostemps? Ultimately, they both maintain the idea of one lady and one
lover. Tostemps places a higher value on absolute loyalty than on
pleasures and favours of love. They both stress the importance of the
merit and worth of the lover and lady. The major themes of courtly love,
transformed into problems or hypotheses, usually provide the subjects
for debate. In this example, the dilemma can be reduced to the questions: are rivals to be tolerated? must love be expressed openly by signs
and favours? The debate on these questions touches on the principal
themes of loyalty, jealousy, reciprocal love and sensual pleasure. Instead
of the essentially subjective development of the *canso* in which the
poet-lover tries to find equilibrium between contrary forces such as *ben*
and *mal*, *joi* and *ira*, *sen* and *foudat*, the *partimen* offers the nucleus of a
drama in which an individual confronts a real choice, in which one
courtly love situation is contrasted with another. Nevertheless, the
solution of the love-problem is less important than the confrontation
between two poet-lovers. The verdict is sought less for a final judgement
on the right or wrong of the case than on the troubadours' skill in verbal
parry and thrust and clear thinking. The fact that the verdicts were
seldom recorded (only four exist) bears this out. On the other hand, it
cannot be said that content is subordinate to form, that the question is a
mere pretext for a display of poetic virtuosity, for subject and poetic art
are here in harmony: the co-existence of opposites, the refusal to
eliminate either of two contrary tendencies is endemic in courtly love, a
subject which therefore lends itself so easily to debate and which, by
definition of its paradoxical nature, eschews a final conclusion.

This *partimen* conforms to the definition of the genre: a bipartite
question, the regular alternation of opposing arguments which are at

times subtly linked to one another, the summing-up, the request for a verdict. The poem is clearly not the work of one poet (i.e. Folquet de Marseille is not discoursing with his *alter ego*) but of two poets, each of whom takes delight in trying to dislodge his opponent. The internal evidence suggests that, while it is not improbable that Tostemps is Raimon de Miraval, there is no positive proof of this. It might seem surprising that in an early example of a *partimen*, the instigator seems to flout the conventions of the genre. Forced by the rules, Folquet had to assume an attitude contrary to his own; by his *volte-face* in the *tornada* he unmasks himself and redresses the situation.[36] A verdict is therefore required on the better argument or defence, rather than on the better of the alternatives proposed.

The poem reveals the rivalry which existed between poets, their knowledge of one another, the amusement they derived from trying to outdo one another in a trial of poetic eloquence and a battle of wits. Because Tostemps' personal involvement is kept to the fore, the gnomic style is less apparent here than in some debate-poems, but it is clear that the poets argue with reference to general courtly principles.

In the *partimen* genre the rhetoric of the courtly love lyric, enhanced with touches of irony and disconcerting personal allusions, was combined with an essentially dialectical process, as two poets vied with one another to expose the true but undefinable nature of love, in a manner which would delight a courtly society.

NOTES

1. A. Pillet-H. Carstens, *Bibliographie der Troubadours* (Halle, 1933), pp. xx–xxi, xxv; C. Brunel, *Bibliographie des manuscrits littéraires en ancien provençal* (Paris, 1935), pp. 56–9, 92; G. Bertoni, *Il Canzoniere provenzale di Bernart Amoros (Complemento Campori), Edizione diplomatica* (Fribourg, Collectanea Friburgensia, n. F., XI, 1911), pp. 416–18.
2. S. Stroński, *Le Troubadour Folquet de Marseille* (Cracovie, 1910), XV, pp. 68–71. See also pp. 44*–45*, 130–1.
3. For example, VII, 5–10.
4. R. Lejeune, 'L'Évêque de Toulouse Folquet de Marseille et la principauté de Liège', *Mélanges Felix Rousseau. Études sur l'histoire du pays mosan au moyen âge* (Bruxelles, 1958), pp. 433–48; see pp. 433–7.
5. Folquet de Marseille names two: Marsan (I, 55), Palais (XIV, 46).
6. J. Boutière et A.-H. Schutz, *Biographies des troubadours, édition refondue* (Paris, 1964), pp. 65, 311.
7. VIII, 56–7, IX, 39, 41, X, 41, XI, 41, 42, XII, 45, XIII, 46, 47, XIV, 46, 47, XVIII, 67, 72.

8. L. T. Topsfield, *Les Poésies du troubadour Raimon de Miraval* (Paris, 1971), pp. 31–2. He uses the term once more than Topsfield lists: VII, 2.

9. W. T. Pattison, *The Life and Works of the Troubadour Raimbaut d'Orange* (Minneapolis–London, 1952), II, 7, III, 19, VI, 39, 42, 44, VIII, 15, XII, 39, XIV, 10, XIX, 6, 56, XXII, 41, XXIII, 47, 109, XXXVI, 7, XXXVIII, 28.

10. L. T. Topsfield, *Les Poésies*..., pp. 334–6 (P.- C. 454.1). Poem XLII (P.-C. 406.30) is Raimon de Miraval's reply to Uc de Mataplana.

11. J. H. Marshall, *The Razos de trobar of Raimon Vidal and Associated Texts* (London, 1972), pp. 95–8, ll.4, 90, 135; pp. 101–3, ll.1, 11–18.

12. 'Tensos es dictatz on tensona/Cascus per sa part e razona/Per mantener o dig o fag' (A *tenso* is a composition in which each party disputes according to his own opinion and argues in defence of words or deeds); 'Partimens es segon romans/Questios dos membres portans/Contraris donatz ad algu/Per so que defenda la.I.' (a *partimen* is according to the vulgar tongue a question containing two opposite parts proposed to someone in order that he defends one of the laternatives), *Las Leys d'Amors*, ed. J. J. Anglade (Toulouse, 1919), t.2, pp. 182–3. Recent studies on the *partimen* genre are: E. Köhler, *Trobadorlyrik und höfischer Roman* (Berlin, 1962), pp. 89–113, 153–92; S. Neumeister, *Das Spiel mit der höfischen Liebe. Das altprovenzalische Partimen* (Munich, 1969); *id.*, 'Le Classement des genres lyriques des troubadours', *Actes du VIème Congrès international de langue et litterature d' Oc et d'études franco-provençales, Montpellier, septembre 1970* (Montpellier, 1972), pp. 401–15. For this *partimen*, see *Das Spiel*..., pp. 149–51.

13. 'Qui enim disputat, verum discernit a falso', quoted by E. Köhler, *op. cit.*, p. 279, n. 32. 'Vera sequestrat a falsis', *Institutiones* II, Praef. 4.

14. 'Dialectic teaches one how to argue, contend, dispute and to compose questions, answers and defence in opposition to one another and to show by sound reasoning and by truthful argument the truth and the correct opinion about the question set', *op. cit.*, t.1, p. 81.

15. 'Through Dialectic I know how to present a case and reply and falsify arguments by reasoning, to use sophistries, to conduct and lead my adversary quite cunningly into discomfiture.' Quoted by L. M. Paterson, *Troubadours and Eloquence* (Oxford, 1975), pp. 26–7.

16. J. J. Murphy, *Rhetoric in the Middle Ages. A History of Rhetorical Theory from Saint Augustine to the Renaissance* (Berkeley and Los Angeles, 1974), p. 102.

17. William Fitzstephen's description of London scenes, c. 1170, bears this out. See R. Barber, *Henry Plantaganet* (London, 1973), p. 5.

18. *Les Chansons de Guillaume IX duc d'Aquitaine*, ed. A. Jeanroy (Paris, 1927), V, 8–9.

19. *Poésies complètes du troubadour Marcabru*, ed. J.-M. Dejeanne (Toulouse, 1909), V, 43–4.

20. 'Entre dos volers sui pensius' (Raimon de Miraval, XXVI, 1); 'e sui aissi meitadatz:/que no.m desesper/ni aus esperans' aver' (Folquet de Marseille IV, 8–10).

21. I. Frank, *Répertoire métrique de la poésie des troubadours* (Paris 1953), p. 146, n° 650: 1. See also J. Klobukowska, 'Contribution à l'étude de la versification et du rythme dans les chansons de Folquet de Marseille', *Actes du 5ᵉ Congrès international de langue et litterature d'Oc et d'études franco-provençales, Nice, 6–12 septembre 1967* (Publications de la Faculté des lettres et des sciences humaines de Nice, 13; Paris, 1974), pp. 414–18; see pp. 416–17.

22. For example 'Ara.m digatz, Gaucelm Faidit,/cals val a bona domna mais . . .'
(P.-C. 167, 8); 'N'Albert, chausetz al vostre sen . . .' (P.-C. 10, 3).
23. For example, Folquet de Marseille XIV, 5–8.
24. Cf. 'En Raimbaut, d'aqest joc partit/pren lo miels, e.l sordei vos lais!' (P.-C.
167, 8); 'N'Aimerics, pauc a d'ensien/qui non sap triar lo meillor, a guissa de
fin amador' (P.-C. 10, 3).
25. *Companho*, 'compagnon, amant' (*Lexique roman* IV, 406–7). Raynouard
quotes one analogous example: 'et ab mi maintas vets *compaignos* / q'ieu volria
mais totz soletz estar' (we give the text according to the edition of J.
Mouzat, *Les Poèmes de Gaucelm Faidit*, Paris, 1965, XVII, 43–4). *Confraire*, 'confrère,
associé, compagnon' (*Lexique roman* III, 383).
26. *Faire col e cais*, 'embrasser' (Levy, *Petit Dictionnaire*, p. 82); *col*, 'neck', *cais*, *cays*,
'cheek, mouth'. In some instances, the expression is used pejoratively, hence
the meaning proposed by A. Jeanroy 'minauder en jouant du cou et du visage,
faire d'engageantes minauderies' ('Prov. *far col et cais*', Romania, XLII, 1913,
pp. 79–83; see pp. 81–2) and by J. Linskill 'to try her simpering ways' (*The
Poems of the Troubadour Raimbaut de Vaqueyras*, The Hague, 1964, XXIII, 23 and
p. 257 note).
27. Cf. Guiraut de Bornelh, *Sämtliche Lieder des Trobadors Giraut de Bornelh*, ed. A.
Kolsen (Halle, 1920–35) XXXIII, 70; Raimon de Miraval XXXIV, 18–19.
See also G. M. Cropp, *Le Vocabulaire courtois des troubadours de l'époque classique*
(Geneva, 1975), pp. 190–2.
28. Cf. 'C'amat ai lonjamen/Tal don' ad essien/C'anc servirs ni plazers/No mi
poc esser bos,/Ni preiars ni chansos/Ni celars ni temers,/Qu'ieu no-i trobes
enguan;/Et ieu, sofren mon dan,/Saup l'enguanar totz enguanatz/E remaner
ab liei en patz' (For I have for a long time used my knowledge in loving such a
lady whose deceitfulness was not prevented by the service, compliments
entreaties, songs, discretion or timidity I devoted to her; enduring my injury, I
knew how to deceive her while being deceived myself and to stay peacefully in
her company), Raimon de Miraval XIV, 20. Elsewhere Raimon declares he
has abandoned ruse (I, 9–16) or that he is devoid of deceit and guile (XVII,
26, XVIII, 31).
29. Cf. 'Qu'el gen parlar e-l avinen solatz/E-l amoros visatge/Cug que me son del
cor verai messatge', Raimon de Miraval VII, 34–6; cf. V, 32.
30. II, 29, III, 14–16, V, 1–8, VI, 1–20, 33, 41–4, IX, 39, XII, 44–6, 49–50,
XXXII, 49–54. See L. T. Topsfield, 'Raimon de Miraval and the art of
courtly love', *Modern Language Review*, LI (1956), pp. 33–41.
31. Cf. III, 36–8, VII, 41–3, IX, 56–8, X, 31, XVII, 3, 25–32, XXVIII, 1–16.
32. Cf. André le Chapelain, *Traité de l'amour courtois*, trad. etc. by Claude Buridant
(Paris, 1974), p.183, XXXI.
33. Raimon de Miraval expresses in a probably much later poem(XXXII) a
more mature attitude, informed by experience and reminiscent of Folquet de
Marseille's line of argument in the *partimen*, allowing for the use of strategy in
love. For example: 'Ben aia qui prim fetz jelos,/Qe tant cortes mestier saup
far;/Qe jelosia-m fai gardar/De mals parliers e d'enojos,/E de jelosi' ai
apres/So don mi eis tenc en defes/Ad ops d'una c'autra non deing,/Mais de
cortejar m'en esteing./E val mais bella tracios/Don ja hom non perda son
par,/C'autrui benananss' envejar' (Blessed be he who first acted out of
jealousy for knowing how to behave in such a courtly manner; for jealousy
makes me beware of slanderers and troublemakers and has taught me to

concentrate entirely on one lady, so that I do not care about another and I even refrain from courting her. A nice act of betrayal by which one does not lose one's prestige is preferable to envying someone else's happiness), vv. 33–43. Three points are to be noticed: jealousy (cf. André le Chapelain, *Traité de l'amour courtois*, pp. 153–4, 182, II), the successful use of deceit and, foremost still, the lover's devotion to one lady. There is tension throughout the poem between general principles and Raimon's own feelings and behaviour as he defends both excesses of behaviour committed under the influence of love and tactics which might ordinarily be considered anti-courtly employed to assure success in love. When compared with Raimon de Miraval's other lyrics, the poem shows the sinuous interpretation to which courtly love was at times subject. Or is it an argument of expediency?

34. Cf. VIII, 1–20, XII, 20–1. Love requires the full application of the mind: III, 8–12, IV, 65, V, 23.

35. Cf. 'Aras cuiaran maldizen/Qu'en loc d'autra cobertura/Fassa de midons rancura,/Et qu'ieu ame seladamen,/Car me sabon *ginhos d'amar*' (Now the slanderers will imagine that instead of some other ruse I am complaining about my lady and that I love her secretly for they know me to be cunning in love), Raimon de Miraval II, 25–9.

36. Cf. 'Mantenen tort e zo don non ai cura,/Vos ai vencut, Luchetz, don sui ioios,/Car ai mostrat q'eu sai tan plus de vos,/C'ab tort conten miels qe vos ab drechura' (Defending wrong and a matter which is of indifference to me, I have defeated you, Luquet, which makes me glad, for I have shown that I know so much more than you that I can dispute on the side of wrong better than you on the side of right), Bonifazio Calvo and Luquet Gatelus, *Luchetz, se.us platz mais amar finamen* (G. Bertoni, *I Trovatori d'Italia*, Modena, 1915, pp. 430–3. P.-C., 101.8a), vv. 61–4.

I am grateful to Terence H. Newcombe, Department of French, University of Edinburgh, who read and commented on this essay which was written while I was a Visiting Research Fellow at the Institute for Advanced Studies in the Humanities, University of Edinburgh.

5   *'Ab joi mou lo vers e'l comens'*

JOAN M. FERRANTE

Provençal is a language that lends itself by its very structure to ambiguity. Its vocabulary developed from Latin with a strong tendency to [word-play] abbreviation: a word with two unstressed syllables at the end usually lost both (e.g., Latin *nitidem* gives Provençal *net*); intervocalic consonants often disappeared (*regem* gives *rei*, *bonum* becomes *bo*, 'good', which is only distinguishable from *bo*, 'ox', by its context). The loss of the last syllable, combined with vowel shifts, can reduce a series of different Latin words to the same Provençal monosyllable: *sensum, sentio, cinctum,* and *signum* all become *sen*. As a result, the language is filled with homonyms, a factor which encourages various kinds of word-play. A line of poetry made up mainly of monosyllables, or of longer words which can be subdivided, might be understood in more than one way, so an audience that wished to catch the poet's meaning would have to listen attentively to a performance. That means that a poet could indulge in rich sound effects with the expectation that at least a part of his audience would appreciate them.

Many of the early poets engage in intricate plays with language and sound, but no one takes advantage of the built-in ambiguities as Bernart de Ventadorn does.[1] His rhymes are rarely based on difficult sounds or polysyllabic words, as Raimbaut's and Arnaut Daniel's are. He relies more on simple words with many possible meanings, and simple rhyme schemes with heavy emphasis on the same sounds; a few distinct sounds usually dominate a given poem. Of the forty-four extant poems,[2] thirty-two are *unissonans*, with the same rhyme sounds throughout the poem, ten are *coblas doblas*, the same sounds through two stanzas; only one is *singolars*, with different sounds in each stanza, and one is a variation which introduces a single new rhyme in each stanza.

The intentional use of homonyms is one of Bernart's most noticeable effects, since they often appear as rhyme words: in 'Non es meravelha s'eu chan', the *d* rhyme, 'mes', means 'put in' in the first stanza, 'month' in the second, 'placed' in the third, and 'is to me' ('m'es') in the fourth. The first line of another poem, 'Bel m'es qu'eu chan en aquel mes', uses two of the same forms in an intentional pun. In 'Pois preyatz me, senhor' (A.36, L.18), the *b* rhyme, 'sai', means 'I know' in the second stanza, 'here' in the third, and is contained within 'essai', 'I attempt' in the first; even more obviously, Bernart uses the word three times in three successive lines, with two meanings:

...qu'eu o *sai*.	...that I *know*.
mas eu sui *sai*, alhor,	But I am *here*, elsewhere,
e no *sai*... (ll. 13–15)	and I don't *know*...[3]

The well-known 'Can vei la lauzeta mover' (A.43, L.31), which is filled with word-plays of different kinds, contains a homonym rhyme: 'fon', a *d* rhyme, means 'dissolve' in I, 'fountain' in III, and, as 'cofon', 'confound', in stanza IV. The word *sens* is similarly treated in 'Can l'erba fresch' e'lh folha par' (A.39, L.20): as a *d* rhyme, it means 'girded' in I, both 'directions' and 'sign' in V, where it rhymes with itself, and 'signs' again as part of *entresens* in VI. The use of the same rhyme word with a different meaning within one stanza is striking; it also occurs in 'Lo gens tems de pascor' (A.28, L.17), stanza VII, where 'dos', 'two', rhymes with 'dos', 'gifts'. 'Sen' is also a rhyme word in 'Era'm cosselhatz, senhor' (A.6, L.25), meaning 'sense' or 'wisdom' in stanza I and 'one hundred' ('cen') in VII; a pun is probably intended in the first instance with 'senhor', the lords who have the 'sen' he is relying on ('Era'm cosselhatz, *sen*hor/vos c'avetz saber e *sen*', 'Now advise me lords,/you who have the knowledge and wisdom'). In 'Non es meravelha', 'sen' appears as a rhyme word three times with different meanings: 'sense' or 'wisdom' in I, 'feels' in II, and 'a hundred' in stanza IV.

There are also instances of inner rhymes using homonyms, as in 'Tant ai mo cor ple de joya' (A.44, L.4):

mo *cor* ai pres d'Amor,	I have my *heart* close to Love,
que l'esperitz lai *cor*,	for the spirit *runs* there,
mas lo *cors* es sai, alhor (33–5).	but my *body* is here, elsewhere.

The play on 'cor' is emphasized by the other rhyme words, 'Amor', 'alhor', as well as by the other inner rhyme: 'cor *ai*, *lai* cor, cors es *sai*'. In a sense, 'cor' encloses the poem, as 'heart' in the first line and as 'run' in the first line of the envoi. In the phrase, '*mas mas* jônchas', '*my hands* joined' ('Can vei la flor, l'erba vert e la folha', A.42, L.7), Bernart puts the homonyms together.[4] In 'Can vei la lauzeta', he uses two meanings of two different words within two lines:

tout m'a *mo* cor, e *tout* m'a me   She has *taken away* from me *my* heart and me
e se mezeis e *tot* lo *mon* (13–14)   and herself and *all* the *world*.

But Bernart's interest in sound is not limited to this kind of word-play. A few examples will illustrate the kinds of effect Bernart can achieve. The first, from 'Pois preyatz me', has already been quoted in part for the use of *sai*. Here is the whole second stanza:

Gran ben e gran onor   Great good and great honour
conosc que Deus me fai   I know God does me
qu'eu am la belazor   for I love the most beautiful one,
et ilh me, qu'eu o sai.   and she me, and this I know.
mas eu sui sai, alhor,   But I am here, elsewhere,
e no sai com l'estai!   and I don't know how it is with her.
so m'auci de dolor,   This kills me with sorrow,
car ochaizo non ai   for I do not have the opportunity
de soven venir lai (10–18).   to come there often.

The importance of the *ai* sound throughout, not only in the *b* rhyme, 'fai', 'sai', 'estai', 'ai', 'lai', but also in the inner rhymes, 'sai' (ll. 14, 15), 'ochaizo', is clear. The repetition of 'sai' in three successive lines is central to the shift of tone in the stanza from the affirmative statement of the first four lines to the plaintive sense of the last five; this is achieved mainly through the words which precede 'sai' and stand out because of the insistence of the sound that follows them: 'qu'eu *o* sai', 'mas eu *sui* sai', 'e *no* sai' ('for I know *this*', 'but I *am* here', 'and I *don't* know'). *O* is an important sound in this passage, because of the contrast between *o* and *no*, but it is also central to the stanza, beginning with the 'onor'/'conosc' juxtaposition, carrying through the *a* rhymes ('onor', 'belazor', 'alhor', 'dolor'), the 'So' and 'dolor' at the beginning and end of line 16, the alternation with *ai* sounds in line 17 ('ochaizo non ai'), to 'soven' in the last line, a word further emphasized by the repetition of *ven* in 'venir' (and by a homonym two lines later, in the third stanza, 'can de leis me sove' 'when I *remember* her').

'Non es meravelha', a poem which has already been cited for examples of homonym rhymes, is similarly rich in other effects, inner rhymes, plays with words, and patterns of sound repetitions. In the lines 'Cor e cors e saber e sen/e fors' e poder' (5–6), there is the inner rhyme of 'cors e saber' with 'fors' e poder', which breaks or overlaps the pattern of paired nouns, an alliterative pairing, in the first two cases. The first pair, 'cor' and 'cors', are also virtually homonyms, often hard to distinguish in Provençal poetry. Bernart returns to this sound in lines 54–5, 'francs *cors* umils, gais e *cortes*!/*ors* ni leos non etz . . .' ('fine, humble *body*, gay and *courtly*! You are no *bear* or lion . . .'); the repetition of sound throws the unexpected 'ors' into especially high relief. 'Cor' also appears as part of a pattern of inner rhymes:

Ben es mortz qui d'amor no sen	en . . . or . . . or . . . en
al cor cal que dousa sabor (9–10)	(a) or a . . . . (a) a or.

Line 10 is virtually repeated in the fourth stanza (l. 26), where it is part of a similar pattern of sounds. Here again, because of the variety of sounds and the intricacy of their patterns, I quote the entire stanza:

Aquest'amors me fer tan gen	a . . a or . . a *en*	
al cor d'una dousa sabor:	a or . . . . a a or	
cen vetz mor lo jorn de dolor	*en* . . or . . or . . or	
e reviu de joi autras cen.	a *en*	
Ben es mos mals de bel semblan,	*en* es os als . . (an)	b m m b b
que mais val mos mals qu'autre bes;	. . al os als . . . es	m m m b
e pois mos mals aitan bos m'es,	. . os als . . os es	m m b m
bos er lo bes apres l'afan (25–32).	os . . es . . es a (an)	b b

The two quatrains are concerned with the same idea, that the ills of love are really good, but in different terms, and with different sounds. The first quatrain relies on the *or* and *a* sounds of love ('amor') in the language of death ('mor') and rebirth; the second quatrain, completely dominated by *b*'s and *m*'s and the conflict between good ('ben', 'bos') and bad ('mals'), with the focus on 'me' or 'my' ('mos'), ends with a positive statement (that the good which comes after the anguish will be good), and a return to the *a* sounds that began the stanza.

Sometimes Bernart uses the repetition of a sound simply to create a mood, as in the self-pitying opening stanzas of 'En cossirer et en esmai' (A.17, L.40), which are dominated by the lamenting *ai* sound.

> I En cossirer et en esm*ai*
> sui d'un'amor qu'm lass' e'm te
> que tan no vau ni s*ai* ni l*ai* (1–3)
>   . . .
>
> II *Ai* las, ch*ai*tius! e que'm far*ai*?
> ni cal cosselh penr*ai* de me?
> qu'ela no sap lo mal qu'eu tr*ai* (9–11).
>   . . .

III E doncs, pois atressi'm morr*ai*,
   dir*ai* li l'afan que m'en ve?
   vers es c'ades lo li dir*ai*.
   no far*ai* ... (17–20)

In each case, these are the opening lines of the stanza and they set the
tone which is carried through the last line of stanzas I and II in 'fa*i*h'
(l. 8) and 'la*i*sses' (l. 16). In the fifth stanza, other sounds become equally
noticeable:

E doncs, ela, cal tort m'i fai	d
qu'ilh no sap per que e'esdeve?	de
Deus! devinar degra oimai	de de de
qu'eu mor per s'amor! et a que? (33–6)	mor mor

Here the *ai* sound is complicated by juxtaposition to *oi* in 'oimai', and the
hammerlike repetition of d's from the second to the third line, which
gives the third line a particularly harsh sound. The poet's self-pity
reaches its climax in these four lines, after which he takes a different tack.

   The use of *ai* as a lament also occurs in the first stanza of 'Can vei la
lauzeta', a complicated poem about which so much has been written that
I will limit my comments to a few elements which are particularly
relevant to this discussion. The first stanza offers several examples:

   Can vei la lauzeta mover
   de joi sas alas contral r*ai*,
   que s'oblida e's la*i*ssa chazer
   per la doussor c'al cor li v*ai*,
   ai! tan grans enveya m'en ve
   de cui qu'eu veya jauzion,
   meravilhas *ai*, car desse
   lo cor de dezirer no'm fon.

'Ai las!' is the first word of the next stanza, drawing together all the
implicit laments in these lines. In the first quatrain, where the poet
speaks of the joy and oblivion of the bird's flight, he makes a rather
intoxicating use of *al* – 'la *l*auzeta', '*al*as contral', '*al* cor' – along with its
reverse, *la* 'la *l*auzeta', 'la*i*ssa', *la* doussor'. But probably the most
interesting play is in the *ve* words, where the same sounds have very
different meanings: 'can vei' ('when I see'), 'enveya m'en ve' ('envy
comes to me of it'), and 'eu veya' ('that I might see'). The pun on 'see'

and 'envy' has a counterpart in stanza III, in the words 'miralh', 'mirror', and 'mirei', 'I looked':

> que'm laisset en sos olhs vezer
> en un miralh que mout me plai.
> miralhs, pus me mirei en te (19–21).

This passage has other echoes of the first stanza in the words 'laisset' and 'vezer', and the phrase, 'en te' (cf. 'en ve'). 'Olhs' is also connected with vision – her eyes are the mirror in which he sees himself. In another poem about a mirror, 'Lancan vei la folha' (A.25, L.38), 'olh' is important both for meaning and sound.[5] In the sixth stanza, it is the *b* rhyme, occurring once as 'eyes' and within five other words, 'orgolh', 'solh', 'colh', 'volh', 'tolh'; all but 'orgolh' are first person verbs. *Orgolh*, 'pride', appears twice in the stanza, once as a rhyme word, and once as inner rhyme:

> ...v*olh*.   ...I desire
> org*olh*s, Deus vos franha,   Pride, may God crush you,
> c'ara'n ploron mei *olh* (68–70)   for my eyes now weep because of you.

The eyes weep because of the pride, but their weeping is a sign that the pride is broken and indeed, in the next stanza when the word occurs (l. 77), it refers to the pride of others. (The sound *olh* also recurs in this stanza (VII) within a pair of very important pronouns: 'e man *lo'lh* ostatge' 'I send *it* [my heart] *to her* as a hostage'.)

Since sound does play such an important part in Bernart's poems, it should be useful to take one poem and investigate the language from that perspective, looking at rhyme sounds, inner rhymes, and any other distinctive sound patterns, to see how they contribute to the meaning as well as to the poetic effect. I have chosen a poem which has not received much critical attention, and which does not turn up in anthologies, 'Ab joi mou lo vers e'l comens' (A.1, L.3).[6] It does, nonetheless, treat themes which recur frequently in Bernart's poetry – the problem of writing a poem, the threat of hostile outsiders, the beauty and power of the lady – and it offers many examples of the techniques I have been describing. My emphasis on sound does not indicate that I consider the meaning less important, but rather that, since the sound effects are so striking, they should be the poet's signals of where the meaning lies.[7]

The first stanza is about beginning and endings, of a poem, apparently, but also, by implication, of love:

I Ab joi mou lo vers e'l comens,
   et ab joi reman e fenis;
   e sol que bona fos la fis,
   bos tenh qu'er lo comensamens.
   per la bona comensansa
   mi [me] ve jois et alegransa;
   e per so dei la bona fi grazir,

   car totz bos faihz vei lauzar al
      fenir.

With joy I start my poem and begin it
and with joy I end* and finish it;
and as long as the end is good,
I hold that the beginning will have been.
Through the good beginning,
joy and happiness come to me;
and for that reason, I should welcome
   the good finish
for I see all good deeds praised at their
   conclusion.
      * or 'continue'

The meaning of these lines seems to be clear, and yet there is a great deal of potential ambiguity in the sounds, as so often in Bernart's poetry. Few of the possible readings I am about to suggest should be taken seriously, nonetheless they are possible, and it is well to be aware of their quantity, at least. It is not, after all, inconceivable that an audience, hearing a poem sung, might lose an occasional word or phrase or, momentarily distracted, might hear a phrase that was not intended by the poet. The large number of variant readings in different manuscripts suggests that the scribes, at least, heard different words.[8] In the first line, 'mou' can mean 'I move' or 'I begin' or 'it moves', and 'vers' can be 'true' as well as 'poem'; the words might be divided differently, so that the line could be heard as: 'ab joi mou lo ver sel com ens', 'the true heaven moves with joy as within'. In the second line, the words as they stand are capable of two interpretations, since the verbs might be either first person (as in the translation above) or third person, and 'reman' can mean 'continue' or 'end'; the line may thus mean 'and with joy it continues (or 'ends') and finishes'. This confusion suggests that despite the apparent clarity of his statement, we cannot be certain where the poet is going, as indeed the poem bears out.[9]

Although the context normally establishes the intended reading, and the existence of literary clichés would lead an audience to hear some words or phrases rather than others, one does have to be attentive; sometimes it is not until the end of a line that one can be sure of the meaning.[10] That demands an attention to the sound that might well make the audience responsive to sound plays which occur frequently in this poem. The rhyme scheme is *abbaccdd*, *unissonans*, the same rhyme sounds in the same positions throughout the poem. The metric scheme follows the rhyme scheme in that the lines of the first quatrain are the same length, eight syllables; the two couplets are seven (the *c* rhyme is feminine) and ten syllables. The rhyme endings are echoed in various ways within this stanza: the *a* rhyme, *ens*, or *mens* in this case (which becomes an important element in the third stanza) is doubled in the second *a* word, co*mens*amens, and recurs in the first *c* rhyme, 'co*mens*ansa'; the *en* sound within the *a* rhyme occurs in the first *b* word, 'f*en*is', and the last *d* word, 'f*en*ir':

comens	(mens)
fenis	(en)
– – –	
comensamens	(mens . . mens)
comensansa	(mens)
– – –	
– – –	
fenir	(en).

The two *b* words, 'fenis' and 'fis', alliterate with the *d* word, 'fenir'. There is a certain pattern in the opening consonants of the rhyme words:

$$
\begin{array}{cc}
 & c \\
 & f \\
 & f \\
 & c \\
 & c \\
(g/c) & - \\
 & g/c \\
 & f \\
\end{array}
$$

and in the vowels of the rhyme words as well:

$$
\begin{array}{cccc}
o & e & & \\
 & e & i & \\
 & & i & \\
o & e & a & e \\
o & e & a & a \\
a & e & a & a \\
 & & a & i \\
 & & e & i. \\
\end{array}
$$

The various sound patterns described here do not overlap the pattern o the rhyme scheme except in the first four consonants, c/f/f/c, which reinforce the abba rhyme. Thus we have at least four kinds of sound pattern: rhyme, inner rhyme, assonance, and alliteration, operating in the last word of each line, connecting and distinguishing the lines in a variety of ways.

There is yet another kind of connection and contrast going on as well, that of meaning: of the eight words, six have to do with beginning and ending in an *A B B A A — — B* pattern, which reinforces the rhyme scheme in the first quatrain:

a	*A*
b	*B*
b	*B*
a	*A*
c	*A*
c	*—*
d	*(B)–*
d	*B*

The *a* rhyme words and one of the *c* words have the same stem ('comens') as do the two *b* and one *d* word ('fenir'). And in the seventh line, the word 'fi' ('end') appears just before the rhyme word. The only other rhyme word which does not fit this pattern, 'alegransa', is a synonym for 'joi', a word which forms a pattern towards the beginning of the lines, paired with 'bos' or 'bona', 'good'. Although the latter occurs in the middle of the line more often than at the beginning, its recurrence in alternating lines makes the pattern clear:

joi
joi
bona
bos
bona
jois
bona
bos.

If we put the two word patterns together, we get still another pattern:

joi	comens
joi	fenis
bona	fis
bos	comensamens
bona	comensansa
jois	(alegransa)
bona	fi (grazir)
bos	fenir.

In other words, joy at the beginning means joy at the end; a good end implies a good beginning, which leads to redoubled joy, and a double affirmation of a good end.[11]

The beginning and ending refer apparently to the poem ('lo vers', l. 1), but the inspiration and persistence of joy make it clear that the poet is also talking about his love. It is that, more than the poem, which must come to a good end, and which, if it does, will justify its beginning; that is the good end which will bring joy and praise at the conclusion. The praise may be both a metaphor for his reward in love and an allusion to the expected response to his poem, leading us back at the end of the stanza to the subject of the first line. Joy in love is the source of the song, but the song is also the beginning of love; the beginning is good, but we will learn how good the song is only by its end, the completed poem, and by its success in achieving the end of love, the consummation. It is only at the end ('al fenir') that we can judge the real worth (the 'good') of any deeds or songs.

But a problem arises in the second stanza, precisely from the joy which inspires the first:

II Si m'apodera jois e'm vens:	Joy so overpowers and conquers me,
meravilh'es com o sofris	it is a wonder how I endure it,
car no dic e non esbruis	for I do not say or proclaim
per cui sui tan gais e jauzens;	the one through whom I am so gay and rejoicing;
mas greu veiretz fin'amansa	with difficulty will you find true loving
ses paor e ses doptansa,	without fear and without doubt,
c'ades tem om vas so c'ama, falhir,	for one always fears that he will fail what he loves
per qu'eu no'm aus de parlar enardir.	which is why I don't dare make bold to speak.

Of the words that dominated the first stanza, only 'jois' appears in this, and then only in the negative sense of an enemy force which overwhelms; there is no good, no beginning or end. The word 'fin' occurs in the fifth line, but with the meaning of 'pure', 'true', certainly a play on the 'fis' (l. 3) and 'fi' (l. 7) of the previous stanza.[12]

This 'fin'amansa', the 'pure loving', which replaces both beginning and end, and which is all, is apparently to be found only with difficulty or rarely, so line 5 leads us to believe; actually, as we learn in line 6, it is not to be found without fear. The whole stanza has a negative tone, from the effect of 'jois' in the first line, to the poet's inability to speak, in the last. The tone is conveyed not only by the negative conjunctions, 'no'/'non' in l. 3, 'ses'/'ses' in l. 6, and 'no' in l. 8, but also by the meanings of other words: 'apodera' ('overpowers'), 'vens' ('conquers'), 'sofris' ('endure'), 'greu' ('with difficulty'), 'paor' ('fear'), 'doptansa' ('doubt'), 'tem' ('fears'), 'falhir' ('fail'). The poet's fear, which is the result of his love, is mentioned three times in two lines ('paor', 'doptansa', 'tem'); boldness is alluded to twice in the last line ('aus', 'enardir'), but in the negative, hence it simply reinforces its opposite, fear. The love in l. 5, like the joy in l. 1 which had been the source of the poem in the first stanza, now makes it impossible for the poet to speak – or so he tells us. In fact, he says everything twice: 'm'apodera . . . e'm vens', 'no dic e non esbruis', 'gais e jauzens', 'ses paor e ses doptansa', 'aus enardir'. Either he is emphasizing the difficulty he feels in communicating, or he is showing up his own claim. The only affirmative repetition is the 'gais e jauzens', but since that brings us back to the 'jois' in line 1, we know that it too has a negative connotation; the triple assertion of joy in the first quatrain is quickly countered by the triple fear in lines 6 and 7.

This stanza lacks both the word patterns and the complicated sound patterns of the first, as if the poet's inability to speak meant a loss of the power to play with language, though certainly not the loss of vocabulary, as we have seen. The rhyme words have echoes, but all outside the stanza (see below, pp. 132–3). The only striking sound effects are the hissing s's and the almost stuttering repetition of certain sounds: 'com o sofris'; 'esbruis/. . cui sui'; 'greu veiretz'; 'tem om vas so'; 'parlar enardir'. Several of these are uncomfortable to mouth, forcing the performer to make the kind of effort to express himself which the poet is claiming he has to make. The stanza has many diphthongs which require more effort to mouth than simple vowels: jois, esbruis, cui, sui, gais, jauzens, greu veiretz, paor, eu aus. Diphthongs did not occur often in the first stanza, except in the last line and the repeated joi.

The poet is back in control in the third stanza. Now he is able not only to speak, but also to lie effectively in order to conceal his love, a complete turnabout from what seemed to be promised in the first stanza, and his language is full of the effects noted in I;

III D'una re m'aonda mos sens: My sense aids me in one way:
    c'anc nulhs om mo joi no'm enquis,   no man ever asked me about my joy
    qu'eu volonters no l'en mentis;   to whom I did not willingly lie about it;
    car no'm par bos essenhamens,   for it does not seem good breeding to me
    ans es foli' et efansa,   but rather folly and childishness[13]
    qui d'amor a benanansa   when one has the fortune of love
    ni'en vol so cor ad autre descobrir, to wish to reveal his heart to another,
    ni no l'en pot o valer o servir.   if it can't help or serve him,

Once again the rhyme words are related to each other by sound and meaning, not so dramatically as in I, but much more than in II;

sens	sen
m'enquis	men
mentis	men
essenhamens	sen men
efansa	
benanansa	en.

– – –

– – –

'Sens', the first *a* rhyme, is repeated in the second *a* rhyme, 'essenha-mens', and is connected both by sound and by meaning to the rhyme sound in the same word, 'mens', which echoes the two *b* rhymes, 'm'enquis' and 'mentis'. That 'men' by itself means 'mind' is no coincidence, particularly since the poet contrasts his sense and educa-tion with folly and infancy (l. 5), and since he uses his mind, he tells us, to lie ('mentis') willingly and regularly.[14] *Sens* is further emphasized by the fact that it is the first noun to occur as the first *a* rhyme; the other two were verbs. Since the words in the same position in different stanzas tend to be the same grammatical form throughout the poem (dictated at least partially by the endings), the exceptions or changes in pattern stand out.[15]

The rhyme words are also connected by alliteration, though not so much as in I:

s	sens
m	m'enquis
m	mentis
s(m)	essenhamens
	efansa
	benanansa
s	descobrir
s	servir.

The *en* sound which dominates the *a* and *b* rhyme words is echoed in the second *c* word, 'benanansa'. The sound *m* is emphasized in the first two lines, '*m*'aonda *m*os . . . / . . o*m m*o . . no'*m*', drawing attention to the 'me' it usually indicates. There are other kinds of sound echo within the stanza, from the beginning to the end of a line: in line 5, '*ans* . . . e*fansa*'; l. 7, '*ni* . . . descob*rir*'; l. 8, '*si* . . . servi*r*'; some inner rhyme: 'am*or*' (l. 6) with 'so c*or*' (l. 7), and 'ni'n v*ol*' (l. 7) with 'si no l'' (l. 8), all of which help to create a sense of harmony, albeit a false sense.

The 'joi' that dominated stanza I is mentioned only once, as in the second stanza; it is the source here not of the lover's poem, but of his lies.

Or perhaps the poem, since it is the product of his 'joi' (and his mind, 'men') is all a lie. The 'bos' with which 'joi' was paired in I occurs once in III to modify 'essenhamens', but good breeding to the poet means hiding his love except when it will serve a purpose to reveal it. If that purpose is the 'bona fis' (the 'good end') he spoke of in the first stanza, or the 'bos faihz' ('good deeds') which would only be praised at their outcome, it is something of a let-down from what they seemed to promise.

In the fourth stanza, which returns to the negative tone of the second, the poet attacks those who try to find out about his love, as though he had completely forgotten the mood in which he began the poem:

IV Non es enois ni falhimens
   ni vilania, so m'es vis,
   mas d'ome, can se fai devis
   d'autrui amor ni conoissens.
   enoyos! e que'us enansa,

   si'm faitz enoi ni pesansa?
   chascus se vol de so mestier formir;
   me cofondetz, e vos no'n vei jauzir.

There is no annoyance or fault
or villainy, it seems to me,
greater than that of a man who would spy
on another's love or learn about it.
trouble-makers – and what good does it
   do you
if you trouble or harm me?
everyone wants to succeed at what he does;
you confound me, and I don't see you
   enjoying it.

This stanza is the low point of the poet's moods in the poem. It is full of negative particles ('non', 'ni'), five of them in six lines, and negative words: 'enois' ('annoyance'), 'falhimens' ('fault'), 'vilania' ('villainy'), 'enoyos' ('trouble-makers'), 'enoi' ('trouble'), 'pesansa' ('harm'), 'cofodetz' ('confound'), and a good number of potential ambiguities.[16] The dominant word in the stanza is some form of *enois*, which replaces 'joi' – this is the first stanza in which 'joi' does not appear at all – both in sound and meaning. *Enois* is what is caused by those who are curious about his love to no purpose, and it effectively dispels 'joi' from the poem; 'alegransa' is mentioned in the second envoi, but 'joi' never reappears. 'Enois' is contrasted with 'jauzir', the last word of the stanza, in the very negative sense: you bother me, but you get no pleasure from it. 'Jauzir', the last rhyme word, and 'falhimens', the first, both echo rhyme words from the second stanza, the first time this has occurred in the poem: 'jauzens' was the second *a* rhyme, 'falhir' the first *d* rhyme. In that stanza, the poet was concerned with his inability to speak because of the joy he felt; the 'jauzens' was real, although its effect was negative, and the 'falhir' was the failure he feared but had not yet known. In stanza IV the 'falhimens' has apparently been committed, often and the 'jauzir' is non-existent.

'Falhimens' picks up the *men* sound that was so important in stanzas

III and I, and its rhyme-pair, 'conoissens', contains the other *a* rhyme from the third stanza, *sens*, but in reverse order:

III	*sens*	IV	falhi*mens*
	essenha*mens*		conois*sens.*

Sens in stanza IV is connected with learning for the wrong reasons, which may also be true of *men*, though *men* certainly still carries the sense of lying. There are other connections among the rhyme words: the two *b* rhymes, 'vis' and 'devis' contain the same word, and the first *c* rhyme, 'enansa', begins with the *en* sound of the *a* rhyme (which was echoed in one *c* rhyme in both I and III, and in a *d* rhyme in I), but the last three rhyme words of the stanza are unconnected to others within the stanza. 'Vis', the first *b* rhyme, is a past participle in the passive mode – rather than an active verb, as the first *b* rhyme has been heretofore, which is not surprising since in this stanza the poet is more acted upon than acting. 'Enansa', the first *c* rhyme, is the only verb in that position in the entire poem; it is a verb normally connected in Provençal lyric with the exalting nature of love, but here it is used in a very negative sense. The activities of the trouble-makers cannot exalt them, but can prevent the poet's being exalted.

The dominant sound effects in the stanza, apart from the rhymes, emphasize the same ideas. There is a kind of inner rhyme involving the central word 'enois': 'Non es enois' begins the first line; 'conoissens', which turns the same sounds around ('s en ois / oissens'), ends the first quatrain. A second reversal of those sounds occurs in the very next word, 'enoyos', which also begins the second quatrain. 'Enoyos' alliterates with 'enansa' at the end of the line, but contrasts with it in sense, and seems to surround it with the repetition of 'enoi' in the following line. In the last line, there is an internal rhyme involving the repetition of four sounds: 'me cofondetz e vos non vei' (*e o on e / e o on e*). The alliteration of the v's also occurred in the second line, 'vilania . . . vis', connecting the enemy 'vos' of line eight with the villainy described earlier; the v's provide the link between the object of the third person description in the first quatrain and the direct attack of the second. The *vi* of 'vilania' and 'vis' is echoed in the rhyme word of the next line, 'devis', which alliterates with 'd'ome' in the same line, and with 'd'autrui' which begins the next line, linking the enemy, his activity, and his object. All of the sound effects, along with the insistence of *i* sounds in five of the first six lines:

                    ni . . lhi
              ni vi . . . vis
                         vis
          ui . . ni
          – – –
          si . . . ni

and the alliteration of *en* and repetition of *s* sounds[17] (e.g. 'enoyos . . . us
enansa') serves to give the stanza the effect of a chanted attack, with the
nasty sing-song quality of children's taunts, on the trouble-makers. And
the music seems to heighten that effect. (See below, pp. 136–7.)

W hat is needed against these enemies is courage, not the poet's but his
lady's:

V   Ben estai a domn' ardimens   Courage sits well with a woman
    entr'avols gens e mals vezis;   among base people and evil neighbours;
    e s'arditz cors no l'afortis,   and if a bold heart does not fortify her,
    greu pot esser pros ni valens;   she can scarcely be valiant or worthy;
    per qu'eu prec, n'aya membransa   which is why I pray that she be mindful,
    la bel' en cui ai fiansa,   the beauty in whom I have placed my trust,
    que no's chamje per paraulas ni's vir, not to be changed or diverted by words,
    qu'enemics c'ai, fatz d'enveya morir.   to make the enemies I have die of envy.

This is a fairly straightforward statement and, poetically, it is one of the
least complicated stanzas. There are some ambiguities in language,[18]
and a certain amount of inner rhyme and alliteration, but they are used
simply to reinforce the surface meaning, not to extend or undercut it.

The rhyme words are linked by alliteration, as in I;

a	ardimens
v	vezis
a f/v	afortis
v	valens
m	membransa
f/v	fiansa
v	vir
m	morir.

'Ardimens' and 'afortis' are connected by meaning, as well as by
alliteration, reinforced in both by 'arditz' in line three. ('Valens',
rhyming with 'ardimens', is also connected by meaning.) 'Ardimens',
the first rhyme word in the stanza, and the dominant idea, echoes the last
rhyme word in stanza II, 'enardir', where the poet spoke of his own loss

of courage to speak. In this stanza, he is working himself up to addressing the lady directly, as he will do in stanza VII, by encouraging her to ignore those around them. Two of the rhyme words are exceptions in the pattern of parts of speech (cf. fn. 15); 'vezis' is a noun where we have heretofore had a verb and it emphasizes the enemies to be fought; 'vir', l. 7, is an active verb where we have always had an infinitive, and always in a rather general observation that certainly applies to the poet but never describes him directly. Here it describes, in an active manner, the action he does not wish the lady to take.

The *en* sound which recurs so frequently in this poem in inner rhymes, as well as in the *a* rhyme, begins the stanza: 'Ben' at the beginning of the first line, 'mens' at the end; 'entr' begins the second line; 'gens', which falls in the middle of the line clearly rhymes with the preceding rhyme word, 'ardimens', fittingly, since it is the object against which the lady's courage must be exercised; 'valens', describing her as he hopes she will be, picks up the same rhyme. *En* occurs again in the last line both at the beginning, 'enemics', and towards the end, 'enveya'; it is by envy that the poet hopes his enemies will be killed. The double rhyme in lines 5 and 6 is also connected in meaning: 'n'*ay*a membr*ansa*/*ai* fi*ansa*', 'let her be mindful', as 'I have faith in her'. The gentle alliteration of *p*'s, not a common sound in the poem, in lines 4, 5 and 7, also underlines his request: '*p*ot esser *p*ros/... *p*er qu'eu *p*rec.../*p*er *p*araulas no's vir' ('she can be worthy' 'I beg her', 'not to be changed by their words'), although he clearly hopes to influence her with *his* words.

Having disposed of the external problem, the poet reveals his own need:

VI   Anc sa bela bocha rizens   Never would her beautiful laughing mouth,
      non cuidei, baizan me träis,   I thought, betray me kissing,
      car ab un doutz baizar m'aucis,   for she kills me with a sweet kiss
      si ab autre no m'es guirens;   if she does not heal me with another;
      c'atretal m'es per semblansa   for it is exactly, it seems to me,
      com de Peläus la lansa,   as it was with Peleus' lance:
      que del seu colp no podi' om garir, one could not be cured of its wound
      si autra vetz no s'en fezes ferir.   unless one were struck by it again.

This is an even more affirmative stanza than the last – the mood improves consistently from the low point in stanza IV to the unadulterated praise of the lady in VII. There are again few ambiguities.[19] The rhyme words are connected by meaning more than sound: 'rizens' with 'guirens', since her laughing mouth provides the healing kiss; 'guirens' with 'garir', connected by stem and coming on either side of the wounding weapon, the 'lansa' (which is contained in 'semb*lansa*'); 'träis' with 'aucis', betrayed and killed; and, finally, 'garir' with 'ferir', curing with wounding, since it is the same weapon which does both and the poet's only salvation from death is continual wounding, quite different from the death by envy he wished to inflict on his enemies at the end of the preceding stanza. 'Rizens' is the only rhyme word which breaks the grammatical pattern in any way: it is an adjective where there have heretofore been two verbs and three nouns, and it announces that this stanza will do something new: it will describe the lady. (There is a second pattern in the initial *a*-rhyme word which is not based on the parts of speech: in the first three stanzas, it refers to the poet, in the fourth, the low point, to the enemies, and in the last three, to the lady.)

The dominant sound in the first quatrain is the *b* of 'bela', 'bocha', 'baizan' and 'baizar', impressing the image of the mouth and the kiss on us aurally as well as visually. The sound is echoed in the *ab* in lines 3 and 4, and 'sem*b*lansa' in 5, and recalled in the *p* of 'Peläus'. The *l* in 'Peläus' alliterates with 'la lansa', and its blow, 'de*l* seu co*l*p' (l. 7), the softer sound being connected with what is traditionally a male sex symbol, the lance, although here it is a metaphor for the female feature and symbol of the mouth, which is characterized by the stronger sound, *b*. It is as if the poet were relinquishing his part in the sexual game to the lady, in the same way he made up for his own lack of courage (cf. II, l. 8), by exhorting her to be brave (V).

A poem that purported, at the beginning, to be about the poet's joy and accomplishments, now turns out to be about the lady who presumably inspires them:

VII Bela domna, 'l vostre cors gens
    e'lh vostre belh olh m'an conquis,
    e'l doutz esgartz e lo clars vis,
    e'l vostre bels essenhamens,
    que, can be m'en pren esmansa,
    de beutat no'us trob egansa:
    la genser etz c'om posc' [posch']
      el mon chauzir,
    o no i vei clar dels olhs ab que'us
      remir.

Lovely lady, your noble body
and your beautiful eyes have conquered me,
and the sweet look and the bright face,
and your lovely manners;
when I reflect upon them,
I find no equal to you in beauty;
you are the noblest woman one can find
    in the world
or I do not see clearly with the eyes
    with which I look at you.

The poet has finally returned to the positive, self-confident tone with which he began the poem. The poetry is rich in harmony of sounds, plays with meaning, and connections with other stanzas. The language, apparently simple, is not without possible ambiguities.[20] Among the rhyme words there are two which play on homonyms that appeared earlier in the poem: 'gens', the first *a* rhyme, meaning 'noble', meant 'people' in V, 2, the 'avols gens' the poet encouraged the lady to ignore in order to prove her own worthiness; *vis*, the second *b* rhyme, means 'face', but in IV, 2, it was the past participle of 'to see'. This is particularly important since stanza VII is concerned with eyes and sight: 'olh', ('eye'), 'esgartz' ('look'), 'vei' ('I see'), 'olhs' ('eyes'), 'remir' ('I look'). 'Remir' is emphasized because it breaks the strong grammatical pattern of infinitives in the *d* rhymes: it is the only time the second *d* rhyme is an active verb.

In some way or other, all the first four rhyme words have connections with other stanzas: 'conquis', the first *b* rhyme, reminds us by meaning rather than sound of 'vens', the first *a* rhyme in stanza II; in II, it was 'joi' that conquered the poet, here it is the much more specific eyes of the lady. 'Essenhamens', the second *a* rhyme, was the second *a* rhyme in the third stanza, where the poet was concerned with the bad behaviour of those who spied on his love; 'no'm par *bos* essenhamens' has been replaced by 'vostre *bels* essenhamens'. *Bels* is the key word in the seventh stanza, as 'bos' was in the first. 'Bela' is the first word in the stanza, emphasized by alliteration with 'belh', 'bels', 'be', and 'beutat', and by inner rhymes like 'e'lh . . . belh' (l. 2), and 'e'l . . . bels' (l. 4). It also picks up and contrasts with the *b* alliterations in the previous stanza, 'bela', 'bocha', 'baizan', 'baizar'; here, in stanza VII, the poet emphasizes the beauty of the lady's eyes and bearing, which seem to have no negative side, rather than her mouth and kiss which both wound and heal. The poet may also be consciously echoing the *p* sounds ('Peläus', l. 6, 'podi', l. 7) of stanza VI, in his 'pren' and 'posc', particularly the latter: the negative seventh line in VI, 'que del seu colp *no podi'om* garir', '*one could not* be cured of its wound', is countered by the strongly affirmative seventh of stanza VII, 'la genser etz c'*om posc*'el mon chauzir', 'you are the noblest woman *one can* find in the world'. The poet seems to have overcome all the anguish he expressed in the middle stanzas of the poem, and his language echoes the harmony of his thoughts: the repetition of *o* sounds at the beginning and end of the stanza: 'd*o*mna, 'l v*o*stre c*o*rs gens / e'lh v*o*stre belh *o*lh m'an c*o*nquis' (ll. 1–2), and 'c'*o*m p*o*sc' el m*o*n . . . / e n*o* . . . dels *o*lhs' (ll. 7 and 8); and the frequent occurrence of the very soft *l* and *lh* sounds, *bela, elh, belh olh*, in the first quatrain and in the last line.

The two themes of the last full stanza, beauty and vision, combine in the senhal of the lady in the envoi:

VIII Bels Vezers, senes doptansa	Lovely Sight, without doubt
sai que vostre pretz enansa,	I know that your worth grows,
que tantz sabetz de plazers far e	for you know so well how to please in
dir:	word and deed,
de vos amar no's pot nuls om sofrir.	no man can help loving you.

There is inner rhyme here: '*Vezers*', 'pr*etz*', and 'sab*etz*'; 'dopt*ansa*', 'en*ansa*', and 't*antz*'; 'f*ar*' and 'am*ar*'. There is an insistence on *o* sounds in the last line: 'v*os* .. n*o*'s p*ot* .. *om* s*o*frir', as there was in the last stanza. And each of the rhyme words is or has an echo in other parts of the poem: 'doptansa' is the second *c* rhyme in II, 6, where the poet says there can scarcely be 'fin'amansa' without fear and doubt – here he no longer has any doubt; 'enansa' is the first *c* rhyme in IV, 5, where the poet asks what use the trouble-makers' curiosity can be to them – here the lady's worth is of benefit to him and to others. Both instances of 'enansa' are exceptions to the grammatical pattern: each is the only verb in a series of nouns, the first and second set of *c* rhymes. 'Dir' is the last word of the second envoi, where it refers apparently to praise of the lady, but presumably also to the poet's words; in the first envoi it refers to the lady's speech, which seems to cure the poet's fear of speaking and enable him to complete the poem and her praises. 'Sofrir', the second *d* rhyme, in the form 'sofris', is the first *b* rhyme in II, 2, where the poet was astonished that he could endure the 'joi' he felt, presumably from his love, because he could not express his feelings; now everyone submits to the lady's power and the poet gives voice to the phenomenon for all of them.

The envoi which is given by the three editors as the second appears in only one manuscript. Appel, followed by Lazar, but not by Nichols, expresses doubts about its authenticity and adds that if it is authentic it should precede the other envoi.[21] I will discuss it as genuine, since it seems to me to round off many of the themes introduced earlier in the poem, and leave it at the end where it is usually printed. The order of the envois does not affect what I have to say about them since, whichever way they go, they both come at the end of the poem.[22]

IX Ben dei aver alegransa,
    qu'en tal domn'ai m'esperansa,
    que, qui'n ditz mal, no pot plus
        lag mentir,
    e qui'n ditz be, no pot plus bel
        ver dir.
	I should certainly be happy
	that I have my hope in such a lady,
	of whom who speaks ill cannot lie
	    more foully,
	and who speaks well cannot utter a
	    lovelier truth (poem).

The 'Ben' and 'alegransa' that begin and end the first line recall the 'bos' and 'jois' of the first stanza, which involved the poet's beginnings and endings, explicitly of his poetry, only implicitly of his love. Here the connection is made: praise of the lady is the 'plus bel ver', both 'the most beautiful truth', as opposed to the foul lie ('lag mentir') that an attack on her would constitute, and 'the most beautiful poem', the 'vers' he began in 'joi' in the very first line of the poem. Although there are few ambiguities in this envoi,[23] the pun in 'ver' carries a lot of weight. The question of speaking well or ill and telling lies or beautiful truths occupied the poet in his first three stanzas. Three of the rhyme words in this envoi echo rhyme words in other stanzas: 'alegransa' occurs in I, 6, where it is the joy the poet feels from a good beginning; here, in stanza IX, it derives from his hope in the lady, which should be his proper beginning. Hope ('esperansa') is the only rhyme word in the envoi which has no counterpart in another stanza, but that is not unusual of *c* rhymes in the poem, see chart on p. 133. 'Mentir' is connected by stem to 'mentis', III, 3; in stanza III, the poet lied to deceive the curious, here he condemns speaking ill of his lady as a lie and affirms his 'bel ver'. That 'dir' should be the final word of the envoi seems fitting, since the poet has been so concerned with his speech; its connection to the second *d* rhyme in the other envoi has already been mentioned.

I have noted the recurrence of rhyme words or stems in individual stanzas, but there are also observations to be derived from an overview of the connections throughout the poem. First I shall list all the rhyme words which have echoes in their own or other stanzas to show the quantity, and then, for clarity, I shall list the correspondences outside the stanzas separately. (The words in parentheses indicate echoes of meaning alone.)

In the first stanza, all but one of the connections fall within the stanza, which underscores the self-confident and self-contained quality of its statement – it is both beginning and end in itself. Only 'alegransa' (the synonym for 'joi', which is the inspiration of the first stanza but becomes a negative force in the second, where it overpowers the poet, and in the third, where it elicits the destructive curiosity of others) has an echo outside the stanza; it recurs in the envoi where it once again expresses a positive feeling. In the second stanza, where the poet finds himself overpowered and speechless, there are no inner connections; all the echoes are external. In III, once again, they are all internal, but they express the confusion in the poet's mind ('men') because his sense ('sen') teaches him to lie ('ment-') about his love. The fourth stanza, the attack on the trouble-makers, is the most negative in the poem; the words with external echoes all have a more negative sense in this stanza than in the others: in stanza II the poet was only afraid of failing ('falhir') his lady, here he condemns real faults ('falhimens') in others; the enemies here derive neither benefit ('enansa') nor enjoyment ('jauzir') from their activities, whereas in the envoi the poet benefits and in stanza II he rejoiced ('jauzens'). 'Morir', in V, has a counterpart in 'aucis' in VI, but the first is the wished-for death of the enemies, the second the figurative,

	I	II	III	IV	V	VI	VII	VIII	IX
	comens	(vens)	sens	falhimens	ardimens	----	----	doptansa	alegransa
	fenis	sofris	m'enquis	vis	----	----	(conquis)	enansa	----
	fis	----	mentis	devis	(afortis)	(aucis)	vis	dir	mentir
	comensamens	jauzens	essenhamens	conoissens	----	guirens	essenhamens	sofrir	dir
	comensansa	----	----	enansa	----	semblansa	----	(doptansa)	
	al-gransa	doptansa	----	----	----	lansa	----		
	----	falhir	----	----	----	garir	----		
	ferir	enardir	----	jauzir	(morir)	(ferir)	----		

alegransa..alegransa

vens..............
sofris...sofrir
jauzens.................jauzir
doptansa..doptansa
falhir...................................falhimens
enardir.......................conoissens..................ardimens
sens..............
mentis..............
essenhamens...essenhamens..mentir
                                                                vis
                                                enansa
                                morir..............aucis
                                                        dir..............dir

and clearly desirable, murder of the poet by the lady's kiss. Stanza VI is essentially self-contained, with echoes in sound or in meaning ('guirens', 'garir', both meaning 'cure', and the paired opposites, 'garir' and 'ferir', 'cure' and 'wound'). In VII, all the echoes are external, and more positive than their correspondences: 'conquis', the victory of the lady's beauty seems to strengthen the poet now, whereas the victory ('vens') of joy hindered him in II; 'vis' is one of the aspects of her beauty here, whereas in IV the homonym had little meaning; 'essenhamens' is another aspect of her beauty, while in III it was the childish behaviour of one who would reveal his love. In the envois, as we have just seen, all the rhyme words are echoes of others, except 'esperansa', and they are all more positive, as befits the rising mood at the end of the poem. it is significant that 'esperansa' should occur only once, at the end of the poem, when one of the aspirations the poet voiced in the first stanza, the good end of the verse, has virtually been accomplished, and the other, the fulfilment of his love which was tied to the fortune of the poem, seems within his grasp; 'esperansa' thus means not so much hope as assurance.

In a discussion that concentrates so much on the sounds of a poem, it would not be altogether honest to neglect the music to which it was performed. It may, however, be reckless to attempt to talk about the music without expert knowledge. I do so with great reservations. There is an added complication with the music of this *canso* – it exists in three manuscripts (W, G, R), each of which has a somewhat different version. But all three move the same way, for the most part; they have the same high and low points, and the same phrases end on the tonal centre.[24] The differences are mainly in the first four notes, the number of embellishments, and the pitch (the melody is set higher in W). Since the G version seems to have more in common with both R and W than either has with the other, and there is no way to determine the authentic melody, I shall base my remarks on G.[25] The modern transcription reproduced here is the one given by Appel.[26]

The four phrases of the first quatrain have certain similarities which reinforce the poetic structure. The regularity of the four octosyllabic lines is matched by the predominantly syllabic setting, by the tendency to hover around and return to the tonal centre, and by the repetition of the first notes of the second phrase (efg) in phrases three and four, a motive which picks up the last two notes of phrases one and three; the fourth phrase, however, moves up one pitch beyond that figure, to the highest note in the quatrain, the note on which the second quatrain begins.[27] The two inner phrases (*bb* in the rhyme scheme) begin with the same five notes; the first phrase begins with an insistent repetition of the

tonal centre (f), and the last four syllables of the fourth phrase fall on that same note by itself or in a group. All of this gives a steadiness, perhaps even a dullness to the melody of the first quatrain of each stanza, relieved only rarely by enjambement, which modifies the structure of the melodic lines to the extent that the first part is tied by the meaning of the words to the previous phrase (e.g. IV, 3–4, where heavy stress is laid on the phrase 'd'autrui amor', 'on another's love'). Only the second phrase has real variety, three embellishments and the ending a fourth below the tonal centre (the other three end on it).

In contrast, the melodic phrases of the second quatrain are quite varied: all begin and end on different notes; even repeated patterns are modified. The opening figure of the first phrase, a b a g a, begins one note lower in the second phrase, g a g e f, and drops an extra step for the last two notes; the scale pattern that begins the third phrase is broken in the middle by a jump and a brief descent, e f a g a b c, while it moves steadily up in the fourth phrase, c d e f g a. The metrics of this quatrain also vary, and also in pairs: one couplet of seven syllable lines (because of the feminine rhyme, though there are eight in the music), one of extended (decasyllabic) lines. The first couplet has a lightness about it, partly because of the feminine rhyme, partly because it precedes the longer lines, but mainly because of its melodic structure: it begins on the highest note of the previous quatrain and plays with it in a sing-song way in the first phrase, and somewhat more gently (and a step lower) in the second. In the other couplet, the added syllables plus the embellishments make the last few notes in each phrase seem an after-thought, a trailing off. This is particularly true in the seventh line of each stanza; the eighth syllable coming as it does after the highest note in the piece, carries the greatest weight, leaving the ninth and tenth hanging and sometimes superfluous in meaning as well (e.g., V, 'ni's vir', and VIII, 'e dir').

Because the music is repeated for each stanza, and the mood of the words changes, the melody cannot always be equally appropriate to the meaning. Nonetheless, there is a clear relation more often than not and some interesting effects: the melody can undercut as well as enhance the apparent meaning of the words, just like any other poetic technique. In the first stanza, as one would expect, the relation between music and words is quite close. The stanza is about the connection between beginnings and endings, and the music reinforces that connection particularly in the first quatrain, by concentrating so markedly on the tonal centre which begins the first phrase, ends the first, third, and fourth, and dominates all but the second. But for a brief moment of questioning in the second phrase, where *fenis*, 'finish', wanders away from that tone and lands on the low note of the phrase, the music ends where it began, on the tonal centre of the piece. That centre was firmly established at the very beginning (in the G version) by the fourfold repetition, which also serves to emphasize the *joi* in which the poem begins and must end. The music introduces a question about that end in the second phrase by moving away from the centre; in the same way, the words introduce a question in the third and fourth phrases with the subjunctive ('fos') and future ('er') forms of the verb, but the music reassures us by returning each time to the centre. Once again, in the fifth phrase, however, the music undercuts; it begins on the high note of the previous quatrain (a), moves up and down from it (a b a g), and then repeats itself, creating a rather shrill sing-song effect (cf. remarks about lines 5 and 6 in the fourth stanza, above p. 127). Thus, although the poet speaks of the joy he derives from his good beginning, the music conveys a different mood and indeed leads us downwards to the low point once again. In the last two phrases, it must work up, by steps, in scale patterns, first to the high point of the piece, 'la bona fi' and then, in the final phrase, back to the tonal centre. 'Bona' falls on the high notes; 'fi', the accented word which follows them, returns to the tonal centre, but the phrase ends suspended on the note above; 'faihz', 'lauzar', and 'fenir' all fall on the f, but the first two in a motion away from it (fg), the last finally coming to rest on it only after some difficulty – it takes six pitches to conclude the two-syllable word.

In the second stanza, the melodic line seems to follow the meaning: in the first phrase, the emphasis in both is on the words of conquest ('si m'apodera, vens'); the questioning tone of the words in the second phrase ('it is a wonder how I endure it') is reinforced by the music; the last two phrases are simple, definite statements. The undercutting in the fifth and sixth phrases is directed at the lover himself, who should know there can be no true love without fear, while the last two lead upwards, in scales, by way of an aphorism, to an understanding if not acceptance of his situation. In the third stanza we return to a conflict between words and music in that the reassuring music of the third and fourth phrases accompanies the poet's boasts about his lies, and the struggle upward to reveal his heart to others (in the seventh phrase) is folly unless it serves his purposes – this is the folly which is pointed up in lines five and six. The conflict is echoed in the syntactic structure: the break in the text occurs after the third line, making what is normally the concluding melodic phrase of the quatrain function also as the beginning of the next section.[28] Thus there is particular emphasis on 'bos' which falls on a, the high note of the fourth phrase and the first note of the fifth, in which the opposite of *good* breeding is defined. But in the fourth stanza, once again, the assurance of the music in the first quatrain is used to strengthen the poet's words, here a condemnation of those who interfere in his love; the undercutting sing-song of the fifth and sixth phrases is directed at the trouble-makers, and the striving in seven and eight contrasts each man's desire to succeed with the enemies' attempts to hinder him, which succeed but do them no good.

The first quatrain of the fifth stanza uses the music to persuade the lady to be strong against the enemy. The plea to the lady which fills the entire stanza affects the tone of the fifth and sixth lines so that they sound more plaintive than mocking. The high point falls on the word 'paraulas' ('words'), which calls attention to it and forces us to recall that although the poet wants her to remain unmoved by others' words, he expects her to be persuaded by his. The change in tone in the second quatrain continues through the rest of the poem: in VI the fifth and sixth phrases still have a plaintive quality; the seventh line reaches its peak on a negative phrase, 'no podi' ('one cannot'), and tries again in the eighth ('unless . . .'). In VII, which is entirely in praise of the lady, the fifth and sixth phrases take on a boastful aspect. The seventh rises on the positive word 'posc' ('that one *can* find'), and the eighth is a pale reflection of it, a scale on a lower level for the throw-away phrase, the redundant 'or I don't see clearly with the eyes with which I look at you.' The envois, which use the music of the last four phrases, continue the boasting sound and (in VIII) the praise of the lady on the rising scales which no longer suggest struggle but rather exaltation.

Thus the music reflects the various moods of the poem: it can be stubbornly affirmative or critical, mocking or plaintive, pessimistic or striving. It adds another dimension to the sound effects which the poet so brilliantly achieves in his words.

NOTES

1. For a study of the homonyms in some of Bernart's poems, see M. L. Hansen, 'A Linguistic Analysis of Selected *Cansos* by Bernart de Ventadorn', unpub. M.A. thesis, University of California at Berkeley, 1975. Cf. M. S. Regan's statement about 'Chantars no pot gaire valer', 'the apparently simple diction conceals a network of difficulties in the sense, ambiguous references, paradoxes, reversals', '*Amador* and *Chantador*: The Lover and the Poet in the *Cansos* of Bernart de Ventadorn', *PQ*, 53 (1974), 23. For a general study of sound and word repetition in Provençal lyric, which includes Bernart, see Nathaniel B. Smith, *Figures of Repetition in the Old Provençal Lyric*, North Carolina Studies in the Romance Languages and Literatures, 176 (Chapel Hill, 1976).
2. Appel actually gives 41 as definite, 3 possible; Lazar gives 44 and Nichols 43. The number in Appel's edition is 45, but the texts of four poems are omitted, while three others of uncertain attribution are given but not numbered. Two of these are accepted by Lazar and Nichols. The one which Nichols omits and Lazar includes, 'Can lo dous temps comensa', had been attributed to Raimbaut de Vaqueiras in one manuscript, but the recent editor of Raimbaut, J. Linskill, attributes it to Bernart, *The Poems of the Troubadour Raimbaut de Vaqueiras* (The Hague: Mouton, 1964), pp. 45–6, as Appel was inclined to.
3. The text is taken from C. Appel, *Bernart von Ventadorn, seine Lieder*, mit Einleitung und Glossar (Halle: Max Niemeyer, 1915); variations in M. Lazar's edition are noted in brackets, *Bernard de Ventadour, Troubadour du XIIe Siècle, Chansons d'Amour* (Paris: C. Klincksieck, 1966). S. Nichols, *The Songs of Bernart de Ventadorn* (Chapel Hill: University of North Carolina Press, 1962) follows Appel's edition in text and numbering. The number of a poem will be given according to both Appel and Lazar, designated by (A) or (L), so that the reader may refer to any of the editions. The translations from Provençal are my own; I give them where the meaning is relevant to my analysis and omit them when I am only concerned with the sound.
4. The same word, 'mas', is used in three senses in 'Lo tems vai e ven e vire' (A.30, L.44), as 'my' in l. 25, 'but' in l. 34, and 'hands' in l. 53.
5. Here the word for mirror is 'mirador', and the lady sees herself in it, 'ela's mire'. Nichols makes an interesting point about this poem, suggesting that since the poem is the mirror in which the lady will see herself, the poet himself is the enemy who made the mirror, 'Toward an Aesthetic of the Provençal *Canso*', *The Disciplines of Criticism*, ed. P. Demetz, T. Green and L. Nelson, Jr. (New Haven: Yale, 1968), pp. 360–1.
6. There is, of course, a translation of it in Nichols' edition of Bernart, and a brief discussion in his introduction.
7. I prefer not to get into the controversy between those who believe in the autonomy of the stanza in Bernart's poems and those who see a clear progression within a poem. However, although I think it makes sense to look at the poem stanza by stanza, the result of such investigation indicates, to me at least, that there is a definite shape to the poem. For recent discussion and approaches to the question see P. E. Bondanella, 'The Theory of the Gothic Lyric and the Case of Bernart de Ventadorn', *Neuphilologische Mitteilungen*, 74

(1973), 369–81; F. R. P. Akehurst, 'Les Étapes de l'amour chez Bernart de Ventadorn', *CCM*, 16 (1973), 133–47; Nichols, 'Toward an Aesthetic', pp. 349–74, and 'Toward an Aesthetic of the Provençal Lyric II: Marcabru's *Dire vos vuoill ses doptansa*', *Italian Literature, Roots and Branches*, ed. G. Rimanelli, K. J. Atchity (New Haven: Yale, 1976), pp. 15–37; F. Goldin, *Lyrics of the Troubadours and Trouvères, An Anthology and a History* (New York: Doubleday/Anchor, 1973), pp. 108–25, and 'The Array of Perspectives in the Early Courtly Love Lyric', *In Pursuit of Perfection*, ed. J. Ferrante, G. Economou (Port Washington: Kennikat, 1975), particularly pp. 51–78.

8. See Appel edition for the variants.

9. There are many other possible ambiguities in the stanza: in the third line, a different division of words could give, albeit somewhat awkwardly: 'sol que bon afos l'afics', 'the sun which sank the good effort', one might hear the fifth line as 'perla bona co m'en(s)ansa', 'how the good pearl exalts me'. In l. 2, 'reman' could be 're man', 'I send something'; l. 3, 'fis' can mean 'pure', 'true', and 'son', as well as 'end'; l. 4, 'bos' can mean 'ox'; 'tenh', 'colour', 'powder', 'holding'; 'er', 'yesterday', 'heir'; 'ensamens', 'equally'; l. 6, 've', 'comes' or 'sees', 'ven', 'wind'; the words might be run together thus: 'veg oi se tal(e) gran s'a') ('I see today if there is such a large . .'). L. 7, 'so' can mean 'sound' and 'his', 'fi', 'faith'; 'figa' is a fig; 'razir', 'to take root'; l. 8,'toza', 'a young girl'; 'faihz', 'exile'; 'fais', 'burden'; 'l'auzar', 'the daring'. I will give the English translation only for the first occurrence of a word in the footnotes; thenceforth, I will simply cite the Provençal.

10. The music can determine the lines for us, but not necessarily the words, since each syllable gets at least a note. For an analysis of the music in relation to the text, see below, pp. 134 ff.

11. Other sound patterns reinforce these connections, cf. particularly l. 3, 'sol que bona fos la fis', the repetition of the o, a, f (and s) sounds: (s) o o a f o (s) a f (s), which are picked up in l. 7, 'so dei la bona fi', (s) o a o a f.

12. There are other possible ambiguities of the kind described in the first stanza, but none so obvious: l. 1, 'si', 'so', 'fi'; 'vens', 'conquers', 'wind'; l. 2, 'm'era vilhes' c'om', 'it was (seemed) a villainy to me that one . . .'; l. 3, 'c'ar', 'for now'; 'es bruis', 'is a noise'; l. 5, 'mas', 'but', 'more', 'hands', 'my'; 'fin', 'end', 'until', 'true'; 'm'an sa', 'they have me here'; l. 6, 's'es', 'if it is'; l. 7, 'cad'es', 'each is'; 'adesc', 'bait', 'lure'; 'te'm', 'it holds me'; 'vas', 'towards', 'vain', 'tomb'; 'tem om va so', 'a man fears a vain sound'; l. 8, 'nom', 'name'; 'noma us', 'he names you'; 'aus', 'fleece'; 'ausar' 'raise', 'ausir' and 'aucire', 'kill': as in VI, 3. Because I am analysing each stanza as a separate unit, at first, and will be referring to corresponding lines in other stanzas later, I have chosen to number the lines anew from one to eight, rather than consecutively.

13. 'Efansa' in Latin is connected with the inability to speak; cf. Isidore, 'dictus autem infans quia adhuc fari nescit, id est loqui non potest', *Etym.* XI, ii, 9.

14. There are a good number of other possible ambiguities in this stanza: l. 1, 'rema', 'remain', 'oar'; 'onda', 'wave'; 'mos', 'moss', 'move', 'my'; 'sens'; l. 2, 'somo' 'call', 'rebuke'; 'no men', 'I don't lie'; 'nom'; l. 3, 'volon', 'desirous'; 'ters', 'third', 'thrice'; 'len', 'slow', 'gentle', 'far'; l. 4 'con nom', 'dear name'; 'par', 'seems', 'equal', 'bos', 'es senha', 'it is a sign'; 'sen'; 'mens', 'mind', 'less'; l. 5, 'an', 'they have', 'year'; 'ans', 'rather', 'years'; 'ses', 'without'; l. 6, 'cuida', 'I think', 'he thinks'; 'quita', 'acquit', 'remit', 'cede'; 'mor', 'death'; 'mora',

'delay', 'ripe'; 'ben', 'well'; 'anan', 'going'; l. 7, 'vol', 'he wishes', 'will', 'flight'; 'so'; 's'o' 'if this'; 'cor', 'heart', 'runs', 'horn'; 'socor', 'help'; 'adaut', 'adroit', 'please'; 're'; l. 8, 'si', 'thus', 'if'; 'olen', 'smelling'; 'pot', 'draught'; 'val', 'valley', 'it is worth'; 'os', 'you', 'bone'; 'ser', 'serf', 'evening'; 'vir', 'turns' (cf. V, 7).

15. The grammatical forms of the rhyme words are:

	I	II	III	IV	V	VI	VII	VIII	IX
a	verb	verb	noun	noun	noun	adj*	adj		
b	verb	verb	verb	verb	noun	verb	verb		
b	noun	verb	verb	noun	verb	verb	noun		
a	noun	adj*	noun	adj*	adj*	adj*	noun		
c	noun	noun	noun	verb	noun	noun	noun	noun	noun
c	noun	noun	noun	noun	noun	noun	noun	verb	noun
d	infin	infin	infin	infin	verb	infin	infin	infin	infin
d	infin	infin	infin	infin	infin	infin	verb	infin	infin

* present participle

16. L. 1, 'no n'es'; 'no ne sen oi' 'I don't feel it today'; 'ni falha mens', 'nor do I fail less'; l. 2, 'ni vil lania', 'nor did I complain basely'; 'so'; 'mes'; 'somet', 'at the surface'; 'vis', 'sight', 'look', 'face'; l. 3, 'mas'; 'domec', 'domaine'; 'c'an'; 'ans'; 'e fai'; 'faid', 'exile'; 'devis', 'devizar', 'relate', 'derive', 'divide'; l. 4, 'aut', 'high'; 'n'i'; 'co' no i sens'; l. 5, 'enoy', 'annoyance'; 'os'; 'o se'; 'us', 'one', 'you', 'custom', 'gate'; l. 6, 'si'm fais sen oi', 'if I feel myself an exile today'; 'pes', 'weight', 'pesa', 'piece', 'space of time', 'thinks', 'weighs', 'breaks'; l. 7, 'chasc'us', 'each gate'; 'se'; 'vol'; 'so'; 'des', 'since'; 'om'; 'o me'; 'mes'; 'omes'; 'tier', 'series'; 'for', 'law', 'custom', 'outside', 'would be'; 'mir', 'I look'; l. 8, 'co fon', 'how they were'; 'detz', 'fingers', 'ten'.

17. There are more 's' sounds (26 which are either 's' or 'z') in this stanza than in any other. Cf. the high number in II (24, as opposed to 19 in I and 16 in III), a stanza resembling IV in the repetition of rhyme words and the negative mood.

18. L. 1, 'Be n'es'; 't'ai'; 'di mens'; l. 2, 'en trav', 'fettered'; 'vol'; 'gen', 'noble', 'cleverness', 'people'; 'sem', 'incomplete', 'sowing', 'race'; 'als', 'other'; l. 3, 'es ar', 'is now'; 'ditz', 'words', 'you say', 'cors'; 'for'; l. 4, 'pot'; 'es ser'; 'pro', 'enough', 'much', 'advantage', 'good'; 'val ens'; l. 6, 'l'abelen', 'they make it pleasing'; l. 7, 'nos', 'knot'; 'par aulas' ('avols'); l. 8, 'Me nemis' (var. in MS. Q); 'fatz', 'face', 'figure', 'fools'; 'den', 'tooth', 'crag'; 'vey amor ir', 'I see love go'.

19. L. 1, 'sa be la'; l. 2, 'nonc videi bai san metr'aïs', 'I never saw a healthy kiss make for ease'; l. 3, 'c'ar'; 'arab', 'take away'; l. 4, 'sia'; 'baut', 'bold', 'joyful'; 'nom es'; l. 5, 'a tre tal'; 'espers', 'expert'; 'pers', 'blue'; 'emblan', 'stealing'; l. 6, 'comde', 'count'; 'c'om'; 'pe', 'foot'; 'pel', 'skin', 'hair'; 'laus', 'praise'; 'aus', 'fleece', 'I dare'; 'l'an'; 'sa'; 'l'ansa', 'handle'; l. 8, 'autr avetz'; 'nos', 'sen'; 'fets', 'fetid'; 'fe rir', 'made laugh'.

20. L. 1, 'al vos tre'; 'cors'; 'gens'; l. 2, 'vos tre'; 'trebelh', 'trouble'; 'man', 'hand', 'command', 'morning', 'I send'; 'c'on quis'; l. 3, 'el doutz (toutz)' 'he took'; 'es'; 'ses'; 's'es'; 'gartz', 'boy' ('Garsio' is a senhal in 'Era'm cosselhatz', 'senhor', l. 61); 'se el'; 'vis'; l. 4, 'el vos tre', 'trebels', 'els', 'ses', 'es sen', 'senha', 'mens'; l. 5, 'c'an'; 'men'; 'enpren', 'undertake'; 'es man'; 'mans', 'sweet'; l. 6, 'us', 'nous', 'new'; 'trob', 'find', 'compose'; l. 7, 'la gens er et'; 'compos', 'compose'; l. 8, 've i'; 'arde', 'burns'; 'solhs', 'mud', 'filth'; 'solhel', 'sun'.

21. Appel, 'Diese Verse stehen nur in C. Sie sind so matt, dass man an ihrer Echtheit zweifeln darf', p. 9; cf. Lazar, 'Appel la [the tornada] considère comme douteuse', p. 240. Nichols simply reports that this tornada is found only in MS. C, 178.
22. There are several double envois in Bernart's poems. See A.4 (L.27), 6 (25), 7 (5), 8 (16), 15 (2), 16 (15), 19 (30), 22 (36), 26 (29), 29 (23), 35 (21), 36 (18), 41 (24), 42 (7), 45 (33), uncertain (22).
23. L. 1, 'Be'n'; 'a ver'; 'gran'; l. 2, 'domnai', 'I courted'; 'mes per ans'; l. 3, 'm'al'; l. 4, 'ben'; 'o d'ir'. In the previous envoi, there are more: l. 1, 'vetz', 'habit', 'time'; 'ers'; 'se n'es'; 'sen es'; l. 2, 'sai', 'here'; 'vos tre'; 'trep', 'game', 'dance', 'trouble'; 'ret', 'net'; 're'; 'sen'; 'an sa'; l. 3, 'quetan', 'quieting'; 's'abetz' ('avetz'); 'de plazers far e dir', '(you know) how to do things to please and anger'; l. 4, 's'amar'; 'nos'; 'nul som'; 'so'm'.
24. There is one exception: in R, all four phrases of the first quatrain end on the same note, the tonal centre. According to G. Scherner-van Ortmerssen, Die Text-Melodiestruktur in den Liedern des Bernart de Ventadorn (Münster: Aschendorff, 1973), the modifications in the melody among the versions are structurally irrelevant (35).
25. According to Appel, the music in G was written by the same hand as the words, while six hands are involved in the melodies in R, Die Singweisen Bernarts von Ventadorn, nach den Handschriften mitgeteilt von C. Appel (Halle: Max Niemeyer, 1934), 1–2. He transcribes all three melodies and seems to prefer R and G to W, although W is earlier. Sesini notes that R has time markings which are probably not authentic, 'Le melodie trobadoriche nel Canzoniere provenzale della Biblioteca Ambrosiana', Studi medievali n.s. 12 (1939), 13.
26. This is the modern transcription of G given by C. Appel, Die Singweisen, pp. 11–12. The words are those of Appel's edition of the poem, which differs slightly from the text given in G, but not in a way to affect the discussion.
27. In R, the same figure recurs in all four phrases. Phrases one and three begin e f g e, phrases two and four begin e f g a; in this version, the high note, a, occurs in both the second and the fourth phrase.
28. Scherner-van Ortmerssen points this out, p. 55.

6 A *Reading of a* Ballade *by Jean Meschinot*

PAUL ZUMTHOR

Beneath my eyes which look at it, and in my consciousness which reads it and communes with it, the text is both object and action. When it is put back in its own time-scheme, it is both situation and product. The term 'production', by the very imprecision of its suffix, can comfortably comprehend all those characteristics. But production is at the same time both a process and the various moments within it, right up to the last one, which can be identified with consummation. It implies a multiplicity of factors, which, though by no means constituting 'levels of analysis', nonetheless produce sufficient points of view to enable a choice to be made.

    1. The events or series of events at whose point of juncture the text is created.

    2. The intertextual zone, whose projection is to be observed in the text and which, to a certain degree, provides it with its dynamic force and organization.

    3. An axis, which I would call desideral, rather than communicative, possessing two boundaries, from which there appear a writing-subject, at one and the same time committed to the discourse and scattered throughout it, and another potential subject who will endow it with his own fantasies, to a degree which cannot be determined, during his reading.

    4. The materiality (linguistic and translinguistic) of the text-object.

Each of these factors possesses its own marks of historicity. Some of them are perhaps not conspicuous: factor 4 at least implies all the others and, in a way, provides the key to them. In the case of most medieval texts it is, in our present state of knowledge, the only one available to us.

The Text

I follow the Trepperel printing (Paris, 1499), reproduced by D. Huë in his mimeographed thesis (University of Aix-Marseille, 1975), 'Pour une étude des "Lunettes des Princes" de Jean Meschinot et de la poésie des rhétoriqueurs' (Appendix I, Section V). The original has no accents and hardly any marks of punctuation. I have added both, and mention in the notes to what extent my action may introduce an occasional ambiguity. I have made some emendations as well, which are explained in the notes, and I have translated two or three barely comprehensible words.

I.	Homme mortel, ceste leçon recorde:	1
	Quant tu es né, droit à jeunesse cours;	2
	L'aige moyen bien tost après s'acorde	3
	T'avoir des siens, et te promect secours;	4
	Et, lorsque tu arrives à ce cours,	5
	Vieillesse vient tantost, pleine de goute,	6
	De touts, de bouts, de gale: somme toute,	7
	Le vieil languist. Estre mort luy fust mieulx;	8
	Mais les aultres ne sont pas hors de doubte	9
	Car aussi tost meurent jeunes que vieulx.	10
II.	La mort maine toutes gens en sa corde,	11
	Et si les faict convenir à ces cours.	12
	Quel remède? Crie miséricorde	13
	A Dieu, voyant tes jours estre trescours.	14
	Es-tu mondain? En fuyant les grantz cours	15
	Des haultz princes, je te pry, ton cas gouste:	16
	Se tu y fais bon guet et bonne escoute,	17
	Tu ne seras vain, fier ne envieulx.	18
	Trop méchant est qui la fin ne redoute	19
	Car aussi tost meurent jeunes que vieulx.	20
III.	Or fay doncques ta paix et ta concorde,	21
	Vifs sainctement et à bonté recours;	22
	Ou pour certain, je te dy et recorde,	23
	Besté seras mieulx que cingue ne qu'ours;	24
	Brof finira de la vie le cours.	25
	Tes jours passent sans retour; or escoute:	26

    Ou jeune ou vieil tu suys de mort la route.   27
    Advise toy d'y penser se tu veulx: 28
    Tes sens, vertu et diligence y boute   29
    Car aussi tost meurent jeunes que vieulx.   30

E. Prince, ce que d'y penser nous déboute,   31
    Le monde aymons tant que n'y veons goute;   32
    De nos plaisirs sommes trop curieulx.   33
    Hélas, servons à Dieu quoi qu'il nous couste   34
    Car aussi tost meurent jeunes que vieulx.   35

Notes

Line 7: 'touts' = toux; 'bouts' cf. Tobler-Lommatzsch, *Wörterbuch* s.v. *bot, boteille* and *enfler.* literally 'barrel', figuratively 'swelling'.

Line 13: The question-mark after 'remède' is my own conjecture. Strictly speaking, it would be possible to regard 'remède', allegorically, as the grammatical subject of 'crie', in which case the question-mark would have to be moved to a position after 'trescours': but this interpretation seems to be a little forced.

Line 15: I have inserted a question-mark after 'mondain' in order to indicate the hypothetical quality which I feel is present in this part of the sentence: 'Si tu es . . . alors . . .'

Line 22: The original gives 'à bone recours', which makes no sense; I propose to put a *t* before the *e* in *bone*.

Line 23: The reading 'cerain' in the original, obviously an error for 'certain', justifies by comparison the correction made in line 22.

Line 24: The original gives 'bestu', which is probably an error. 'Bastu' (for *battu*) is a possibility; I prefer to read 'besté' (for *bêté*), cf. Tobler-Lommatzsch s.v. *beter* 'morde, in talking of dogs baiting a bear'; this is a hunting term well suited to the context.

In order to avoid any disturbance of the analysis by extraneous material, I have deliberately chosen this apparently routine *ballade*, which cannot be connected with an external event by any detail in the text. The indications of historicity which it must, of necessity, contain cannot be deciphered as a result of facts or ideas drawn from the 'chronicle history' of the period.

    In other words, we are set before a poem which obliges us to leave out of consideration the 'circum-text'. By this I mean the sum of circumstances, alien to the text as such, which may have contributed to its production: political, religious, and biographic. Such circumstances did, perhaps, exist. The text does not refer to them explicitly. At most they become perceptible at a deep level as the analysis proceeds, but they cannot be assumed *a priori*.

On the other hand, the law of intertextuality, the importance of which in the process of the creation of a text is generally agreed upon, induces us to define what I would call the discursive 'context', involved in the actual forms of discourse and embraced by them without being subordinated to them. To a certain degree, one could put forward as an initial hypothesis that the 'circumtext' is here completely taken over by the 'context'.

Now, the intertextuality appears in different focus according to certain historical parameters arising from the typology of cultures. It is not necessary here for me to refer to the passages in my *Essai de poétique médiévale* and then again in *Le Masque et la lumière* (1978), in which I defined the functions of tradition in the civilization we call medieval. Even if it is true that, towards the end of the fifteenth century, the elements of that tradition, once tightly compacted, were beginning to disintegrate, the disintegration had barely begun. It may be perceived less in the elimination of traditional paradigms than in the strengthening of the tendencies to parody, irony and 'carnival', and by the introduction of ambiguities which undermine a discourse which is itself incontestable. It would be rewarding, within this perspective, to set Meschinot's *ballade* side by side with some passages from Villon's *Testament* (in the first 700 lines) on old age and death. The discourse, in its constituent parts, is identical in this regard. The difference lies in the manner of their manipulation. In Villon, the argument-surface is shattered by a syntactic syncope into a breakup of semantic continuity, phonic disharmonies, and the quick pace of the lines. In Meschinot, the enunciation remains continuous; the forms of syntax and versification continue to their full flowering, rhetorical figures reign supreme in a closely knit argument. But, as we shall see, this opaque discourse is enriched at a sub-surface level by subtle plays which are not easy to see at a first reading and which depend on hidden recurrences in word, phrase and line. The result is a new level of discourse underlying the first, whose effect is to disturb the 'plain sense' of the former to some extent. In Villon, the poem flows on riotously and is riddled with gaping flaws. In Meschinot, nothing is so badly chopped up or contradictory; all that can be noted is an unobtrusive but profound reserve, and one could very well ask whether that reserve may not conceal a threat.

Whatever the diversity of these manifestations, the discourse in question does exist, and its mode of existence is tradition, in the powerful sense which I attribute to the term – a collection of matrix-forms, sometimes providing a medium for the fossilized debris of former ideologies. This is one of the levels of medieval intertextuality, the most obvious and the most rewarding. Its importance in the creation of medieval texts is so decisive that all other intertextual effects usually seem negligble by comparison, whether they are incorporated in it or not. At its level, one can assemble within their common context long series of texts laid out in diachronic succession, and yet synchronic at any given point in this time-sequence. If we were to deal with discourse (of the text, in the collective, abstract sense of an entity made up of a selection of possible utterances) on the subject of old age and death we would collect hundreds of French poems, from the *Vers* of Hélinand de Froimont in the twelfth century to contemporaries of Meschinot, such as Villon certainly and his successors like Guillaume Cretin, but equally didactic works and sermons, pictural motifs such as the Dance of Death, and a large number of proverbs. The same is true of all the Western languages. It is not a matter of 'influences' or 'imitations' or any other of the pseudo-phenomena so dear to nineteenth-century critics. This is the reality, at one and the same time of one object and of many, potential but instantly realizable, of a common discourse whose generative rules determine the main structures of its concrete forms.

However, at the heart of such a cultural model, intertextuality must be understood on another level as well, that of the actual continuity of the utterances delivered by a particular subject. This is a continuity within which cumulative relationships are established, to enrich it, to bring about harmony or eliminate redundancy, together with more or less allusive correspondences, oppositions, conversions or inversions of themes. This is the very continuity which can be observed, from the *Lais* to the *Testament* of Villon and, in the latter, between the two parts of which it is apparently composed under the cover of a single title. It is thus that Meschinot's *ballade* can be read in continuity with the beginning of his great work, *Les Lunettes des Princes* (ed. Christine Martineau-Genieys, Geneva: Droz, 1972, especially pp. 36 ff.) and more precisely in that of the group of five '*ballades* on the Ages of Man' (Huë, Appendix).

I shall not go into detail on these points. It would be possible, if I were to write at great length, to draw a figurative plan of this double level of intertextuality. Elements would be observed in it which embrace all levels of discourse: thematic ones, of course, but even more rhetorical, lexical, and sometimes syntactical elements, regrouped and to some extent organized according to predominant trends, so that they act as transformational rules: what I have called, in another context, a 'register'. This register shows rather loose ties in collective continuity; sometimes, but not always, tighter ones in the individual continuity. In every way the power of this intertextual dynamism, when observed at the level of individual texts, offers us a first indication of historicity. It is, in fact, the perception of such a power which forces us to admit a degree of contradiction between the surface conventionality of the discourse and the production of the poem as such. In our eyes this contradiction brings about a kind of alienation of the subject. Was this the case in the fifteenth century? The asking of the question is in itself the first indication that there is a historicity. Before any reply is made, the principle must be admitted that it is in this perspective that the functioning of the text must be read and appreciated in its concrete detail. That the general theme may come from somewhere else is of little importance. Once it has been authenticated in the 'context', it finds itself being reauthenticated in an original way each time it appears, because of the materiality of that individual manifestation. It is this materiality which is important: it alone 'contains' whatever contradictions there are, in the double sense that it determines their form and sets its limits.

Functionally, this materiality can be defined from two viewpoints which are different from each other, but the second of which is determined by the first: the genre point of view (the *ballade* as such) and the individual point of view (*this ballade*).

The *ballade* is classified among the 'fixed forms' which were very popular in the fifteenth century, so much so that with some authors they take over the formal aspects of poetic endeavour almost completely. I shall not repeat here the views on this subject which are put forward in *Le Masque et la lumière*. On the subject of rules, I shall refer rather to H. Châtelain, *Recherches sur le vers français au XVe siècle* (Paris: Champion, 1907; rpt. 1974) and for their aesthetic significance to D. Poirion, *Le Poète et le prince* (Paris: Presses Universitaires de France, 1965).

In the poetics of the period, the central position, in itself indicative of a particular concept of what is 'poetic', is given to the 'chant-royal' and to the *ballade*, which are closely related, to the *rondeau* and to 'genres' which are close to it, such as the *virelai*. All these forms are strictly limited in their dimension and precisely organized in the distribution of their constituent parts. Even when the poet works on a large scale with poems whose dimensions are not predetermined, for most of the time he composes them in very regular strophes and this reproduces, at the microtextual level, the basic conception of the fixed form. There are thus

groups of eight, twelve and sixteen octosyllables (this latter, in Meschinot's work, in the *Lunettes*, pp. 36 f.) and of ten or twelve decasyllables
(this latter also in the *Lunettes*, pp. 26–32).

In the *ballade* and the *chant-royal* the demands of the strophic form are
integrated with the basic conception. With few exceptions, the strophe is
'squared', that is, there are as many lines in it as there are syllables in the
line: eight, ten, or twelve; the even numbers are by far in the majority.
But every strophe, as well as the *envoi*, whose structure is the same as that
of the second half of a strophe, ends in a refrain-line, generally of gnomic
character, which defines the *theme*, in the sense in which this word
designates the initial statement from which the *rheme*, the argument,
proceeds. As a result of this, the strophes with an apparently even
number of lines are in fact reduced to an uneven number and vice versa.
A rhythmic balance thus emerges which is important for the definition of
the genre. The rhymes are identical in the three strophes (five in the
chant-royal) and in the *envoi* and are distributed in accordance with a
limited number of possible combinations. The order *ababbccdcd*, which
is exactly symmetrical, is the most common in the decasyllabic strophes.
Furthermore, it is possible to observe the same kind of rhythmic balance,
of deliberate hesitation, of reserve, in the structure strophe + *envoi* as in
the three- or five-number combinations and in the four- or six-groups
which are obtained by counting the *envoi* – or, more accurately, groups
of three and a half or five and a half. It is here that I see the first possible
level of ambiguity which, under certain circumstances, determines the
structure of the discourse.

The rigidity of the model (which is in any case relative, since it leaves
to the poet the choice of rhymes and line-length), appears to me to be a
compensatory factor for the loss of vocal and instrumental music, from
which poetry in the fifteenth century had broken away. Instrumental
music, which Eustace Deschamps, about 1400, called 'artificial', is to be
distinguished from the 'natural music' which language produces on its
own; and by *music* let us understand a harmony which reproduces by
analogy that of cosmic movements. Language as such does, indeed,
constitute a crude metaphor of the universe, but only poetry, properly
regulated, makes the metaphor effective (cf. R. Dragonetti, *Fin du
Moyen-Age et Renaissance*, Mélanges R. Guiette, Antwerp: Nederlandse
Bockhandel, 1965; and *Aux Frontières du language poétique*, Ghent: Presses
Universitaires, 1961, ch. 1). The stricter the regulation, the more
harmony it shows. Harmony is seen as the object, never quite attained,
because it is, by its nature, inaccessible and constantly shifting, of all the
rhythms indicated in the poem, whether they are prosodic, musical, or
semantic.

This genre-structure of the *ballade* and what it implies impose a particular point of view on the reader of the text. The definition of the genre (its 'rules') determines the strategic areas which, it is reasonable to believe, act as points of departure for its overall organization. Whatever the substance of the message and whatever combination of materials is chosen by the poet, these factors can do no more than lend substance to a model, in order to produce a concrete realization of harmony, itself a merely approximate and temporary realization (for the duration of one reading) of the *musica mundana*, the music of the universe, eternal and immutable. From this there arises a twofold demand on the reader: to grasp fully the point from which this reading must start, with all its implications, and to pay the closest attention to the smallest details of the realization, details which can be grasped only by a microscopic examination of the linguistic tissue, less for its own sake than as a vehicle of 'meaning'.

I shall distinguish three features as starting points, the uniformity of the strophes, the refrain, and the rhymes.

The uniformity of the strophes is perfect here, according to the rules governing the *ballade*, which regulate the number of lines and of syllables. But although this uniformity is clear on the surface, on a more profound level it hides a great deal of diversity. Beneath the surface of invariable numbers (three and a half times ten decasyllables) shifting combinations can be worked out, subject, apparently, to no laws except those of unending divergences in an unclear gradation. They can be observed in the syntactical groupings and in the structure of the line.

Each of the three strophes, ending with the refrain, forms an independent nucleus of discourse. Their order of succession is not entirely fortuitous, in as much as the first line of the first strophe announces the exposition ('ceste leçon'); and the first line of the third strophe ('or . . . doncques') its conclusion. Apart from that, they could be considered interchangeable, with the *envoi* excluded from consideration. The transition from one to the next is carried out contextually, with the same traditional theme producing a proliferation of varying motifs which are also traditional as such, though their order of succession remains free.

Within these strophic units, a continuous discourse of demonstrative type is enunciated. But the clauses of varying length, of which it is composed, form syntactical groups which can be more or less clearly delimited – in a way which differs from one strophe to another.

Strophe I: a syntactical triptych: line 1, then lines 2–7 middle, and lines 7–10; the central element can be further divided into line 2, lines 3 and 4, and lines 5–7. Except for the sub-group of lines 3–4, these combinations bring about a predominance of odd numbers and incomplete forms: 1, 1, (2), 2 1/2, 3 1/2. (The regular progression in the size of the discourse should be noted.)

Strophe II: syntactical square: lines 11–12, 13–14, 15–18, and 19–20. Predominance of even numbers: 2, 2, 4, 2 (four elements); but if a break between lines 16 and 17 is posited, there are five groups of two lines each (even/odd).

Strophe III: a series of two odd, and two even groups framing them: lines 21–2, 23–5, 26, and 27–30.

Envoi: lines 31–3 and 34–5, an odd group followed by an even group.

Thus the clause-organisation, which is the determining element in the uniformity of the strophes, rests upon the fundamental numerical disparity between even and odd and its ability to produce movements within the text: a tendency to extablish progressively, as the discourse unfolds, a regular alternation between the two. If this alternation has any significance, it can only be in its own right, not by any relation to what a semiotic analysis would reveal. At best it would be a *signal*.

An equivalent of this *signal* is to be found in the structure of the lines. They are, according to fourteenth-century norms, regular, and I shall look at two elements in them which are also dependent on the poet's own decisions: correspondence between line of verse and clause and, correlatively, the nature of the caesura.

There are several occasions on which a line forms a complete sentence: lines 1, 2, 11, 12, 21, 22, that is to say, at the beginning of each strophe. There are also three such lines in strophe III, 25, 27, 28 as well as line 33 in the *envoi*. Elsewhere a sentence is made up of two lines, each of which contains a complete statement: lines 9–10, 19–20, 29–30, and 34–5, that is to say, the ends of the strophes and of the *envoi*. In addition, there are lines 17–18. On the other hand, there are seven occasions on which the sentence spreads over two lines without any correspondence between the syntactical structure and the line-length ('enjambement' in the broad sense): lines 3–4, 6–7, 7–8, 13–14, 15–16, 23–4, and 31–2, that is to say, three times in strophe I, twice in strophe II, and once in strophe III and in the *envoi*. Is this intended to be a diminishing progression? Finally, there are three sentences which occupy only a part of a line: lines 8, 13, 26. This structure can be found elsewhere as a deliberate system in the 'ballades en dialogue' of Meschinot and several other poets of the fifteenth century (cf. O. Jodogne, 'La Ballade dialoguée', in *Mélanges Guiette*, pp. 271–85). Line 13 could be read as a fragment in dialogue, with the reader asking 'Quel remède?' and the author replying 'Crie . . .'.

Thus an interesting distribution may be observed. Each strophe begins and ends (and the *envoi*, in conformity with its structure, ends) with the same scheme, in which line and sentence conform precisely. I shall call this scheme 'frame of identification' and shall distinguish between two variants of it: the absolute (one line = one sentence), a variant which twice appears at the beginning of a strophe; and the relative (two lines = two distinct propositions in the same sentence), which appears at the end.

In the body of the strophe (from the third to the eighth lines), the absolute variant of identification appears only in strophe III (three times) and once in the *envoi*. I see here a kind of gradation from difference to identity.

Apart from these lines, two other types of structure follow one another in irregular order within the fixed frame of identification. One of them occurs once in each strophe: sentence = part of a line. The other, 'enjambement', shows diminishing frequency from three times in strophe I, through twice in strophe II, to once in strophe III and in the *envoi*.

Thus several factors join in bringing into the discourse categories of like and unlike, singular and multiple, agreement and opposition. But the elements by means of which these categories are presented are linked in such a way that an overall movement can be traced which would lead to a final realization of the like, the singular, and agreement.

So far as the caesuras are concerned, it is worth noting that eight lines out of thirty-five (or, if we count the refrain only once, out of thirty-one different lines, i.e. more than a quarter) show the 'lyric' type, with the caesura occurring after a 'mute' *e*, not elided and necessarily unstressed: lines 9, 11, 13, 16, 21, 26 on the one hand, 5 and 31 on the other. This proportion of twenty-five per cent corresponds to the frequency of occurrence of mute *e* in the whole text, if feminine rhymes are not counted: seventy-three syllables out of 350. I hardly think this fact is accidental. The delicate harmonic plays in which fifteenth-century poets indulged with this sound, before the gradual imposition of the constricting rules of so-called classical usage, are well known. It is a sliding, fleeting sound, difficult to handle, and it constantly seems to be on the verge of shattering the model, of breaking through the 'square' form, of upsetting the distribution of the stresses. Further, the irregular distribution of the 'lyric' caesuras in our *ballade* is set against a very regular distribution of feminine rhymes (rhymes *a* and *c*, that is, five out of ten lines in each strophe, three out of five in the *envoi*). There is the same effect of alternation, a more diffused *signal*.

All the lines but three make the caesura coincide with the end of a syntactical group. The lines are thus divided 4+6. The three exceptions call for divisions as follows: 2+8 (or 2+4+4) in line 14 and 7+3 in line 5. Lastly, line 31, which is a special case because it begins with the word 'Prince', in accordance with *ballade* tradition, can apparently be divided only 2+5+3. There might be some doubt about lines 6, 12 and 17, in which the fourth syllable comes after an accented monosyllable: it would be possible to divide 6+4 (a common type in decasyllables) in lines 6 and 17, but 7+3 in line 12. In any case, at this level of consideration, there is a predominance of even rhymes, even if it is disputable or even occasionally negated.

Once the *theme* as such has been removed from consideration, the refrain is defined according to its lexical and syntactical composition.

Syntactically, the refrain-statement, introduced by *car,* has an explicative-causal value. *Car* coordinates it with the preceding line, which acts as a main clause; hence a modality of relative identification, repeated four times in the *ballade.* The causal function is at one and the same time 'final', in the double sense in which it brings a unit of discourse to an end and determines the issue of 'ceste leçon'.

Outside the refrain, no conjunction or equivalent expression indicates such a connection. Strophe I sets up time relations (simultaneity, in lines 2 and 5), opposition (line 9). Strophe II twice sets up a condition (lines 5 and 17). Strophe III sets up a consequence (line 21). In the *envoi* there are relations of a logical order (lines 32 and 34), the first of which remains ambiguous (time and/or result).

The refrain is modalized by a sententious, even proverbial tone. The semic paradox it contains, of which there is no other example in the *ballade,* indicates this: the use of the word 'jeune' shows that the seme referring to the shortness of time is involved; 'vieux' refers to the length of that time. But 'aussi tost' establishes equality between these two times and the image thus introduced authenticates in a different way what I have called the 'frame of identification'. The idea contained in the verb 'meurent' makes this concept of equality explicit, although it is *a priori* absurd. The line thus has great rhetorical force, which the connecting word 'car' exploits by coordinating and subordinating to the argument of each strophe in turn. In doing so it elevates this argument to the plane of universality. A knowledge of the extra-text would perhaps tell us that the *ballade,* as an event, referred to the death of some personality who passed away prematurely. Such a discovery could only point up the effect, but it is not necessary to know it to understand the text.

Lexically, the line-refrain forms a cluster whose heavy elements (al the words of which it is composed except the connectives *car, aussi,* and *que*) permeate in one way or another the textual entity to which they thus provide one of the keys.

Formally, these elements are only four in number: 'tost', 'meurent', 'jeunes', 'vieux'. An opposition/contradiction relationship joins the last two, a relationship which the first two cumulatively reverse.

Semically, there are several chains of association connected to these words:

1. quickness, either of time and/or of movement;
2. shortness of time, beauty, pleasure;
3. length of time, ugliness, sadness;
4. end of time and/or of movement, annihilation.

It is on this two-fold level, formal and semic, that the influence of the refrain makes itself felt.

Formally, the evidence is strongest in strophe I: there are seven repetitions of refrain-words, either in their exact form or with morphological variants: 'tost' (line 3), and 'tantost' (line 6), 'mortel' (line 1) and 'mort' (line 8), 'jeunesse' (line 2), 'vieillesse' (line 6), and 'vieil' (line 8). strophe II, on the other hand, picks up only 'mort' (line 11). In strophe III, line 27 repeats the refrain in another form and uses in turn 'jeune', 'vieil', and 'mort'. Three of these terms, 'Jeunesse' (line 2), 'Vieillesse' (line 6), and 'Mort' (line 11), to which should be added 'Aige moyen' (line 3), are the only allegorized names which the poem contains. Although the last two are preceded by the article, which weakens the figure of personification, there is no doubt that in these four cases we are concerned with an allegorical metaphor which has been developed throughout the first seven lines of the strophe. This fact authenticates the terms in question, which dramatically clarify the maxim provided by the refrain.

Seme 1 may be found, in more or less clear-cut form, in a long series of lexemes where it is associated with various other denotative or connotative elements: 'recorde', 'né', 'cours' (from *courir*), 'aige', 'cours' (noun), 'maine', 'jours trescours', 'fuyant', 'vain', 'recorde', 'bref', 'le cours', 'passent', 'suys . . . la route'; to some degree also 'après', 'quand', and 'lors que', which are also distributed throughout the three strophes (but not in the refrain, unless we count 'tant que').

Seme 2: 'droit à', 'secours', 'mondain', 'fier', 'le monde', 'aymons', 'plaisirs'.

Seme 3: the series of ills enumerated in lines 6–7 and in addition 'languist', 'doubte', 'bêté'.

Seme 4: 'somme toute', 'corde', 'miséricorde', 'fin', 'finira'.

Here there is a tightly knit and well organized network starting from a double figure (the refrain and the allegory in strophe I). It brings together, through their form or through their sense, most of the nouns, adjectives, verbs, and adverbs of the text. This network forms an area of dense meaning, both explicit and implicit.

But there are two gaps in it, lexical entities not directly connected with the refrain: one is lines 15–19, which are at the mid-point of the poem in strophe II, the other is lines 21–4 and lines 28–9 in strophe III, as well as line 34 in the *envoi*. The ambiguity of the word 'cours' in line 12 (it could be the plural of *le cours* or *la cour*; see also 'cours', from 'la cour' in line 15), provides a tenuous connection between the main network and lines 15–19; 'vifs' in line 22 (from *vivre*: see also 'vie' in line 25) brings about the same type of connection with the group of lines 21–4 and 28–9; as for line 34, it is attached to line 14 because of the name 'Dieu' and could be associated with lines 28–9.

It would thus appear that we have two subsidiary thematic groups which freely amplify the refrain network. Perhaps these two amplifications are only one, constructed as an opposition: the court of the 'haultz princes' against a life of holiness. The presence of the words 'Dieu' and 'prince' both in the refrain network (lines 14 and 31) and the amplificatory series (lines 16 and 34) would seem to allow such a bipolarization. The motif of old age and death would thus be accompanied here by the no less traditional one of *taedium vitae curialis*, illustrated at the very period at which this *ballade* was composed, by the *Abuzé en court*, at one time wrongly attributed to King René. This motif, however, though less explicit, and subordinated to the other in rather lax fashion, in its turn introduces into the argument an element of hesitation, of instability, of intentional heterogeneity which to some degree corresponds to and functionalizes the variations in the structure of the verse-form and the syntax.

The rhyme and the other sounds in the refrain are made up of very few phonemes: vocalic – *eu* (three times), *o* (twice), *a* and *i* (once each), to which should be added three mute *e*s; consonantal – *c* (twice), *s, t, m, r, j, n,* and *v* (once each), as well as semivocalic *y*. In themselves, these facts have no particular value. Some of them will be incorporated into a later phase of the analysis. In fact, it is not the refrain as such which dictates the selection and distribution of sound effects at the genre level. It is, by definition, the rhyme.

Rhyme of whatever sort is by nature a matter of sound and, indirectly, of sight. Its sound quality and harmonies set up, within the dense nature of the text, a net of phonic suggestions to which it may be expected that other sound qualities and other harmonies, apparently fortuitous but actually authenticated by it, will respond within the body of the poem: thus they are raised to the status of indices, regrouped, if not exactly organized, in a sort of embroidery which brings about as such a diffuse effect of the sense.

In conformity with the external rule (historical label), each strophe is divided, so far as rhyme is concerned, into two parts, M1 and M2, as follows:

M1 = *ababb*
M2 = *ccdcd*

They are exactly symmetrical.

In M1, *a* = -*corde* (rich rhyme); *b* = -*e cours* (disabyllic rhyme, except in line 15, where the -*e* is missing). In lines 1 and 23, the *a* rhyme is itself preceded by a -*e* ('recorde'), which joins it with the *b* rhyme by the identity of the penultimate syllable.

The system in M1 therefore seems to be instable, apparently closed yet open to potential combinations.

M2 forms the descending part of the strophe (the *cauda*) and is repeated at the end of the *ballade*, since it makes up, in succession, the second part of strophe III and the *envoi*. M2 thus has an autonomous existence in the *envoi*: it is syntactically isolated in strophe III, but connected to M1 in strophes I and II. Thus it removes in the course of the poem from fusion with another element to independence.

The *c* rhyme is in -*oute*, the *d* rhyme in -*eux*: these are weak rhymes in themselves, in the interior of each strophe, but because of their connection with the totality of the sounds in the verse-endings, they do function like two themes differently developed. In lines 6, 7, 9 and 19, the -*oute* in the *d* rhyme does merge with a scheme *e* + some consonant + -*oute*, which recalls the M1 system. In lines 17, 26 and 31, the sound correspondence is imperfect but the visual correspondence is clear. The -*eux* in the *d* rhyme is rich, both visually and quasi-phonically, in strophe II: 'vieulx' (monosyllabic) and '-vieulx' (disyllabic). Furthermore, rhyme relationships are established from one strophe to another, which correct the 'poverty' of the phonic theme.

the rhymes in lines 6, 16 and 32 are rich in regard to one another;
the rhymes in lines 9 and 19 are disyllabic;
the rhymes in lines 17 and 26 are disyllabic and that in line 34 is rich in
    relation to them,
the rhymes in lines 29 and 31 are rich in relation to one another.
Ten out of twenty rhymes are so distinguished.

The relatively closed system of M1 is thus contrasted with the much looser but always perceptible structure of M2, whose field of application is the totality of the *ballade* rather than the line in itself.

Rich and disyllabic rhymes demand that the consonants before the last stressed vowel shall be identical. In M1 this consonant is always *c*; in M2 it is *c-* three times, its voiced form *g-* three times, *v-* six times; others are *r-*, *d-*, *b-* (twice each), and *t-* and *m-* (once each). This dispersion is more apparent than real, since the distinction between unvoiced and voiced was often ignored in the sound- and word-plays in which medieval poets indulged, which were always fairly approximate: *c* and *g*, *d* and *t* can, to a certain degree, be grouped together as simple combinatory variants. Thus M2 shows: six velars, six labials, three dentals, and five of various types. In the totality of rhymes in the *ballade*, the velars are completely dominant (twenty-one against fourteen of other types). The unvoiced form *c* alone appears eighteen times: it is not insignificant that this sound is the first sound in the refrain, where *car* echoes the *-cor* of the *a* rhyme, with vocalic variation.

These observations have to be the starting point of any attempt to locate possible echoes of the system in the mass of the text. Nothing gives us the right to proceed any other way, since the historicity of the *ballade* (its contingent definition) does no more than indicate the rhyming sounds. We are not concerned here with a search for anagrams nor for paragrams (cf. Zumthor, *Langue, texte, énigme*, Paris: Seuil, 1975, pp. 55–67).

Three full syllables (vowel + consonant) which are found in the rhymes also appear elsewhere, here and there, in the text:

-*or*, six times: with rhymes, twelve times in the *ballade*;
-*our*, four times: with rhymes, fourteen times in the *ballade*;
-*oute*, once: with rhymes, thirteen times in the *ballade*.

The three groups make up twelve per cent of the 350 syllables in the text.

Two vowel sounds, very close to one another and sometimes hard to separate in fifteenth-century pronunciation, alone make up twenty per cent of the syllables:

o: twenty-six times outside the rhyme-scheme, thirty-two times in all;
ou: sixteen times outside the rhyme-scheme, thirty-one times in all.

But visually the letter *o* (the spherical shape), which can be read in the groups *ou* and *on*, appears seventy-nine times.

The vowel sounds *o* and *ou* are encountered in every line (on an average twice a line), except in lines 18 and 28 (which, incidentally, rhyme in -*eux*). They lay down the basic sound-scheme of the poem.

The sound form -*eu*, rendered significant by its appearance in the *d* rhymes and by the refrain, in which it appears three times, is to be found thirteen times in the body of the text, and altogether twenty-one. Thus, *o*, *ou*, and *eu*, which together occur eighty-four times, make up a quarter of the syllables in the *ballade*.

A similar account reveals the following frequencies of consonants:

t appears visually eighty-six times; if the finals are excluded, since it is doubtful whether they were pronounced, there remain fifty-five *ts* (that is to say, sixteen per cent of the syllables) and with the thirty *ds* this gives a total of eighty-five dentals, approximately a quarter of the syllables;

r fifty-eight times (sixty, if we count the final in 'penser', which occurs twice);

c forty times; *g* six times; total velars forty-six;

v twenty times; *f* eight times; total labials twenty-eight;

m twenty-four times.

Taken together *t/d*, *r*, *c/g*, *f/v* and *m* contribute to the make-up of 199 syllables, that is, four-sevenths of 350, a proportion which cannot be regarded as fortuitous *a priori*, particularly because it is confirmed by the refrain:

car (aussi) *tost meu*rent (jeunes) *que vieulx*

The two words in which the consonants noted do not appear do, on the other hand, contain the vowels noted, *o* (in 'aussi', whatever the exact pronunciation may have been) and *eu*.

It is obvious that nothing in all this need be regarded as the result of a deliberate intention, but rather as that of an empirical search for a specific harmony which can never be totally attained nor truly systematic. I would compare it with the scintillation which can be observed near a light-source, except that this scintillation comes both from the source and from material which the author's hand has put there: the floating sound-themes which may at any time form shifting syllabic cells and substitute one for the other of these cells:

o,	*ou*	/	*r*
		/	
	eu	/	*t/d*, *c/g*
		/	
		/	*m*
		/	
		/	*f/v*

Of all the combinations theoretically possible, the rhymes (the source of light) give most significance to *o*, *ou*, *c/g*, *r*, and *t/d*; the *eu*, *m* and *f/v* sounds are introduced as substitutes.

As a suggestion rather than as a hypothesis, I shall put down the main possible configurations:

1.	*cor* (Latin)	*cour, cour(s)*	*coeur*
	cord(e)	*cou(s)t(e)*	
	roc	*gou(s)t(e)*	
		gout(e)	
2.	*tor(t)*	*tour*	
	dor(t)	*rout(e)*	
		dout(e)	
3.	*mort(t) mor(d)*		*meur(t)*
	mo(t)		
4.	*for(t)*	*four*	*feu*
			veu(x), voeu
			v(i)eu(x)

These are scattered fragments of something. But of what? The rhymes again show not the key to a code (there is no code here), but the way at least to the auditory and visual perceptions. There are actually some monosyllabic rhyme-words in this imaginary list:

cour(s) four times	*cord(e)*
cou(s)t(e)	
gout(e) twice	
gou(s)t(e)	
dout(e)	
rout(e)	
v(i)eu(lx), veu(lx).	

'Cour(s)' and 'cord(e)', which are full syllables (consonant + vowel + consonant) in the *a* and *b* rhymes, appear in this form fifteen times in the text. By comparison the others, even 'v(i)eu(lx)', which appears five times because of the refrain, are negligible.

Thus, by successive stages, the phonemes noted come to be regarded as the products of the wide dispersion of these two master syllable-words and so are scattered throughout the entire range of the discourse. But once again these things must be taken for what they are – empty sound-forms. The procedure which will make them into significant forms will arise from the reading of the poem, which will integrate them into some form of extratextual, contextual, or intertextual discourse, as a result of the concrete possibilities in natural language. Now these possibilities are not indefinite. The sound-group *cour* will be read as '(la) cour', '(le) cours', '(il) court', '(est) court'; 'cord(e)' is never more than a *corde*, but this latter is associated with either the idea of rigidity, absence of freedom, or of death by hanging. The various types of interpretative form which can come about as a result of reading are thus predetermined as a result of semic links:

1. prince's location
2. break-up and movement
3. shortness
4. rigidity
5. violent death

(It should be noted that 1 could be authenticated by the visual omnipresence, in the text, of the spherical shape of *o* – the enclosed court, an analogical image of the universe and its order.)

The relationships which are established between these series appear in a reading as ambiguities.

1 stands in the same relation to 2 as the harmony of astral movements does to the permanence of the Cosmos; but it is at variance with 3 and 5, which represent what is totally foreign to it and hence exclude it; 2 is opposed to 4; but 2 and 4 are related figuratively and, in different fashion, to 3; 2 is related to 5 as a possible end; 4 can, under certain conditions, be identical with 5.

These are simple potential notions which are here made concrete in a pair of complex ideas: the court against death. This is how the apparently digressive lines 15 to 18 are to be explained.

Most of the conceivable configurations suggested above would fit without difficulty into one or the other of the five semic series, except for the first, which is concerned exclusively with the word *cour*:

into 2. *route*; *doute*; *goute*(?); *mot*; *vieux*
into 3. *meurt*
into 4. *roc, tour, dort, veux*
into 5. *mord*.

Coeur could be put, in mutual opposition, either in 2 or 4. This semic distribution, on which I place no particular stress, would, I believe, confirm the validity of my proposals.

There is another probable confirmation: the words which are scattered throughout the body of the text, without any perceptible system, produce the following sounds:

o appears in thirty-two words, which can be grouped in two semic series, except for a few units of little significance: one, made up of rhyme words, refers to notions of remembrance, of (re)union, and of meeting; the other, with an adverbial shading, recalls either the shortness of time, the expulsion from a place or some excess;

ou appears in thirty-one words, which, in their rhymes, form a series connected with ideas of precipitate haste or, on the contrary, of care and fear; non-rhyming words refer to ideas of precipitate collapse or of evils afflicting man;

eu appears in twenty-one words referring on the one hand to ideas of death and moral evil, on the other to the opposition young/old, which is itself opposed to *God*, who neutralizes it;

r appears in fifty-five words which, with few exceptions, are those in which *o* and *ou* appear. The main exceptions are: 'prince', 'finira', 'crie', 'après', 'arrives', 'bref', 'vertu', 'plaisir', which add to the earlier series the elements of a chain opposed to 'evil', whether physical or moral;

t appears in fifty-three words, distributed like those in which *r* appears, except for nineteen instances where the sound occurs in the second person pronoun;

d appears in thirty words, setting up in the rhymes a series 'remembrance, meeting', and in the non-rhyming words 'pleasure' against 'hesitation, fear', 'care' and *God*:

c appears in forty words which, apart from a few insignificant exceptions, are those in which *o* and *ou* appear. There is a characteristic common to *c, r,* and *t,* which gives additional confirmation to my suggestion of a homogeneous kernel of sound;

g appears in six words containing the semes 'evil' and 'negation', 'test' and 'care';

v and *f* appear in twenty-eight words, semically grouped according to ideas of decadence and end, moral evil and moral good, existence, action, and precipitate movement;

m, finally, appears in twenty-four words, in nineteen of which it is the initial sound and which set up a complex and well structured series: death – world – evil – pardon – betterment.

I see no point in further comment. The marked unity of these effects seems obvious to me. They bear witness to a type of independent existence of sounds, in the midst of the text material, without any direct connection with the surface referential meaning, but which under its impact can be read beneath it. It is a level of shifting significance, fleeting and lacking any clear-cut outlines, and one which constantly goes beyond the apparent limits of discourse in one way or another. Semic potentialities are sketched, take on shape, then slip away, around and in reference to a central theme which is simply the succession of phonemes making up the word *cour(s)*, the court of the 'Prince', and the course of human life.

Thus in the substructure the isotopy of the text becomes instable and, in the layers of a discourse on old age and death, another discourse begins on the subject of the *court* at which the poet serves, where the *course* of his life goes by, 'empty, proud, and envious': the court, the round centre of the world, torn by its contradictions, between immobility and precipitation, between evil and forgiveness, between life and death, all under the eye of God.

This second discourse crops out on the thematic level in lines 15–18 but that is scarcely important. It is present from beginning to end in the *ballade*, unorganized, allusive, concealed and concealing, words beneath words, asking for discovery as much as for reading. The feature which delimits the operation (the 'oeuvre') of the poet is less an effort at juxtaposition or thematic interlacing than the actual way in which the elements of an unspoken statement are combined and integrated into those of an enunciation: by harmony alone.

The poet has spoken: from now on he stays silent, not only outside the text, but outside speech and outside the world: his addressee is 'Mortal Man'. If he distinguishes himself from 'Man' it is because he does not belong to this species (but does he need to or on the contrary does he reduce himself to such a universal concept?). He is not God either, the God whom he invokes. The person who is talking, here and now, is Truth. But the 'Mortal Man' apostrophe in line 1 gives way in line 31 to *Prince*, who there takes his place. And with this we are back at Court.

The only traces in the text of the first person who has been eliminated are these apostrophes themselves, the imperatives in lines 1, 21, 22, 28, and 29, as well as the 'je' in line 23. The person addressed, on the other hand, is mentioned nineteen times by the use of *tu* and *te* and the corresponding possessives. The *envoi* unobtrusively joins the one to the other in a *nous*, which recreates from Truth a man like the rest of us, just as the discourse is on the point of giving up.

The two are thus joined grammatically and even more strongly by the discourse itself, which fills in the space between them: it fills it while creating it and at the same time empties it, by the play of its double nature, since it is less space than spacing in the course of which the matter is fragmented and diluted, and within which a new word is born in the word and from the word.

'Spacing', certainly: but we should not slip between the syllables of this word concepts which are too modern, nor a phenomenology which is constructed on the basis of other models of writing. A space that is crossed, lived in (like a countryside that one travels through) but perceived as mere decoration, as embellishment that provides security. The 'first person' has passed by this way. He fades away, departs along a road known only to himself, to the beyond. He is calm: he has played his part for a little while, on the stage where traditional discourses make their speeches, and also far behind the scenes, hidden in the opacity of the work which was in course of being created: in turn or all at once, naïvely repeating what he has been taught to say and cunning in his tricks of paradox, always alert to double meanings. He has left us this object: some letters on paper, written as a true statement but a statement which other marks, not so quickly readable, wipe out and change into riddles. The solution of the riddles is not an urgent matter: time will tell and we shall be surprised, no more than that.

The real question asked by a text like this has thus to be formulated at the level of the contradictions, apparent or real, which it transcends even while producing them. The poet is the prisoner of a language which is not his own. He makes no claim to it as such and, guided only by his own perception of the material nature of this language, he gropes towards a discovery which is important only to himself: the discovery that he actually has control over this material. He tries to make use of this power: sometimes he is intoxicated with it, as Meschinot is in the admirable beginning passages of the *Lunettes*; on other occasions he uses it with care. But in every way this experience transforms the great game of poetry for him; there is, somewhere, a freedom in the very action which sets up the text. Without, perhaps, expressly intending to do so, he gnaws away at the material, under the guise of using it in his rhetoric, doubles the surface sense by means of ambiguities, equivocates, and, at the end of this long effort, if he ever were to get there, he would deprive its signs of any significance. It is true that this *ballade* is a less striking example in this respect than, for instance, a highly stylized poem of Molinet, of the same period. But this text, which is all fire under its coating of dull grey, reveals all the better the nature of the tendencies which were destined to triumph in the two succeeding generations of *grands rhétoriqueurs*.

7 Dietmar von Eist XII: 'Nu ist ez an ein ende komen'

PETER WAPNEWSKI

1. The Text

1. Nu ist ez an ein ende komen, dar nâch mîn herze ie ranc,
   daz mich ein edeliu vroûwe hât genomen in ir getwanc:
   der bin ich worden undertân
   als daz schif dem stiurman,
   swanne der wâc sîn ünde alsô gar gelâzen hât.
   sô hôh ôwî!
   si benimet mir mange wilde tât.   C 29; MF 38, 32

2. 'Jâ hoere ich vil der tugende sagen von einem ritter guot.
   der ist mir âne mâze komen in mînen staeten muot,
   daz sîn ze keiner zît mîn lîp
   mac vergezzen', redte ein wîp.
   'nu muoz ich al der welte haben dur sînen willen rât.
   sô hô ôwî!
   wol ime, wie er daz gedienet hât!'   C 30; MF 39, 4

3. Wie möhte mir mîn herze werden iemer rehte vruot,
   daz mir ein edeliu vrouwe alsô vil ze leide tuot,
   der ich vil gedienet hân
   als ir wille was getân.
   nu wil si gedenken niht der mangen sorgen mîn:
   sô hô ôwî!
   sol ich ir lange vrömde sîn!   C 31; MF 39, 11

II. The Text-Tradition

'Kaum von Dietmar,' says Carl von Kraus pontifically.[1] The judgement is valid enough if we are referring only to Kraus's Dietmar, that is, to the artificial result of his highly refined process of selection, which results in the designation of three-quarters of the extant material connected with the name Dietmar as 'not genuine'.

The latest revision of *Minnesangs Frühling* by Moser and Tervooren[2] dispenses with the dubious distinction between 'genuine' and 'not genuine'. The text I present here differs only in details from their version (see the remarks made on the passages concerned). The fact that the poem occurs in only one manuscript (C) helps to make many expressions seem uncertain and many passages seem obscure – and, as we shall see, remain so.

Any attempt to understand the poem is naturally closely bound up with the strophic order which determines the sequence of sense-expression. Since their connection with each other has at various times been regarded as either close or loose and their logical arrangement variously interpreted, it has on occasion been suggested that strophe 3 should be set off from the others and further that the order of strophes should be changed. Kraus followed the latter suggestion and put them in the order C31, C30, C29, that is, 3–2–1. His reasoning is indicative of the attitude of this phase of self-satisfied 'reconstruction-philology': 'Thus we in fact produce a logical sense-sequence'.[3] As if there were any way of determining what seems logical to one period and what does not, except by looking at the surviving work of the period and at its original state. Quite aside from the fact that in this case neither the one arrangement nor the other presents to a non-contemporary reader the degree of 'continuity' which he expects to find there or experience, Moser and Tervooren were quite right to leave the original order intact, that is, put them back as they were. What disturbs people today may have been regarded as perfectly logical eight hundred years ago; indeed, the principle of logical continuity may have been unknown and inconceivable. (Details on the setting-up of the text are to be found in Section IV).

III. The Form

Kraus devotes two and a half pages to the metrics of the *Ton*, since the first, second and fifth lines at times allow 'various interpretations'.[4] Lachmann printed these lines (1, 2, 5) with no break, thus treating them as seven-stress lines, whereas later research has preferred to insert caesuras, admittedly in different places according to each individual's choice. The result of this procedure argues against it, that is to say, the necessity of amending the text in various places. Once again we have to agree with Moser-Tervooren in keeping the manuscript readings, taking the three long lines (with Lachmann and Vogt) as seven-stress lines and simply accepting a hiatus at two points (strophe 1, 5 and strophe 3, 2), which can be tolerated when a work is sung.[5] If only those stressed syllables are counted which are actually realized in speech, according to the principle currently accepted, the following metrical pattern can be established without any forcing:

7a
7a
4b
4b
7c
2W
4c

The rhymes are pure. This is true even for the apparent difference in quantity in strophe 1, 3–4, since in the Danubian-Bavarian speech-area the *-man* is pronounced long and slightly rounded, with a little nasalization.[6] The number of rhymes available is clearly limited. In a total of twenty-one lines, there are only the rhyme-sounds *-a-*, *-i-*, and *-uo-*. The *-uot-* rhyme introduces both the second and the third strophe, and the *-ât* rhyme closes both the first and second and does so furthermore by reintroducing the rhyme-word 'hât' (strophes 1, 5 and 2, 7). The last observation is of significance in regard to the fact that the last rhyming pair in strophe 1 'hât'/'tât' appears again as grammatical rhyme in the last strophe and furthermore in the prominent final rhyme position 'hân'/'getân' (lines 3 and 4). This gives us reason to think that it is not the clumsiness of an unconscious repetition that is at work here but the artistic necessity to join the strophes by means of rhyme connections and variants of them. If that is correct, however, then it must be deduced from the demonstration of such a structural principle that all three strophes are to be understood as tightly knit with each other and must be so interpreted.

There is in addition within the strophe a three-part sequence: lines 1 and 2, as well as lines 3 and 4 respectively are made into pairs both by the rhyme and the metre. Lines 5 to 7 then prove to be a rhyming unit, at one and the same time extended and thrown into relief by the unrhymed refrain. Consequently, this type of three-part division, which rejects exact correspondence of the *Stollen*, does not correspond with the classic *canzon* structure and its question–answer character.

IV. Special Points in Setting up the Text

1, 1.   Lachmann, Vogt and, following them, Kraus changed the order for the sake of the metre: 'dar nâch mîn herze ie ranc', and Moser-Tervooren are in agreement in indicating their preference for this version by the use of a paragraph-sign ¶. In my opinion, this very cautious emendation is justified by its practical results, for the double unaccented syllable ('ie mîn') markedly slows up the line.

1, 2.   Lachmann notes at this point: 'besser *in ir gewalt*', a remark which is as laconic as it is enigmatic.

1, 5.   The 'alsô' of the MS. sets up the seven-stress line. Kraus's substitution of 'sô' in the text is due to his own quite different conception of the metre.

1, 7.   Here occurs the one really important conjecture. The MS. has 'benement' (with the *n* suspension mark), which one would gladly retain if it made any sense whatever. Probably the scribe was misled into writing the plural by the group of nouns which immediately precedes, 'schif', 'stiurman', 'wâc', 'ünde'. What must be borne in mind is that this conjecture, 'benimet', makes a great deal of difference. It puts into the text a piece of strict doctrine, the confession of 'being well behaved' because of love. Nevertheless, the change does seem necessary, and thus we can record here one of the relatively rare cases where a conjecture has made its way unchallenged from Lachmann through Vogt and Kraus to Moser-Tervooren – until now, when Schweikle constitutes the exception. He lets the MS. reading stand on the ground that it is impossible to understand it as a 'general sentiment' and to make it refer to 'the refining society of all ladies'. In accordance with this, he translates: 'They restrain me from many senseless (*unbesonnen*) acts'.[7] Incidentally, Schweikle goes back to the manuscript order, as in *MF* 77. To do so is indeed an essential part or rather precondition of his interpretation. (Grimminger had made the same proposal as early as 1969. See below, p. 171 and note 10.)

1, 7.   'wilde tât': when Lachmann asks 'etwa *missetat?*', he destroys the connection in the image-sequence of ship, calmed sea, and calmed *Mannesmut.*

2, 3. Lachmann's change of the line from a quite unobjectionable version into 'daz ich sîn ze keiner zît', that is, the deletion of the 'pure' rhyme word *lîp* in favour of the artificial creation of an 'impure' rhyme, i.e. an assonance, coupled with the *addition* of the personal pronoun *ich* seems to me to be quite uncalled for, even though Moser-Tervooren, by their use of the paragraph sign here, do raise the question of a presumptive variant. But surely it is pushing mistrust of Manuscript C's regularizing tendency to absurd lengths to be suspicious on principle of pure-rhyme situations which have actually come down to us and to 'primitivize' them into assonances whatever the chance is offered by a text to which an early date can be assigned. I am in complete agreement with the warning 'ohne eine Parallelüberlieferung ist die Richtigkeit der Überlieferung nicht auszuschliessen.'[8] I would rather phrase it positively: in such a case correctness is to be assumed.

2, 7. MS. 'wol ime wie schône er daz gedienet hât'. The line is overloaded. Lachmann, Vogt and Kraus lightened it by eliminating the prothetic 'wol ime'. I agree with Moser-Tervooren and their elimination of 'schône'. Their version is probably based on the assumption that a scribe would be more likely to have added mechanically a comfortable adverb to the verb 'dienen' than to have invented a free-floating 'wol ime'.

Str. 3. *MF 77* has rightly restored the original text as against Kraus's two changes (line 2, Kraus 'sô' for MS. 'alsô'; line 5, Kraus 'niht gedenken' for MS. 'gedenken niht').

V. Explanatory Notes on Individual Passages

1, 1. The image-formula 'mîn herze ranc' is to be found in Bernger von Hornheim, in Hartmann von Aue and in the *Nibelungenlied*. See *MFU*, p. 96. This would thus be one of the earliest instances of the phrase.

1, 5. MF77 notes in the translation aids on 'lâzen': 'loslassen'. But the image is not clear. It could mean 'When the sea has left the power of its waves completely in peace', that is, the sea is smooth. But it is also possible to see in it the thought that the sea has let its waves go, let them free. Moser-Tervooren seem to have this image in mind, and it is, in fact, nautically plausible. Wave movement is the result of wind; only when there is wind can the steersman make his [sailing] ship 'submissive to the wind'. Nevertheless, this interpretation does run counter to the confession in the last line of the strophe: the 'vrouwe' has calmed the man, has tamed his wild desire for action, has brought about calm in the soul. My decision, therefore, is to understand the passage like this: 'When the sea makes the power of its waves come to rest'.

2, 2/3.   Kraus puts a comma after 'muot' and this seems right in view of the following consecutive 'daz' (= *so dass*). However, see below on 3, 4 on the subject of the first rhyming couplet as a syntactical unit.

2, 4.   The *inquit* formula sounds old-fashioned or archaized. See below, Section VI.

3, 4.   'als' can be taken quite simply as an abbreviation of *alsô* or *alse* and thus as the adverb with demonstrative or the conjunction with modal-comparative function. Both Wehrli ('I have served her for a long time, as was her desire') and Schweikle ('to whom I have given much service, as was her desire') do, in fact, translate this way. As a result, Moser-Tervooren puzzle the interpreter with the aid to translation which they give: '*als* Nf zu *allez* immer' (*als* as a by-form of *allez* 'always'). They thus take lines 3 and 4 each as an independent syntactical unit and probably intend to translate, 'She whom I have constantly served – her desire was always fulfilled!' The editors' terseness in not supplying their reasons for this interpretation leaves it up to the reader. It obviously has to do with Moser-Tervooren's conception of the rhythmical-syntactical structure of the poem: they attribute syntactical independence and completeness to the first metric grouping. That is the reason for the exclamation mark after 'tuot' in strophe 3, line 2 and the presumption of a new start in strophe 2, line 3 ('daz sîn . . .'), with the result that the passage is to be taken as conditional rather than consecutive and is to be prolonged beyond the inserted 'redte ein wîp.' (Thus this middle part of strophe 2 would read, according to Moser-Tervooren: ' "So that I don't forget him at any time," said a woman, "I am forced to do without anyone else for his sake." ') Such a rigid syntactical and structural system, which is not even hinted at by the situation in strophe 1, for the demonstrative connection with line 3 totally minimizes the effect of the break, cannot be regarded as a rule of

Middle High German strophic patterning, and there is thus no reason for not keeping the accepted meaning in strophe 3: take 'getân' in the adjectival sense of the participle as is normal in Middle High German. (The meaning is 'shaped', 'having an appearance', and 'constituted'; see the numerous instances in connection with an adverb [of the type *wol getân*] and absolutely [of the type *wie er was getân*] in Benecke-Müller-Zarncke, III, 143. Thus we have not 'semper [omnis] voluntas eius performata erat' but 'ut voluntas eius erat.' The appropriate handbooks on Middle High German phonology and syntax, incidentally, give no encouragement to the idea of regarding this *als* as the adverbial genitive *alles*, or even the adverbial accusative *allez* in its short form *al(s)*. See Behaghel, *Deutsche Syntax*, I, 722f.; Grimm, *Deutsches Wörterbuch*, Vol. I, column 246f.; Benecke-Müller-Zarncke, p. 20 (where there is warning against overhasty interpretation of the common scribal form *als* as the adverbial *alles*); Michels, *Mittelhochdeutsches Elementarbuch* (1921), para. 322; the examples in Ingeborg Schröbler, *Mittelhochdeutsche Syntax*, para. 357,2; and the appropriate paragraphs in Moser, *Mittelhochdeutsche Grammatik* (1969): in this latter, furthermore, the by-form *al* is given for the fixed adverbial forms *alles* and *allez* but not *als* (which is, however, given as still in use in Hessian dialect in this form, but otherwise designated as 'antiquated': does this mean that it was already dying out in the Middle High German period?)

VI. Interpretation

This song is one of the most puzzling in the whole corpus of *Minnesang*. It convinces by irrationality; it makes its impression by means of a poetic dynamism which appears in lively images and compelling sound-effects, particularly in the refrain. This extraordinary *sô hôh ôwî!* is vaguely reminiscent in sound of the old sailor's cry 'Ahoy' and like every refrain it possesses its own force of speech-magic. There are also some surprising turns of phrase which sound as if they had been translated from modern German into Middle High German: 'Now it has reached a conclusion for which my heart always strove', and 'How can my heart ever become sensible. . . . These are the utterances of a reflective pathos which sounds more like the age of sentiment or like expressionism than the early stages of *Minnesang*. In addition, there is the intensity of the metaphors; the well known topos of the ship of life is transferred to the world of erotic imagery, the lover shows the dependence and subjection to the will of the beloved lady in imagining himself to be a ship steered by her and under her command. (The metaphor may be inspired, incidentally, by memories of a crusade.) Such a choice of imagery gives evidence of an already 'mature' attitude determined by the Romance idea of love: the lady has taken the singer 'in ir getwanc' (into her power), as her servant into her 'overlordship', and she calms his unruly and boisterous nature (strophe 1). He has served her and has broken down the resolution of her sense-system so that she is forced to ignore everyone else and think constantly of him (strophe 2). Finally there is the classic *Minne* attitude: although he has served her with complete devotion, she causes him nothing but suffering, she takes no notice of his misery and makes him afraid that he will still be separated from her for a long time (strophe 3). There are also formal indications, in addition to linguistic-stylistic, metaphorical, and ideal forces which correspond to a level of consciousness of mood which bears the imprint of the attitude in the *Song of Songs*. There is the determining function of rhyme, already noted in Section III, which acts as a link throughout the three strophes. There is the art of the tripartite structure, which does not, however, correspond to the question and answer and repetitive scheme of the *canzon*, but produces its effects 'more freely' and hence with more originality. There is the subtlety of the refrain, whose wordless singing quality produces an extraordinary effect of mood-impression by its figure of repetition. And, finally, there is the striking correspondence between the first and third strophes. They are constructed like one another and integrated with one another even in detail. Both begin with the misery of the 'herze' in the first line and with the sorrow brought about by the dominance of the lady in the second: 'edeliu vrouwe' in both cases. Finally, in the *coda*, 'mange' (*wilde tât*) as against 'mangen' (*sorgen*); and in the introduction of 'wilde' and 'vrömde', that is, of words which are closely allied in the same concept-field.

That is highly developed art, even artistry, and the elements of archaism and clumsiness stand out in sharp contrast to such maturity: the naïve 'ritter guot', the adjective 'vruot', the ponderous indication of direct speech by the narrative *inquit* figure 'redte ein wîp'. (Cf. Der von Kürenberg, II, 3 and 4 in *MF*, 8, 16: 'sô sprach daz wîp'; Dietmar [der 'alte'] likes this comfortable formula: see 1, 3; 2, 3 in *MF* 32, 3 and 32, 7 and also Kaiser Heinrich 1, 5 in *MF* 5, 6). This middle strophe, incidentally, contrasts noticeably with the other two in its entirely old-fashioned dramatization of word, image, and thought. In the distribution of roles the 'modern' part is, or seems to be, assigned deliber-

ately to the man and the old-fashioned part to the woman, something
which may also be observed in other strophes in the earlier stages [of the
Minnesang], e.g. Dietmar IV, 14 and V. 6 and 8. The sub-genre to which
this poem belongs, the *Wechsel*, is old-fashioned too. (It has an additional
third strophe; see *MFU*, p. 95) Kraus is right: 'The poem is a mixture of
older and later elements'.⁹ It is the classic *Minne* attitude, adjusted to the
old *Wechsel* form; modern, even recent, thought-groupings and word-
sequences worked into the simplest kind of formulaic material and
archaic formulation; artistic correspondences in word-setting, artful
linking of strophes by rhyme repetition, with refrain, and added to these
simple groups which are their own *raison d'être*. It is a strange creation,
put together of disparate elements and owing some of its charm to
precisely this picturesque confusion. We must agree with Grimminger's
extension of Kraus's judgement:

> Obviously two basically different conceptions overlap. Dietmar is
> adapting the new Provençal love-scheme to the old one, even though
> they are in basic contradiction. The song progresses from glorification
> of companionship to its dissolution according to the patterns of
> hopeless love. Consequently, not only the metrics and the treatment of
> the rhymes . . . but also the content are indebted to different *Minnesang*
> traditions. The totality [of the poem] should thus perhaps be ap-
> proached as an experiment which attempts to connect the old Min-
> nesang with the new, Provençal oriented *Minnesang* without being able
> to reconcile the contradictions, perhaps even without wishing to do
> so.¹⁰

But what about the 'logical sequence' of the execution? Are we to
abandon it completely as an unfair demand?
Strophe 1: The singer expresses his thanks. His struggle has attained its
goal; the lady he has wooed has taken him under her seigneurial
protection; he answers to her as a ship on a calm sea does to its
helmsman; and he knows he is purified by her.
Strophe 2: The 'vrouwe' reacts according to the convention of the
Wechsel. She has heard of the man's excellence and feels her inner
stability disturbed because of him. She announces that she thinks of him
constantly and must now renounce the whole world, society and its
opinion in order to reward his 'dienest'.
Strophe 3: What the singer-lover complains about here does not
correspond with the message which strophe 2 has brought him. Instead
of rejoicing about the reward promised to him, he laments over the great

sorrow she causes him, points to his devoted love, blames the lady for paying no attention to his 'sorgen', and in the cry of misery in the refrain outburst he expresses the fear that he could be kept at a distance from her for a long time yet.

This is obviously not a 'logical sequence' in the terms of modern logic, and even for a medieval listener its construction was probably not without contradictions, as was made apparent in the remarks about the 'mixed up' character of the elements of the song. It must be emphasized, however, that the reversed order suggested by Carl von Kraus provides no satisfactory solution. The song then begins with the complaint about unrequited love. There follows the promise of reward – so far, so good. But now comes his song of thanks: he is in her 'getwanc', subject to her. Is that supposed to be the acknowledgement, is that supposed to be the goal towards which his heart has always been striving? That surely presents only the unvarying, completely static love-service attitude from which he started out – without reward. And to be subject to 'her' seigneurial will – he was that from the very beginning. It is a situation which is only the beginning stage for the classical *Minner*, starting from which he wants more, that is, not to be 'vrömde' to her. Thus, no modification of the strophic sequence in the manuscript can be justified from the point of view of a 'self-evident' (in whatever sense) logical sequence. The case for its retention is also strengthened, incidentally, by the fact that only that sequence prepares us for the refrain and provides the key to it; the ship-sea image explains the sailor's shout which follows.[11] Perhaps the following chain of thought will be of further help, although admittedly it presupposes an already highly differentiated state of awareness: the singer believes that he has finally found peace in the service of his lady and that he has won peace in his soul (strophe 1). The lady confirms this (strophe 2). But now the man's heart, which thought it had reached the goal of its desire in fulfilling *dienest* (duty), recognizes in despair that it cannot find satisfaction in such service and cannot feel such an act of service as a reward in itself. But he knows: he wants more. And it is exactly this knowledge which makes clear to him how unwisely his heart has always beaten (strophe 3). That is how I understand Schweikle's commentary: the last strophe seems to draw up a disappointing profit and loss account for the love-service announced in strophes 1 and 2.

In this way the song demonstrates the paradoxical structure of love-service: the heart yearns for calm, for non-problematic involvement in duty. Duty, however, is not content with itself. Like every service operation, it wants its reward – and knows, nevertheless, that it cannot sue for it but only beg for it in a complaint, and in the final analysis must do without it. This is an antinomy on which love-service lives and from which a love-servant can die. Let us grant that the heart grows sensible. For 'Ein leicht-bewegtes Herz/Ist ein elend Gut/Auf der schwankenden Erde' (Goethe, Dritte Ode an Behrisch). Understood in this way, the antinomial elements of the three strophes do not indeed constitute a unity but they do form a correspondence. Nevertheless there remains something unresolved and perhaps unresolvable in this poem, but the scholar should beware of explaining the irrational, mysterious and unclarified elements as peculiar characteristics of poetry, and in particular of lyric poetry. It is quite certain that poetry can be made up of illogical, mystifying, and indeterminable elements; it is also certain that over and over again there is an unexplained residue and a substance which cannot be conveyed by verbal analysis; but, on the other hand, it is certain that the study of literature has to do with the task of explaining and not with that of pointing significantly to what is unexplainable.

But here it is the tension between the archaic and the modern, between clear concept and unclear execution, the mixture of disparate elements, it is the combination of Kürenberg and Morungen and modern elements which constitutes the disturbing charm of these oddly attractive lines. A capricious collage of typical and atypical factors, love doctrine and love complaint – and something else which is lost in the unknowable. It will be recalled that in the miniature of Dietmar von Aist in manuscripts B and C we see a pedlar, a vagrant, offering his trinkets for sale. Is this a picture of his role? Or pure misunderstanding on the part of later illuminators? A game of mistaken identity? It is quite possible that even those charmingly strange 'Ahoi' lines are a disguise and that they playfully slip away from the critic's approach, at least to a considerable degree.

VII. Translation

The aim of a translation is to give a summation of what has been understood and to present one's understanding. In order to achieve the total clarity we are aiming at, it must renounce 'beauty'. The beauty is in the original. We must look to it, for it cannot be imitated. It should be stated in advance that the refrain appears to me to be untranslatable; even in the original it has no meaning which can be syntactically determined. But this 'sô hôh ôwî' contains on the one hand the upswing factor of the 'high' wave, luck, pain. On the other hand it contains a sound element, which gives it the charm of the exotic: far-off seas, far-off sounds, enticing sing-song. Wehrli's understanding[12] of the refrain as 'O bright sorrow' attempts to integrate the factors named, but in doing this he slips into a pathetic, stylized strain characteristic of modern 'I-lyricism'. (Walther Fischer is far worse with his 'So laut ohoi').[13] Schweikle, on the other hand, has confined himself to reproducing the Middle High German version.

1. Nun ist endlich das Ziel dessen erreicht, worum mein Herz von je
                                                              rang:
    dass eine edle Herrin mich in ihren Dienst aufgenommen hat.
    Der bin ich nun untertan
    wie das Schiff dem Steuermann,
    wenn das Meer seine Wogen still ruhen lässt.
    sô hôh ôwî!
    Sie sänftigt gänzlich meinen wilden Tatensinn.

2. 'Viel Vorzügliches höre ich reden über einen tüchtigen Ritter.
    der hat mein doch so festes Herz über alles Mass erschüttert,
    so dass weder Tag noch Nacht ich
    ihn aus meinen Gedanken entlassen kann', so sprach eine Frau.
    'Nun muss ich um seinetwillen mir alle Welt gleichgültig sein
                                                              lassen.
    sô hôh ôwî!
    Wohl ihm, wie sehr er sich das erdient hat!'

3. Wie könnte mir denn mein Herz jemals wirklich vernünftig
                                                              werden,
    wo mir doch eine edle Herrin derart viel Schmerz zufügt,
    sie, der ich all den Dienst geleistet habe
    wie ihr Wille verlangte.
    Nun aber will sie sich nicht kümmern um meine viele Sorge.
    sô hôh ôwî, – weh mir,
    wenn sie mich noch lange abwehrt.

NOTES

1. In the *apparatus criticus* to his redaction of *Minnesangs Frühling*, 32nd printing (Stuttgart, 1959).
2. (Stuttgart, 1977). Hereafter abbreviated as *MF 77*.

3. Carl von Kraus, *Des Minnesangs Frühling, Untersuchungen* (Leipzig, 1939), hereafter abbreviated as MFU.

4. *MFU*, p. 92.

5. *MF 77*, vol. 2, Editionsprinzipien, Melodien, Handschriften, Erläuterungen, p. 75, hereafter abbreviated as *MFA 77*.

6. Cf. Karl Weinhold, *Bairische Grammatik* (Berlin, 1867), para. 36 and *passim*.

7. Günther Schweikle, *Die mittelhochdeutsche Lyrik*, I, 'Die frühe Minnelyrik, Texte und Übertragungen, Einführung und Kommentar' (Darmstadt, 1977).

8. *MFA 77*, p. 73.

9. *MFU*, p. 96.

10. Rolf Grimminger, *Poetik des frühen Minnesangs* (München, 1969), pp. 20ff.

11. 'Ältester Refrain der mhd. Lyrik (Neben Hausen und Veldeke), gebildet aus einer Interjektion': Schweikle, p. 403. On the refrain-rhyme, see also P. Habermann in the first edition of Paul Merker and Wolfgang Stammler, *Reallexikon der deutschen Literaturgeschichte*, 4 vols (Berlin, 1924–31).

12. Max Wehrli, *Deutsche Lyrik des Mittelalters* (Zürich, 1955), pp. 66–9.

13. Walter Fischer, *Liedsang aus deutscher Frühe* (Stuttgart, 1939), p. 10 (one strophe only).

I wish to thank Burkhardt Krause and Rüdiger Krohn, who gave me a great deal of help and many ideas in discussing the text.

8 *Meaning in Medieval Spanish Folk Song*

BRUCE W. WARDROPPER

Alan D. Deyermond has well said, 'For educated medieval Europeans, genre rather than the writer's nationality determined which language was used.' In medieval Spain, prose works, epic, and hagiographic poetry were generally written in Castilian, the language which today is standard Spanish. Lyric poetry was written either in Provençal or in Gallaeco-Portuguese: Catalan troubadours gravitated to Provençal, a language very similar to their own; Castilian-speaking poets, including the famous King Alfonso the Wise, used Gallaeco-Portuguese. We should not forget, however, that for obvious reasons in Al-Andalus, south of the states under Christian rule, educated poets wrote in Classical Arabic or in Hebrew.

It was not until the fifteenth century that these marriages of genre to language began to dissolve. Ausias March (1397–1459) was the first poet to write entirely in Catalan. The great anthologies called *Cancioneros* (beginning with that of Baena, compiled around 1445) offer for the first time a considerable body of verse in Castilian, which still, however, suffered competition from Gallaeco-Portuguese. It is true that sporadic examples of learned lyric poetry in Castilian occurred earlier. The twelfth-century *Razón de Amor*, an anonymous narrative poem capped with a debate, contains some lyric passages. In the thirteenth century, Gonzalo de Berceo inserted into his *Duelo de la Virgen* a watch song which he has sung by the Jews who were guarding Christ's sepulchre. In the fourteenth century the Archpriest of Hita included a number of lyrics in his *Libro de Buen Amor*; and Diego Hurtado de Mendoza composed a lyric in the parallelistic form used for the Gallaeco-Portuguese *cantigas d'amigo*, innovatively writing it in Castilian. These few exceptions only prove the rule that in the Middle Ages educated lyric poets avoided Castilian.

There was, nevertheless, an authentic medieval Castilian lyric which was not the product of the literate class. In the thirteenth century, Lucas de Tuy cites in his Latin *Chronicon* these lines in Castilian:

> En Cañatañazor
> perdió Almanzor
> ell atamor.

It was (El Tudense said) a ghostly fisherman – a demon in disguise – who sang this lament at the time of the great Moorish general's death. He interprets the reference to Almanzor's loss of his drum as meaning that he had lost his vigour, and not his life, for at the battle of Calatañazor, in the year 1000, Almanzor was, as always, victorious. More plausibly, Ramón Menéndez Pidal regards the snatch of Spanish verse as a battle cry sung by Christian soldiers who were hopeful of victory. Its importance for literary history is that it shows that songs were being sung in Castilian even though their composition was not scribal but oral. In the Middle Ages such songs by the unlettered were seldom transcribed as this one fortuitously was. There were transmitted orally from village to village and from one generation to the next. Hispanic scholars refer to them as popular or traditional lyrics. Which term is used depends on which theory one holds about their nature. The theories need not concern us here. We may refer to them without prejudice to literary theory as folk songs. The well-known fact that folk song is easy to fake need not detain us. For our purpose the genuine folk song and its pastiche serve equally well: if an educated poet is capable of writing a song indistinguishable from those of the folk, he is himself a part of the *pueblo*, the folk. Like the English word 'people', *pueblo* may refer either to the untutored masses or to all social classes. Such semantic ambiguities, when rooted in the language itself, invite not discrimination but synthesis.

Folk song is generally based on a rural society and an agricultural economy. The only major exception is formed by the *kharjas* of Al-Andalus, which, sung either in Vulgar Arabic or Mozarabic Spanish, thrived in the great cities of the south. The necessary conditions for folk song are in any case a homogeneous view of life, shared by rural peasants or urban house servants, and small, self-sufficient communities. One sang usually to or with a few others. Perhaps for this reason a majority of Spanish folk songs express the feelings and hopes of women, since a man's work on the farm is often done alone. Most frequently the singer is an unmarried girl who is in love.

Until the present century, work on the farm and life in the village changed little and slowly. The songs that accompanied these activities also changed little and slowly. Still in the twentieth century, in remote or backward areas of the Spanish-speaking world, songs may be picked up by a field worker with a tape recorder that are clearly descendants of songs written down or printed in the Renaissance. And in New York, Morocco, and elsewhere, Sephardic Jews still sing in archaic Castilian songs that their ancestors carried in their memories in the diaspora of 1492. Mechanization of farms, rapid transportation, electronic entertainment, and all modern technological advances are only now putting an end to the way of life that sustained Spanish folk song over a millennium.

It was in the fifteenth century that Spanish aristocrats developed an interest in all kinds of folk art, including song. A 'Villancico a unas tres fijas suyas',[1] attributed to the Marqués de Santillana, incorporates four folk songs. In the great *Cancionero musical de Palacio*, compiled for the court of Ferdinand and Isabella, folk songs and courtly songs appear side by side. In the sixteenth century very many folk songs were published in printed books. As the texts of these songs are transcribed, they gain a wider social and geographical acceptance; some – but not all – lose their viability in the oral tradition. What is significant about the collection of folk songs in the Renaissance is that it is medieval lyrics that are being transcribed for the first time.

The antiquity of these texts may be demonstrated in a number of ways. One of the songs in the so-called 'Villancico' ascribed to the Marqués de Santillana reads:

> Dejatlo al villano pene;
> véngueme Dios d'elle.

Although the song is here sung by an aristocratic lady, its words belong to some anonymous peasant girl. The girl, having suffered some wrong from her swain, wishes to let the wretch (*villano*, 'peasant'!) suffer; and she prays God to take vengeance on him. Now, the word for 'him' (*elle*; modern, *él*) was archaic long before Santillana's time; it disappeared from the language about 1250. It could not have been modernized within the poem because the assonantal rhyme with *pene* (*é-e*) had frozen it in its older form. Here is positive linguistic proof that the song was at least 200 years old by the time it was first written down. Similarly assonance prevents the normal and early diphthongization of open *o* in songs such as:

> A mi puerta nace una fonte [for *fuente*]
> ¿por dó saliré que no me moje?

A spring having mysteriously appeared at the door of her house, the singer cannot leave home without getting soaked (*me moje*). Such linguistic evidence of a song's antiquity is common. Occasionally, too, internal historical details may point to a remote date of composition. The hunting song

> Rey don Alonso, rey mi señor,
> rey de los reyes, el emperador

must allude either to Alfonso VI (1085–1109) or to Alfonso VII (1126–57), both of whom eccentrically styled themselves Emperor. Thus there need be no doubt that folk song in Castilian flourished in the Middle Ages; indeed it would be surprising if it had not, for all peoples sing. Many – probably most - of the songs collected in the fifteenth and sixteenth centuries were of medieval origin. This folk song, which Julio Cejador y Frauca has rather polemically called 'the real poetry of Castile' (*La verdadera poesía castellana*), is the lyric legacy of the Castilian Middle Ages.

The difficulty of studying these folk songs lies in their extreme brevity. Like *haikus*, *kharjas*, and *robâ'is*, they constitute what Stephen Reckert has called *lyra minima*. They consist of a nucleus – generally called a *villancico* – of two, three, or four lines. Any development or prolongation ('glossing') of this nucleus is supect: a courtly tone, the expression of courtly love, or courtly vocabulary often betray the interference of a literate hand. We are left, then, with the problem of how to study a miniscule literary text.

Let us consider a sample:

> Con el aire de la sierra
> híceme morena.

A girl is singing that because of the wind (*aire*) blowing down from the mountain range she has become dark-skinned (*morena*). The song raises questions that it does not answer. Is the singer happy or unhappy over the changing of her complexion? Is she right in attributing this change to the mountain breeze? But in the modern reader's mind the main question about the meaning of the song is: So what? From this scepticism about the importance of the singer's statement the reader easily passes to doubt about the value of the tiny poem. An octosyllabic line is followed by a hexasyllable; the lines are connected only by weak assonantal rhyme (*é-a*). It is small comfort to learn that, as long ago as 1920, Pedro Henríquez Ureña showed that metrical irregularity is typical of popular Spanish verse or to know that assonance is common in medieval

Romance poetry. The reader of this one poem can only experience bafflement.

Perhaps a four-line song will give us more to work with.

> ¿Con qué la lavaré,
> la flor de mi cara?
> ¿Con qué la lavaré,
> que vivo mal penada?

The repetition of the first line deprives the reader of some of the additional material for which he had hoped. Even so, in asking herself the same question twice, the girl introduces a significant variation the second time. A comparison of the two questions might conceivably form the basis of a critical method. What, the girl first wonders, will she use to wash the beauty (*flor*) of her face? The second formulation of the question provides the extra information that her life is full of suffering. Because young women habitually sing about love and because the course of true love never did run smooth, it may be surmised that the singer's unhappiness has been caused by her lover. In that case it is hard to understand how washing her face will improve her lot. If she must – for some reason – wash her face, surely plain water is the obvious fluid to use. The slight increase in information supplied by this song compared with the first has done little to reduce the reader's bewilderment at the minimal poem.

In the text of this song, which was collected in the Renaissance, the four-line *villancico* is followed by a gloss consisting of another four lines. Although we know that such extensions of the poetic nucleus are unlikely to belong to the original folk song, we may in desperation be tempted to turn to it in search of some clue:

> Lávanse las casadas
> con agua de limones.
> Lávome yo, cuitada,
> con penas y dolores.

Married women wash with lemon water, which is no doubt sensually pleasant; they may do so with a smug satisfaction with their good fortune at being married. The girl in the song, who had no doubt been looking forward to an early marriage, has been disappointed and so must wash herself with sorrows and pains. Does she mean that her face is bathed in tears? Even with this extra information, whether it be authentic or unreliable, one ends up again asking: So what?

The way to circumvent this defeatist response to a short folk song is to recognize that, while the folk are creative, they are not innovative. In ceramics, for example, folk craftsmen repeat the same shapes and the same ornamental designs over centuries with a rudimentary kind of mass-production technique. The same is true of the ballads of the folk: the narrative plots are relatively few, and they are punctuated by the clichés of formulaic diction. Insofar as folk song expresses the emotions and situations of being in, and out of, love, it necessarily harps on a few themes, for the human experience of being in love is monotonously repetitive. Collating folk songs with the same or similar themes would seem to be a reasonable approach to the study of this *lyra minima*. The homogeneity of folk experience leads one to expect a common expression of it in these medieval Spanish lyrics. Perhaps through a study of the songs of the Spanish folk as song – of the plural as a singular, of the collectivity instead of the unit – it will even be possible to perceive some uniqueness in the experience of the Spanish folk. The medieval poem that I shall discuss will, then, be a conglomeration of brief songs with a similar theme, regarded as a single, more or less coherent lyric expression.

I have chosen to discuss the songs in which a *morena* laments the dark colour of her facial skin, of which our first sample ('Con el aire de la sierra') is typical. The word *moreno* means 'dark' or 'brown'. Older Spanish dictionaries define the colour as being not quite black; sometimes indeed in these poems the *morena* is bluntly called black, *negra* or *prieta*. Today a *morena* is normally a brunette, the colour referring to her hair. In the Middle Ages – and still to some extent among the folk – the colour reference is to the complexion. From the woman's point of view a host of folk songs testifies to the fact that a dark complexion is undesirable. Knowing this, we now realize that the girl who claimed in song that her skin had been darkened by the wind from the sierra was by no means rejoicing in the change. The second of our mysterious songs – about what a miserable girl should use to wash her face – suggests, then, that she is contemplating some way of toning down the darkness of her face.

Washing is a method of whitening the face that occurred to other composers of folk song.

Aunque soy morenita un poco,
no me doy nada;
con el agua del almendruco
me lavo la cara.

Even though she is a tiny bit dark (as she coyly puts it), this diminutive *morenita* doesn't worry at all: she is washing her face, not with the lemon water appropriate to married women, but with water spiced with the juice of the green almond fruit (*almendruco*). Editors of this song invariably cite the seventeenth-century lexicographer Sebastián de Covarrubias to the effect that green almonds were a delicacy much prized by pregnant women. The relevance of this information is unclear; it is unlikely that this girl was pregnant. It is obvious that the girl expects a chemical reaction between the almond water and her skin pigments gradually to bleach her face. A variant of this song reinforces this interpretation.

> Aunque soy morenita,
> no se me da nada;
> que con agua del alcanfor
> me lavo la cara.

This singer is not concerned about her colour because she has faith in camphor as a bleaching agent. This time Covarrubias is more helpful: purified camphor gum is, he says, extremely white (*es blanquissimo*). Camphor is, moreover, a diaphoretic; sweating surely helps cure excessive darkness of the skin.

Travellers get the impression that Spanish peasants are naturally swarthy. Most of the peasant girls in the songs do not share the outsiders' impression. They were not born brown but turned brown. One singer blames wicked fairies for having tampered with her originally white face.

> Hadas malas me hicieron negra,
> que yo blanca me era.

A variant of this song has 'Duelos' ('griefs') for 'Hadas malas', which is a slightly more plausible but still unconvincing way of accounting for the strange change of colour.

Working out of doors furnishes a much more likely explanation. Some country girls must herd animals in all kinds of weather.

> Aunque soy morena
> blanca yo nací;
> guardando el ganado
> la color perdí.

Others must help with the harvesting, unprotected from the sun's rays.

> Blanca me era yo
> cuando entré en la siega;
> dióme el sol
> y ya soy morena.

A Sephardic wedding song, transcribed in the twentieth century but dating at least from the fifteenth, makes the same explanation, or excuse.

> Morenica me llaman;
> blanca nací;
> el sol del enverano   [= *verano*, 'summer']
> me puso así.

The point that all these songs make is that the cross a peasant girl must bear is her upbringing in the country or in a village. If she had been born and raised in a city, with its shaded streets and shuttered windows, she would have retained her God-given white skin and would now be much prettier.

> Criéme en la aldea;
> híceme morena;
> si en villa me criara
> más bonica fuera.

The consensus of these singing girls is that their naturally white skins have been discoloured, if not by some malefic interference, then by the sun and the weather. A tan is not becoming. The only hope is to remove it by chemicals or cosmetics.

One girl, nevertheless, clings to a different hope. The magic power of words in her poetry persuades her that, whatever the cause of her swarthiness, she is marriageable; because the black earth usually produces white bread, her offspring are going to be white.

> Aunque soy morena,
> no soy de olvidar,
> que la tierra negra
> pan blanco suele dar.

By implication the singer suggests that she is genetically white, notwithstanding her present colour. The concessive opening formula ('Although I am dark'), repeated with small variations in so many of these songs, reveals a widespread anxiety. In one way or another, all these dusky girls ardently wish they were lighter in colour.

What they fear of course is that their dark skin makes them unattractive to males. They are certain that, like gentlemen, peasant lads prefer blondes. To some of them an unexpected experience brings a pleasant surprise.

> Aunque soy morenica y prieta,
> ¿a mí qué se me da?
> Que amor tengo
> que me servirá.

Although this girl's complexion is both dark and black, she couldn't care less: miraculously she has a lover. So it does happen that some boys will fall in love with *morenas*. How can this be? Another although-song gives us an inkling.

> Aunque soy morenita
> mi amor me quiere
> lo mismo que si fuera
> como la nieve.

Her sweetheart loves this dark girl as if she were white as snow. What she doesn't realize is that for him she *is* as white as snow. Beauty is not only more than skin-deep; it is in the eye of the beholder. Another dark-skinned singer has no difficulty in recognizing the subjectivity of her lover as he assesses her charms.

> Morenica me llaman, madre,
> desde el día que yo nací;
> al galán que me ronda la puerta
> rubia y blanca le parecí.

An exceptionally realistic *morena*, she is under no illusion that she was born white. All that matters is that her rustic gallant, as he hangs around the door of her house, *is* under the illusion that she is fair-haired and white-skinned. In the crazy logic of love, to be wrong is to be right. Love is notoriously contradictory.

> Morenica me era yo;
> dicen que sí,
> dicen que no.

In this case the gloss is in the spirit of the *villancico*, which it helps us to understand:

> Unos que bien me quieren
> dicen que sí;
> otros que por mí mueren
> dicen que no.

Despite her colour, this girl has a plethora of lovers. Some say yes, they will marry her; others say no, they won't. Though her choice is limited by those who, even if they are in love with her, refuse to marry a *morena*, she can take her pick among a number of less prejudiced, willing suitors. Considering the bleak prospect seen by most *morenas*, her future is an enviable one.

The *morena* of Spanish folk song has discovered that, to a degree, her unappealing skin colour is not necessarily a deterrent to some lovers. Her fate in life may not merely be to wish to love; with luck she may actually love and be loved in return. A *morena's* love affair, nevertheless, is precarious. Once a lover is found, the *morena* fears – with justification – that she may be jilted.

Vanse mis amores;
quiérenme dejar;
aunque soy morena
no soy de olvidar.

Her lover is unfair in leaving her; in spite of her dark colour she is not a woman 'to be spurned' (*de olvidar*). The phrase is constantly reiterated in the songs of the *morenas*. But for whatever reason – military service or male libertinism – the girls are forever being abandoned by the socially dominant males. It is only when the woman takes the initiative in rejecting her lover that the *morena* has fully overcome the anxiety which society's prejudice has inflicted on her. She never expresses her victory in her own songs. The closest she comes to gloating over her triumph in her own words is in *villancicos* in dialogue form.

– Morenica, ¿por qué no me quieres?
– Por verte morir y ver cómo mueres.

The *topos* of the cruel maiden is rarely conveyed in this manner by the woman herself. The malicious glee in the man's suffering is accentuated by contrast with the customary self-denigration of the *morena* in folk song. Here it is a joy for her to watch her would-be lover writhe in humiliation. Her sadism is explained by her having been humiliated herself by a male-dominated society that had repudiated her for what she was, for a factor over which she had no control.

Since society is made up of two sexes, the male attitude to the *morena*, as expressed in folk song, deserves a hearing. In the lads' songs the objection to a dark skin is much less pronounced. The girls seem to have been exaggerating the extent of the male prejudice against brownness. The man in song may be capable of admitting his love for a *morena* and at the same time the absurdity of his bias against her colour. Some of these songs, however, may be ironical.

Linda morena,
moler os vi yo;
y era la harina
carbón junto a vos.

Not only does the unexpected combination of 'pretty' (*linda*) and *morena* strike a false note; it even suggests a seduction ploy. When the singer says that the *morena* who was grinding wheat was so white that her flour looked like coal, we suspect that he may be ridiculing her. Another singer, however, seems to be seriously in love with a *morena*.

> El cielo me falte,
> morena mía,
> si en tus ojos no veo
> la luz del día.

The dazzling bright eyes of the beloved distract the young man's attention from the ugly skin colour. This reaction from males is frequent. They praise the eyes or the hair of the *morena*, ignoring the problem of her skin. Some men are even so unprejudiced that they declare that black is beautiful.

> Morenica, no desprecies la color,
> que la tuya es la mejor.

The *morena* is urged not to despise her colour, for it is the best.

Because it is an insidious force, love will be requited in spite of the social pressures fostering prejudice. With their greater social security, the male singers among the folk realize this more than the women.

> La morena graciosa
> de ojuelos verdes
> es quien mata de amores:
> cautiva y prende y puede.

The ugliness of the girl's brown skin is here offset by the green eyes that are normally associated – especially in courtly literature – with blonde hair and a fair complexion. Perhaps the lover is befuddled; in any event he realizes that this *morena's* beauty is such that 'it captivates, arrests, and has the power to do so'. For other lovers the Nordic trait of green eyes is unnecessary.

> Bella pastorcilla
> de la tez morena,
> no miente quien dice
> que me dais pena.

The shepherdess' beauty and the lover's consequent anguish reside precisely in her dark complexion (*tez morena*), which is seen as paradoxically beautiful. Another male is so sure of his *morena's* beauty that he calls down on her divine retribution in case she should leave him.

Morenita bella,
si me olvidares,
ruego a Dios que te goces
con mil pesares.

Yet another is so confused by being in love with a dark girl that he cannot begin to analyze the complex of personal feelings and social restraints in which he is enmeshed.

No huyas, morena;
duélete de mí,
que no sé qué tengo
después que te vi.

The rhyme in *í* is often one connoting despairing anguish in Spanish folk song. The *morena's* lover calls out both for compassion and for comprehension. He is a victim of her person; external beauty does not enter into his calculations. What is wrong with him since he met her? Love, that irresistible force, is to blame.

Tengan, tengan, señores,
esa morena;
ténganla, que me lleva
mi amor tras ella.

That dark-skinned girl has stolen this lover's heart. 'Stop thief!' (*ténganla*), he cries out. For him considerations of colour prejudice are both impossible and superfluous, since for someone in love social imperatives and taboos are annulled.

However much the men protest their love, the *morenas* persist in their self-prejudicial prejudice. They seem not to realize that thereby they are hurting their lovers as much as themselves.

Morenica, dime cuándo
tú serás di mi bando;
¡ay, dime cuándo, morena,
dejarás de darme pena!

Holding steadfastly to the notion that *morenas are not for the likes of her* lover, this girl refuses to accept his proffered love. And yet these young men love their *morenas* fervently. In vain they seek a rhetoric to persuade them of their ardour.

¡Oxte, morena, oxte,
oxte, morenica!

'Don't come near me!' this lover cries. His *morena's* beauty is so radiant that it will scorch him.

As we have seen, green eyes are an effective distraction from unacceptably dark skin. The courtly ideal of beauty has evidently infected the peasantry. But dark eyes, so deep and mysterious, may serve the same purpose as green ones. The ugliness attributed to the colour in regard to the complexion does not attach to the eyes. Beautiful dark eyes, basilisk-like, can kill.

Ojos morenicos,
irm'he yo a querellar
que me queredes matar.

Alternatively they may set a man beside himself, driving him crazy.

Vuestros ojos morenillos,
que por mi desdicha vi,
me hacen vivir sin mí.

Once again, the piercing assonance of accented *í* indicates the lover's despair. Even completely black eyes captivate the beholder, turning him into a *Minnesklave*.

Unos ojos negros
me han cautivado.
¿Quién dijera que negros
cautivan blancos?

How ironical it is to the singer that, where eyes are concerned, blacks enslave whites! Since the effect of beautiful dark eyes can be so devastating, their possessor is well advised to avert them.

¡Ábalos tus ojos,
linda morena,
ábalos, ábalos,
que me dan pena!

Although the eye colour of this incongruously pretty dark-skinned girl is not mentioned, in the absence of an assertion to the contrary it may be assumed that they are dark.

In several of the songs sung by males we have seen an entranced lover forced to admit to himself and to his beloved that a dark skin is not ugly.

The conflict between social prejudice and individual preference gives rise to some comparatively complex folk songs of extraordinary beauty.

> – Digas, morena garrida,
> ¿cuándo serás mi amiga?
> – Cuando esté florida la peña
> de una flor morena.

The girl who speaks in this dialogue is not taken in by the flattering form of address. She knows that the term of endearment 'beautiful *morena*' is designed to seduce her. Sensibly respecting the prejudice of the folk, she agrees to be the would-be seducer's mistress only when the rock blooms with a dark-coloured flower, when (as it were) he produces the botanically impossible black tulip. The put-down is unmistakable. But some male singers have honourable intentions. For them dark colour mingled with beauty is a fatal combination.

> Viva contenta y segura
> de cuanto pueda dar pena
> la que tiene hermosura
> mezclada con ser morena.

Beauty and dark colour combined hold the promise of happiness and freedom from suffering – presumably in marriage. The prejudice against darkness is gainsaid by the physical beauty of the dark body, the 'cuerpo garrido' of the *morena* in the next song. Bereaved of her lover, she utters frightening mournful shrieks. Because the gloss helps us understand why she does, it is appended to the *villancico*.

> Gritos daba la morenica
> so el olivar,
> que las ramas hace temblar.
>
> La niña, cuerpo garrido,
> morenica, cuerpo garrido,
> lloraba su muerto amigo
> so el olivar,
> que las ramas hace temblar.

The mourning girl – dark but with a lovely body – screams out her terror so that the branches of the olive tree, beneath which she is standing, tremble in sympathy and reverberation. Contrary to the usual expectations of a *morena*, she has been privileged to know what it is to have a lover. Now that he has died, she realizes that her good luck is unlikely to be repeated. Her brief savouring of love, that experience too often denied to *morenas*, has come to a premature end. She is condemned to a lifetime of chastity, which will be all the harder to bear because she has had a sexual partner.

Inconsolability of this sort is characteristic of Spanish women, faced historically with few alternatives to an arranged marriage, conventual life, and dreary widowhood. Seeing their problem, the foreigner sympathizes; but they are not the best of company, and they seem to lack moral fibre. When one of them strikes back at her fate in life, she elicits and deserves the fullest admiration. Such is the case of one dusky folk singer, who either is proud to be what she is or replies truculently to the man who would persuade her that she is something else.

No me llaméis sega la erva
sino morena.

She rejects the euphemistic coinage 'grass-cutter' (*sega la erva*) – which is simultaneously pejorative – in favour of the straightforward term *morena*, not even sweetening it with a diminutive suffix. She will not, as her language-perverting lover tries to do, beat about the bush. While not quite insisting that *morena* is an appellation one should be proud to bear, she fearlessly recognizes its propriety in her case. Any other epithet would be a misnomer.

Pride in dark colour does not appear commonly in folk songs until the great collections which were made in the field in the nineteenth and twentieth centuries. Before then the medieval curse was gradually removed from *morenas*. The shift of attitude began around the middle of the sixteenth century. The association of the Virgin Mary with the dark lady of the Song of Songs may have been responsible. It is certain that some secular folk songs were contaminated by religious allusions, while others were rewritten to give them a religious meaning. In the following example a religious analogy to the lover's experience is misapplied and perverted.

La que me abrasó la fe,
sin tocarme en el vestido,
la morená, morenica ha sido,
la morená, morenica fue.

To the diseased woman who touched the hem of his garment, Jesus had said: 'Thy faith hath made thee whole.' In the poem it is the lover's 'faith' that is kindled, even though she did not touch his clothing, by the *morena*, whose charms are lyrically evoked by the dancing repetition of the epithet with a false accentuation and a diminutive form. More significant is the assimilation of the black Virgin by popular erotic poetry, for her dark colour sanctifies that of all *morenas*. In the manger at Bethlehem, the Virgin Mother sings of her love for the Christ Child in the style of the *morena* songs.

> Yo me era morenica
> y quemóme el sol;
> ¡ay, mi Dios, que me abraso
> y me muero de amor!

The poem usurps the themes of the *morena* songs: the singer's identification of herself as a *morenica*; her assertion that the sun's heat had darkened her complexion; her declaration of love. But there is now no shame attached to the colour, and no suggestion that the singer was originally white. The sun which has scorched her is her divine baby, to whom she addresses the formulas of erotic love in order to express her unfathomable maternal and filial love for the male who is both her child and her God. Increasingly the *morena* songs are exploited by composers of sophisticated religious lyrics to make their doctrine more accessible and familiar. The gloss to the folk song

> Yo me soy la morenica,
> yo me soy la morená

incorporates from the *Canticum Canticorum* the crucial Latin text for the rehabilitation of *morenas*: *Nigra sum sed formosa*. The black Virgin begins to redeem the dark-skinned girls of the Spanish countryside. The sixteenth century was a turning point in the slowly evolving attitudes of the Spanish folk.

Individual Spanish folk songs are often enigmatic and impenetrable. Grouped by themes, they yield their mystery, each one shedding light on the others. The mutual illumination of folk songs is possible only because the peasants shared common responses to human experience and the human condition. I have used a particular set of medieval folk songs to bring into relief an aberration of the Spanish people, their prejudice against women of dark colour.

It would be a mistake to suppose that this prejudice was uniquely Spanish. One finds it, for example, in the poetry of medieval France.

> Por ceu se je suix brunete
> me fai je pas a ranfuseir.

Most European cultures have assumed that black is evil and ugly, the colour of sin.[2] But more than that of other countries, Castilian song offers more examples and shows a fuller development of the plight of women stigmatized by an accident of birth. One can only speculate how this widespread prejudice came about. Unquestionably the presence of large numbers of infidel Moors on Iberian territory in the Middle Ages contributed to the adoption of *moreno* as one of the Castilian words for 'brown'. Its application to Christians of dark colour may have transferred to them some of the religious animus felt for the *moros*. It appears in any case to have been a deep-seated prejudice, keenly felt by its victims, who were chief among its perpetrators. Women, doomed to play a passive role in the serious game of courtship, must have felt the stigma more than men. In the Spanish *Frauenlieder* one detects what amounts to a national neurosis among peasant women. Happiness and marriage, it is assumed, will never be the lot of the *morena*. And yet, in spite of the much vaunted 'blood of the Goths' running in Spanish veins, a dark complexion is normal among Mediterranean peoples. Since the race was perpetuated, a great many *morenas* must have married. The anxiety they express lyrically was clearly unwarranted. In this respect, the men's songs, though far fewer in number, must have been somewhat reassuring. They recognize beauty in a dark skin; or they avoid mention of the skin in order to praise the *morena's* beautiful body or her dark eyes. Hypersensitive, the *morena* in folk song often interprets their compliments as insincere flattery or as a move to seduce her. Singing about herself, she seldom comes to terms with the fact of life her colour represents.

The cult of the black Virgin came too late to help the medieval *morena*. But her descendants would benefit. In the twentieth century, the prejudice occasionally lingers 'on, sometimes tempered by religious considerations, as this song from Extremadura shows:

> Morenita la quiero
> dende que supe
> que morena es la Virgen
> de Guadalupe.

The singer's love for his *morena* did not burgeon until he found out that the famous monastery of Guadalupe contained a black Virgin. It is pleasant to report that such grudging acceptance of *morenas* is now rare. Most modern Spanish folk songs (like the one sung by the medieval girl who saw virtue in black earth), boldly assert that *morenas* are the best kind of girl.

Morena tiene que ser
la tierra para ser buena;
y la mujer para el hombre
también ha de ser morena.

Nowadays no real man would want a woman who is not as dark as the good earth. The spectre of the prejudice has finally been laid to rest in Spain. Or has it? At the risk of ending on a sour note, I must point out that these twentieth-century songs were collected before the invasion of the Costa del Sol by Swedish blondes.

NOTES

1. The term *villancico* ('rustic song') is so ambiguous as to require some explanation. The *villancico* attributed to the Marqués de Santillana is a courtly poem, each strophe of which ends with a rustic song: this use of the term is unique.

Ordinarily scholars mean by *villancico* a poem of a kind associated with the folk but often imitated by court poets. It consists of a short opening refrain followed by a longer strophe (or a set of strophes) known as a gloss, the final line(s) of which revert to the rhyme established by the initial refrain as if to invite its repetition. The refrain either is or appears to be popular; the gloss is usually courtly in style or written in imitation of the popular style by an educated poet. (Such *villancicos*, secular in origin, developed into Christmas carols, *villancicos de Navidad*, which is the meaning of the term in common usage today.)

To compound the confusion, the opening refrain is itself also called a *villancico*. This short *villancico* often survives without a gloss. It is these *villancicos*, whether a gloss has been attached to them or not, that are discussed as folk songs in this essay.

2. In the sixteenth century even as enlightened a man as Saint John of the Cross quite naturally associates darkness with evil. Commenting on his use of the term 'color moreno' in his *Cántico espiritual*, he declares that it refers to 'the ugliness and blackness of sin'.

9 *Movement and Meaning in an Old Italian Poem*

MARK MUSA

If Panuccio del Bagno[1] is usually distinguished from the rest of the little-read poets of the so-called 'Guittonian School', it is only to be blamed for his 'obscurity' and 'artificiality'.[2] In my opinion Panuccio has been underestimated, and in order to show this I shall analyse in some detail one of the most 'artificial' and most 'obscure' of his twenty-two poems:

> Se quei che regna e 'n segnoria empera
> avesse vera in suo stato fermezza,
> serea già questo, al mio viso, mainera
> d' avere spera aver non mai altezza
> omo ch'è basso, ma d' aver misera,   5
> e serea fèra sua vita 'n gravezza.
> Ma noi veggiam che più grandezz' altèra
> conven pur pèra e più affondar s' apressa;
>
> perché di rota ha 'l mondo simiglianza
> che non posanza ha mai [ma] va volgendo;   10
> saggio, tememdo, vive alto, mutanza;
> però chi bass' è non stia in disperanza:
> faccia mostranza, fortuna salendo,
> sé contenendo, allegro in gran possanza.
>
> Sed alcun folle se trova ne l' alto,   15
> senza defalto su' cred' esser fermo,
> poi vesi sper' mo: fa di sotto 'l salto:
> chi è 'n grande assalto, non cre' regni guer' mo.[3]

If those who reign and in lordship rule
had true stability ('vera fermezza') in their position
this would certainly ('giá') be, to my way of thinking, a way
of having hope never to reach a high place
(for the) man who is low, but to have misery,
and his life would be painful and severe.
But we see that the most lofty greatness
must nevertheless ('pur') perish and rush downward all the more;

because the world is like a wheel
that never rests but turns continuously,
the wise man lives on high ('vive alto') fearing change;
therefore, whoever is low, let him not despair,
let him get ready ('faccia mostranza') as fortune moves upward,
restraining himself, happy in great wealth.

If some fool finds himself on high,
he believes his situation ('su' esser') to be without a doubt permanent;
then he will suddenly see himself as a wheel: turn upside down:
whoever is in great affliction, I do not believe it will last long.

This poem, which treats the familiar theme of the ever-turning Wheel
of Fortune, is, unlike most treatments, a poem of hope, since the
movement of the wheel is mainly viewed from below: the poet addresses
himself to whoever happens to be 'in basso', assuring him that this state
will not last forever. This idea will be made explicit in the last verse,
toward which the whole poem has been moving: 'chi è 'n grande assalto,
non cre' regni guer' mo'(l. 18).

The poem can be divided in two ways. According to the rhyme scheme
it falls into three stanzas: 1–8; 9–14; 15–18. According to the division by
sentences, however, we must read: 1–6; 7–14; 15–18. In both cases we
have to do with a tripartite construction. It is with the latter division that
I shall begin.

The first sentence (1–6) opens with the word 'Se': *If* things were static
and never changed, then there would be no hope for the man who finds
himself in unfavourable circumstances ('ch' è basso') to rise from his
misery. The conditional sentence with which the poem opens is of the
contrary-to-fact variety: what is here represented is that which is not
true. Since the poet's aim is to encourage, he has obviously chosen to
accept for the moment the gloomy picture haunting the mind of his
discouraged reader, in order to suggest by the very construction of his
sentence the falsity of what is predicated. And, of the two parts of this

construction, the apodosis is twice as long as the protasis: the poet would dwell on the dire results of the (untrue) condition postulated. The construction of line 4, '*d' avere* spera *aver* non mai altezza', would seem to echo the hopelessness of such a condition. With the affirmative 'd' avere spera aver' hope is first allowed to arise: 'hope of having'; then, however, when it is almost within one's grasp, the 'altezza' is snatched away and replaced by 'never more' ('. . . non mai altezza'). But the momentum generated in 'd' avere spera aver . . .' by the repetition of the infinitive, cannot stop: 'd' avere spera aver (spera aver d' avere spera aver. . .)'.[4]

In the first line of the apodosis, with 'al mio viso', the poet introduces himself into the poem, into the situation of his reader, thereby indicating his desire to establish contact with him, so that his effort to persuade will appear more sincere and carry more conviction. But this intrusion is effected parenthetically, politely: the poet's conviction is presented to his reader as only a personal opinion (as if to say, 'I may be wrong but . . .'). To introduce such a phrase as 'al mio viso' is obviously to limit, to temper the argument; introduced where it is ('serea giá questo, *al mio viso*, mainera') our phrase serves the purpose of modulating the suasive rhythm: the incomplete 'serea giá questo . . .' is an outburst – immediately restrained by 'al mio viso'.

But only in line 5 (i.e., not until after the poet has sympathetically admitted the hopelessness that would result from the 'false' hypothesis he has constructed) does the poet mention this man for whom the poem is intended: 'omo ch' è basso'. And by choosing to place the postponed 'omo' at the beginning of line 5 (i.e., immediately following 'altezza'), the poet has not only achieved a juxtaposition of opposites, but has chosen, as cue to bring 'omo' on stage, the word that represents his goal: *altezza*.

Glancing back toward the beginning of the sentence we have just analysed, our 'contrary to truth' sentence, we may now better appreciate the unusual word order of line 2: 'avesse *vera* 'n suo stato *fermezza*', where the normally indissoluble unit adjective-and-noun has been split. The initial psychological effect produced on us by an adjective in isolation is that of simple shock. (Every adjective must have a noun to modify. Where is the noun?) Then we are forced to analyse the sentence word by word in order to locate the noun. When we find the missing half of 'vera fermezza' we see why the poet has not allowed the phrase *vera . . . fermezza* to remain intact. That he has broken it suggests the act of negating the positive concept represented by the phrase itself. This is no 'true stability'. At the same time, however, the adjective 'vera', in splendid isolation, almost assumes the status of a noun, 'veritá'. And 'truth' is a concept well worth stressing within this 'contrary to truth' protasis.

When from sentence one, with its verbs of unreality, we pass to sentence two, with its verbs in the present indicative, we are passing from truth implied to truth made explicit:

> Ma noi veggiam che piú grandezz' altèra
> conven pur pèra i piú affondar s' apressa;

With the causal 'piú ... piú' construction, height (*grandezza*) itself, which might be a discouraging factor for 'omo ch' è basso', is presented as reason for hope. The first two lines of sentence two counterbalance the first two lines of sentence one: the truth contained in the former destroys utterly the artificially staged contrary-to-fact hypothesis contained in the latter. The opening word 'Ma', in which the force of the refutation to come is already felt, is followed immediately by '*noi* veggiam' which enhances its persuasive quality. Having introduced himself into the poem with 'al mio viso' in line 3 the poet now feels that it would be psychologically appropriate to become one with his reader. And in this way he can present the truth as something already 'seen' by 'omo ch' è basso'.

Lines 9–10 (which introduce the topos of the wheel) express the same truth of lines 7–8, this time, however, in the form of an image, a causal image. These lines, introduced by the word *perché*, offer the cause both for the two lines that precede and the one that immediately follows (hence my punctuation): '*because* the world is a wheel/that never rests but continually turns', *therefore* the truth of verses 7–8:

> Ma noi veggiam che piú grandezz' altèra
> conven pur pèra e piú affondar s' apressa

and *therefore* (line 11):

> saggio, temendo, vive alto, mutanza

With these lines we find ourselves moved into the second half of the poem. And at this point we must reconsider what was said above as to the doubly tripartite division of the poem: three sentences, three stanzas (I and II of each, incidentally, interlocking). Now we see that the division is triply tripartite. Surely our poem must also be divided according to quantitative symmetrical proportions: 1–8; 9–10; 11–18; for lines 9–10 represent exactly the minimum mid-section of the poem's physical structure, and the limits of this central section correspond exactly to those of the concept which has inspired the poem and governed its diction.

Now the third part of the poem so divided (11–18) begins, as we have seen, with the introduction of a new character, the 'saggio' to whom only one line is devoted but whose figure overshadows the rest of the poem. After having simply stated a truth which 'we can see' (7–8) and presented the causal image of this truth (9–10), the poet now offers us a person, the 'wise man' who knows and accepts this truth, which is thereby brought to the effective human level of the reader. The *saggio*, then, is to serve as an example for him to follow – hence the 'però' ('so', 'now', 'therefore') of line 12 (no less effective and forceful than the 'Ma' opening of the entire sentence, which has obliterated the 'Se' opening of the whole poem), introducing the last three lines in which the reader is urged to emulate the wise man's stoical attitude.

But *my* reader may object that since the wise man is represented as on high, he can hardly serve as an example to the 'omo ch' è basso'. The fact is that 'omo ch' è basso' has already started to rise before the sentence ends. Consolation to one in misery is offered only in line 12 ('non stia in disperanza'), in which the man at the bottom is named as such (this is the second time the poet addresses his reader, this time as though he were actually calling out to him: 'chi bass' è!'). The advice of the last two lines of the second sentence, which hinges on the casual phrase 'fortuna salendo', is intended for a man already rising on the Wheel of Fortune – who, if he learns how to rise, will know how to emulate the attitude of the *saggio* when he reaches the top.

The period beginning with *però* ('therefore') has not only presented a logical conclusion; one feels that these lines with their resolution of truth and proper attitude serve as a fitting 'conclusion' to the poem itself, which might have ended here at line 14. This sense of finality is also due perhaps to formal reasons: for the first time sentence and stanza end together,[5] and one is led to feel the first two stanzas as a unit. And this unit would be a sonnet (note the rhyme scheme of these 14 lines: *ABAB ABAB/CDCCDC*).[6]

But instead of ending his poem at this point, with his reader already indoctrinated and prepared for 'fortuna salendo', the poet decided to add an appendix, in order to introduce a new character, one who has not learned the truth of the 'sonnet's' message: the 'fool'. After having shown us the quiet, poised figure of the 'saggio', he brings in the 'folle' to have him take a somersault before our eyes ('fa di sotto 'l salto'). Like the wise man and in contrast to 'omo ch' è basso', he is presented first as riding high on the wheel. But because he is a fool, because he believes the protasis of lines 1–2 to be true – indeed, he is convinced of the *vera fermezza* that our sonnet has denied: 'senza defalto su' cred' esser fermo' – he must be punished. It happens suddenly: 'poi vesi sper' mo: fa di sotto 'l salto'. Because he did not believe in the wheel, he must see himself become a wheel: his metamorphosis is a veritable *contrapasso*.

It is not difficult to understand why the poet brings in the fool: the reader must be offered not only the example of the wise man to be followed, but also the example of the fool to be avoided. Why he chooses to present him in the 'appendix' should also be not too difficult to understand: there is no room in this stately sonnet for the fool with his contumacious attitude and his ridiculous fate.

But while it was necessary for expository reasons to present this poem as a sonnet plus appendix – and surely this device was justified for both conceptual and formal reasons – it is obvious that what Panuccio has written is an eighteen-line poem. Thus, it must be shown that this appendix is, after all, an integral part of the whole poem.

The first two lines (15–16):

> Sed alcun folle se trova ne l' alto,
> senza defalto su' cred' esser fermo

reflect the first sentence of the poem, especially the opening two lines:

> Se quei che regna e 'n segnoria empera
> avesser vera 'n suo stato fermezza,

With the 'Sed' of line 15 echoing the 'se' of line 1 the poem seems to be starting all over again. And not only does sentence three, like sentence one, open with an 'If': it also treats of those in high position, and again the theme of 'fermezza' is raised (the 'senza defalto' of line 16 being parallel to the 'vera' of line 2). Whereas this 'fermezza' is presented as false in sentence one, by virtue of the contrary-to-fact construction, it is presented as something to be true in sentence three – but we are in the mind of a fool. Line 17:

> poi vesi sper' mo: fa di sotto 'l salto:

recalls the second sentence and reflects its movement if only in that the dominating central image of the wheel reappears in the metamorphosis of the fool. In line 18, which concludes the poem:

> chi è 'n grande assalto, non cre' regni guer' mo.

we find 'omo ch' è basso' (represented now as 'chi è 'n grande assalto') and poet side by side. The cautious ('non cre' regni guer' mo', with which the poet expresses his personal opinion to bring the poem to an end, reflects the 'I may be wrong but . . .' technique introduced in line 3 ('al mio viso').[7]

Of the three types of tripartite division into which our poem was said to fall, the first (division by sentences) was chosen to guide us in analysing the contents of the poem; and, in treating the relationship between the sentences, some consideration was also given to form. We have still to see what light can be shed on form by the two remaining schemes of division. The best way to exploit the second (division by stanzas) is to consider the principle that determines such division by stanzas: i.e., rhyme.

The scheme of the end-rhymes has already been given and sufficiently discussed for our purposes. But this poem is based also on inner-rhyme, and if Panuccio showed originality in his treatment of the end-rhymes he outdoes himself in his manipulation of inner (and outer) rhyme, as the reader can see from the following chart:

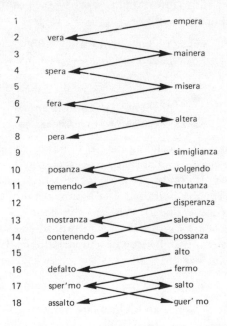

After the relative simplicity of the first stanza, complications appear in the 'sestet' and increase in the last four lines. In stanza one there is simple internal rhyme: the end-word of every odd line is echoed by an interior word (second or third) of every line.

In the 'sestet' the new complication consists of the fact that both end-rhymes are echoes – though only once in each tercet: *mutanza* and *possanza* have no echo. We have not only the progression odd ◊ even but also the progression even ◊ odd, as in lines 10–11 and 12–13. What is more, the original progression (odd ◊ even) is here not always carried through: it is missing in lines 11–12 – obviously in order to separate the tercets.

No new principles of variation appear in the last four lines; the increased complexity is due to exploiting the possibilities given by the additional line that the quatrain offers.

But this complexity which increases and which has been treated, statically, in terms of rhyme alone, must suggest also a complexity more dynamic: an intensification of movement. And it is the movement of this poem which we shall now consider, basing the discussion on the third principle of division: that determined by quantitative symmetrical proportions.

The movement of the poem is suggested by the central image, which constitutes the physical centre of the poem:

> perché di rota ha 'l mondo simiglianza
> che non posanza ha mai [ma] va volgendo;

This image introduces the figure of the wise man on the wheel; he knows the truth implied by the image of the ever-turning wheel, accepts its movement, and turns with it:

> saggio, temendo, vive alto, mutanza

In this line describing the wise man's attitude and his movement, we find a most unusual example of word order in which a verb is separated from its object not by an adverb but by another verb.[8] The dislocation involved brings about a slowing down of tempo: the line, as constructed by Panuccio, seems to push itself along. And as we read slowly, we hear three natural pauses that indent the line into four parts; and of this line describing the movement of the wheel[9] the four quarters surely correspond to the four-fold division of its rotary movement. That is, we would start at the bottom with 'saggio' (the wise man would have been at the bottom as the movement of the line begins), begin our upward movement with 'temendo', reach the top with 'vive alto', start descending with 'mutanza'. Given 'vive alto' as *point de repère*, this can be the only progression possible.

In other words, the wise man who has been at the low point of his fortunes ('omo ch' è basso. . .') will, as the wheel begins to bring him up, already be prepared to enjoy good fortune wisely. When he reaches the top, which is the moment predicated ('vive alto'), he has already accepted the 'mutanza' that is necessary to complete the movement of the wheel.

How different the treatment of movement is in line 17:

> poi vesi sper' mo: fa di sotto 'l salto:

Here is the movement of a fool who does not realize that 'di rota ha 'l mondo simiglianza'. The gradual, sophisticated moving towards 'mutanza' on the part of the 'saggio' gives way to the sudden (*poi*), unexpected (*vesi* . . .) transformation (. . . *sper' mo*): 'fa di sotto 'l salto' (a verbal somersault) of the fool. And between the circular movement of the wise man and that of the fool we have felt the movement initiated of 'fortuna salendo', line 13, as 'omo ch' è basso' enters into the cycle.[10]

But this particular movement of the wheel explicitly predicated in lines 9–10 and allowed to reverberate in the succeding lines had been already suggested in the two lines immediately preceding the central image (the two lines that make the important break in the poem); 'Mą noi veggiam . . .' Indeed, the acoustic effect itself has been anticipated with the correlative 'piú . . . piú' construction mentioned earlier; the two members of this construction echo the two contrary phases (up: 'piú grandezza altèra' and down: 'piú affondar s' apressa'), of the movement of the Wheel of Fortune.

In this poem Panuccio has taken one of the most familiar of all topoi, one that invites to prolixity, and has treated it in a succinct, even epigrammatic, and original way. The 'obscurity' and 'extreme artificiality' for which he has been blamed are perhaps rather grounds for praise. For, if what I have attempted to show above is true, the poetry of this Pisan poet is 'artificial' only in that it is very artistically contrived and 'obscure' only until it has been examined with patience and care, only until the apparent obscurity of a first reading becomes transparent as the poem slowly unfolds its meaning, method and purpose and reveals the necessity of such momentary 'obscurity' as that of

saggio, temendo, vive alto, mutanza.

NOTES

1. Panuccio del Bagno of Pisa, who belonged to an old and noble family, was born between 1215 and 1230 and died before 1276. More is known about Panuccio's family than about the poet himself. See Guido Zaccagnini, 'Notizie intorno ai rimatori pisani del secolo XIII', *Giornale storico della letteratura italiana*, LXIX (1917), 8–13.
2. Guido Zaccagnini, *Rimatori siculo-toscani* (Bari, 1915), p. 253: 'Guittoniano puro, Panuccio è, tra i rimatori pisani, il più oscuro e il più artificioso: la sua poesia è tutta infarcita di forme e di reminiscenze provenzali.' Alberto del Monte, *Studi sulla poesia ermetica medievale* (Napoli, 1953), p. 191: 'Panuccio è il più artificioso dei guittoniani, il più prolisso e oscuro.' Giulio Bertoni, *Il Duecento* (Vallardi, Milano, 1954), p. 139; 'L'artificiossimo Panuccio è autore

di alcuni componimenti amorosi modellati naturalmente sullo stampo di Guittone e tutti pieni di reminiscense provenzali.' Because of such generalisations as the above, as well as unsatisfactory critical editions, the poetry of Panuccio, and that of many of the poets of his time, has been neglected by scholars.

3. See Mark Musa, *The Poetry of Panuccio del Bagno* (Indiana University Press, 1965).

4. Pope in his *Essay on Man* did it somewhat differently:

> Hope springs eternal in the human brest;
> Man never is, but always To Be Blest:

5. As concerns the failure to coincide of sentence I (1–6) and stanza I (1–8), this is perhaps connected with the poet's desire to encourage his reader: before stanza I is allowed to come to an end, sentence II with its message of hope has already begun.

6. It is true that the rhyme scheme of our sestet is neither CDECDE nor CDCDCD, which were the normal patterns for the sonnet in Panuccio's time. Exceptions to these are, however, not lacking: Da Lentino has (perhaps: see Rivers's articles in *Speculum*, XXXIII, 43) two examples of CCDCCD, and in the love sonnets of Guittone we find the pattern CDEDED (cf. 19, 22, 63, 117, 124, 128: ed. Egidi). Still greater variety was afforded by the repetition of one or both of the octave-rhymes; this device, found with the two poets just mentioned, is also used by Panuccio in one of his '14-line sonnets' (*Rapresentando a conoscenza vostra*): CDCDCD with C = A and D = B.

7. Note how the litotes of the poet's opinion contrasts with the dogmatic assurance of the fool's opinion (*senza defalto*); and the parallelism of the two statements of belief is brought to our attention by means of rhyme ('fermo – guer' mo') and rhythm ('. . . su' cred' esser fermo – non cre' regni guer' mo'). It is as though the poet, by rhyming 'guer' mo' of the last verse with 'sper' mo', the central words of the preceding verse, were laughing – perhaps sarcastically – as he looks back at the fool in the previous line who 'saw himself as a wheel'.

8. Note that it is an independent predication ('vive alto') that is made somehow subordinate to a dependent predication ('temendo'). Another, but less striking example of the same type is found in line 20 of Panuccio's canzone 'Dolorosa doglienza in dir m' adduce': 'l' uman lignaggio/*d'aver* fugge *signor* naturalmente'.

9. The reader may object that this line describes not the movement of the wheel but the 'living high, fearing change of the wise man'. It is true that this is all that the line predicates, but in the preceding image of cosmic movement a momentum has been generated which must be allowed to continue for a while.

10. It is perhaps not impossible to imagine that lines 13–14, which describe the movement of 'omo ch' è basso',

> faccia mostranza, fortuna salendo,
> sé contendo, allegro in gran possanza.

are meant to suggest not only the first phase of upward movement but that, with their four-fold division, they imitate the same four phases of the 'saggio'. The 'faccia mostranza' would represent advice to the man still at the bottom, 'fortuna salendo' obviously takes him up, 'Sè contenendo' is that attitude on guard against *hubris* necessary for a man at the top, while happiness (*allegro*) will mark his downward movement, because of his wealth (*possanza*) in which the joys would represent spiritual possessions.

It is true that this possibility would involve an interpretation of both 'faccia mostranza' and 'sè contenendo' different from that suggested above where both injunctions were taken as referring to the upward stage of movement.

10 *The Middle English Court Love Lyric*

ROSSELL HOPE ROBBINS

Just as *le bourgeois gentilhomme* one day realized he had been speaking prose all his life, so students of Middle English may one day realize that much of what they have been reading is court verse. French medievalists are accustomed to the term and accept 'Court Poets' as descriptive of the circle of Henry II and Eleanor of Aquitaine and of the writers over the succeeding centuries serving royalty and nobility.[1] Not having grown up in a tradition of English court poetry, Middle English scholars do not think of Chaucer as England's first and greatest court poet[2] and – specifically as a court poet – the chief influence on English poets in the fifteenth century, even on Wyatt and Surrey and Spenser in the sixteenth.[3] Instead, critics focus attention on Chaucer the civil servant, writing the *Canterbury Tales* for a mixed audience in an increasingly mercantile milieu.[4] Yet the obverse of Chaucer is just as important: Chaucer the page and squire to the old King himself, to his sons, and finally to Richard II;[5] Chaucer on the same royal payroll as the French court poet Froissart;[6] Chaucer the translator of the *Roman de la Rose* and French court poets like Machaut and Oton de Graunson;[7] and Chaucer the recipient of an accolade from the French court poet Deschamps.[8] The image of Chaucer as clerk of the works should be countered with Chaucer as brother-in-law to the Duke of Lancaster, ancestor by affinity (through his sister-in-law) of Henry VII and (through his grand-daughter) of Edward IV, and source of the forty-five noble and even royal coats of arms stemming from his full-length portrait in the sixteenth-century Cambridge University MS. Gg. 4. 27, Part 1, b.[9]

Middle English court verse consists primarily of formal love poetry. The genre comprises some 300 short court love lyrics, either praising the poet's mistress or complaining about an unsatisfactory love situation. In these short poems, there is not much scope for variation, and the lyrics tend to become highly conventionalized. In addition, there are some thirty longer love poems best identified by their corresponding genre in French, *dits amoureux*, largely influenced by Chaucer and hence known generically as the Chaucerian Apocrypha,[10] like the *Flower and the Leaf* or the *Temple of Glass*.

Both the lyrics and the long poems derive from two French lyric forms: the *salut d'amour* and the *complaint d'amour*.[11]

The first English court poem adopting the new French patterns, Chaucer's *Book of the Duchess*, is best viewed as combining an extended *salut d'amour* and a *complaint d'amour*, buttressed with courtly rhetorical loci and topoi and framed with a dream sequence. The basic salutation is an extrapolable little lyric:[12]

> Lord, hyt maketh myn herte lyght,
> When I thenke on that swete wyght
> That is so semely on to see;
> And wisshe to God hit myghte so bee
> That she wolde holde me for hir knyght,
> My lady, that is so fair and bryght.

(BD 175–80)

This has been expanded into a lengthy tribute to the lady's qualities (*BD* 817–1111). The brief complaint is likewise isolable:

> I have of sorwe so gret won
> That joye gete I never non,
> Now that I see my lady bryght,
> Which I have loved with al my myghte,
> Is fro me ded and ys agoon.

(BD 475–9)

This too has been extended into a long lament on the injustice of Fortune (*BD* 598–709).

Expansion of a *salut d'amour* is circumscribed, for the counting of ways to praise a beloved soon comes to a halt. Greater opportunity is offered by the *complaint d'amour*, for numerous factors can interfere with a love affair: jealous relatives, a rival lover, separation by travel, war, family, or the lady's lack of pity, fickleness, and so forth. Consequently, most of the *dits amoureux* (like the *Temple of Glass*, the *Black Knight*, the *Assembly of Ladies*) are elaborations of various facets of disappointment in love.[13] To a core complaint are added rhetorical embroideries – the garden, a plesaunce, a temple, images, an arbitrating god or goddess – to imply some narrative.

In principle, there is no essential difference in circumstances of composition or in style or in point of view between the short lyrics and the extended love sequences. Indeed, the long 'love ditties' very often incorporate extrapolable lyrics in a social setting, and sometimes introduce lyric types and forms not found independently.[14] The longer poems are thus very useful in increasing our understanding of their shorter lyric counterparts. In this essay, however, emphasis is on the shorter court love lyric.

Court poetry is, quite obviously, found in manuscripts owned by noble families. Several dozen mid-fifteenth-century manuscripts survive to indicate the type of courtly collectors and their courtly collections. Only two or three can be mentioned here.

Bodleian MS. Fairfax 16,[15] for example, contains in addition to Chaucer's *Book of the Duchess* and the *Legend of Good Women*, dits amoureux like *La Belle Dame sans Merci*, *Complaint of the Black Knight*, and the *Temple of Glass*, along with the well-known series of shorter love poems linked to the Earl of Suffolk, and copies of two curious courtly games, the *Chance of the Dice* and *Ragman's Roll*.[16] Written about 1450, the manuscript has a heraldic shield (f. 14 verso) of one branch of the famous Stanley family, William Stanley, Esquire, of Hooton (fl. 1440).[17] Obviously, both the owner and the contents are 'court'.

Bodleian MS. Tanner 346 is a more 'modest' manuscript, also dating about 1450, containing Chaucer's *Legend of Good Women*, along with *Complaint of the Black Knight*, the *Temple of Glass*, and other similar fashionable love poems; it belonged to the Yorkshire Greystokes, one of whom, Ethel Seaton suggested,[18] might have commissioned the book. The Greystones, a baronial family, had 'intermarried with Clifford, Beauchamp, and Beaufort', all extremely powerful clans.

Other manuscripts of court poems current in the mid-fifteenth century show fewer 'palace' or aristocratic connections, but nevertheless are still courtly. One such is the Findern Anthology, or the 'Roos Scrapbook' (Cambridge University Library MS. Ff. 1. 6), a commonplace book compiled mainly by young women at a manor-house in Derbyshire, assisted by a few professional scribes, with a web of longer and shorter lyrical court poems.[19] Another court manuscript, Pepys 2006, was owned by John Kiriel, 'a younger brother of the renowned fighting leader Sir Thomas Kiriel', Lieutenant of Calais.[20]

An easy way of identifying other manuscripts with comparable poems is to take an obvious court love poem, like Chaucer's *Parliament of Fowls*[21] (in 14 MSS.) or the *Temple of Glass*[22] (in 8 MSS.), and examine the provenance and contents of all the other manuscripts in which the poem occurs. For example, one such, Cambridge University Library MS. Gg. 4. 27, Part 1, a, contains the non-court *Canterbury Tales*, but in addition has the court *Troilus and Criseyde*, the *Temple of Glass*, and the G-Prologue of Chaucer's *Legend of Good Women*.[23] The peculiarities of spelling (perhaps a Norfolk dialect) have sparked speculation that the collection may have been written for Jacqueline of Hainault or (more likely) for the Duke of Gloucester.[24] Quite apart from these theories, the contents of the manuscript are enough to establish its 'courtliness'.[25]

Throughout the fifteenth century, literary and aristocratic interests centred not on the *Canterbury Tales* but on *Troilus and Criseyde* and Chaucer's other court poems; these were the models for succeeding poets (*Book of the Duchess* begetting Lydgate's *Complaint of the Black Knight*; the *Complaint of Mars*, Lydgate's *Flour of Curtesye*, and Lydgate's *Temple of Glass* suggesting the *Court of Love*).

The court love poems of the fifteenth century are probably the most neglected genre in English literature.[26] The texts are available only in part in Skeat's *Supplement* to the Oxford Chaucer of 1897, and (more fully) in the first volume of Chalmer's *English Poets* of 1810; others may be found in obscure German dissertations.

For this neglect, the poems themselves are partly responsible. Very few equal the *Flower and the Leaf*, praised by Keats for 'its honied lines – what mighty power has this simple story.'[27] So pervasive is the dictum of their alleged literary poverty, however, that some medievalists might well ask: Who would want to read a court poem? This attitude is unfortunate for two reasons: the poems of the court tradition constitute the most important and numerous group written in the fifteenth century; and furthermore, ignorance of what they are and what their authors were attempting obscures the links binding Chaucer to Spenser and hides the position of Spenser as the last poet in an English poetic tradition extending nearly two hundred years.

The other cause of their neglect is the lack of a critical literature that can encompass unfamiliar genres, attitudes, and conventions. Students simply do not know how to read a court poem.[28]

Unfamiliar writing of any kind needs guideposts to help readers know what to expect. The critical assumptions brought to a carol or a closet hymn, each of which genres has its own rules and standards, will not help interpret a court love poem. The *method* of arriving at such criteria, however, is the same, whether for a carol or a closet hymn or a court poem; it consists of seven time-honoured basic questions, on which the whole historical approach to literature rests: Who wrote the poem? For whom was it written? When was it written? Where was it written? Why was it written? Sometimes the answer to the fifth question is implied or subsumed in the answers to the others. The answers to these questions, or approximations to answers, elucidate the final questions: what does the poem say and how does the poem say it?

In reading contemporary literature, many of these questions may be disregarded for we already know the answers. In reading literature of five centuries ago, they can be ignored only on peril of gross misinterpretation.[29] And if the answers are not clear from the texts themselves, they can be found from the manuscripts, the final courts of critical appeal.[30]

The first two questions – who wrote the poem and for whom was it written – can be answered directly. The writers of court verse were men associated with 'courts', either the royal court or palace or some magnate's court; the organization and life in both were the same, the difference lay in size and power. Some court poets were themselves nobility or gentry. James I of Scotland outranks the others, no matter the degree to which the *Kingis Quair* is considered autobiographical.[31] There were also poets like William de la Pole, Duke of Suffolk; Richard Beauchamp, Earl of Warwick; Edward Stafford, Duke of Buckingham; Anthony Woodville, Earl Rivers; and Sir Richard Roos and Sir John Clanvowe.[32] Such men could legitimately take the stance of lover as poet. The Earl of Warwick writes:[33]

> I can not half the woo compleyne
> That dothe my woful hert streyne.
>
> (1–2)

Similarly the Duke of Suffolk speaks for himself:[34]

> I say for me, ther ys no man on lyue
> That more hath cause to playn as in this case.
>
> (9–10)

Otherwise, most of the poems are anonymous, probably written by commoners like Chaucer, who wrote in the guise or persona of poet as lover:

> And thogh the lyke nat a lovere bee,
> Speke wel of love.
>
> (*LGW* 490–1)

Lydgate too, lacking Chaucer's royal connections, also assumed this role, emphasized in Shirley's rubrics: 'Loo here begynnethe a balade whiche that Lydegate wrote at the request of a squyer that serued in loues court',[35] or 'And her filowyng begynnethe a right lusty amerous balade made in wyse of complaint of a right worshipful knyght that truly euer serued his lady enduryng grete disese by fals envye and malebouche made by Lydegate'.[36] No matter what their birth, the authors were educated and sophisticated and knew the conventions of rhetoric and of making love like gentlemen. They knew what was expected of them, and even if from time to time they wrote burlesque (like Chaucer's *Rosemounde* or Hoccleve's *Praise of his Lady*), they reacted within the aristocratic tradition. In theory and practice any 'lewed' would neither understand these poems nor be given the opportunity to understand them.[37]

The audience comprised the nobles and their entourages, and the nucleus of gentle folk living on the estates of most knights of the shire. One would expect to find coteries at the homes of such peers as Bedford, Beaufort, Beauchamp, Clifton, Fawcomberg, Lovell, Montague, Scales, Stafford, Talbot, Vere, Vernon, or Woodville, many of whom owned quite considerable libraries. Out of a population of some two to two and a half million, in the year 1400 or 1425, the total audience was probably not over one or two thousand.[38] Such an insignificant proportion need not shock us; the circulation of even well-established academic journals in America today hovers between 500 and 1,000 subscribers – out of a population of over 200 million. The picture in Corpus Christi College Cambridge MS. 61 of Chaucer reading his *Troilus and Criseyde* seems to me an accurate presentation of his first audience.[39] Court poetry is indeed coterie poetry.

When was the poem written, and where was it written, cannot be answered by the texts alone. A few poems give dates; one lyric mentions the month but not the year:[40]

> For now the god of loue, in gret aray,
> Of feueryere the two and twenty day. . . .

$$(4-5)$$

Where was the poem written? Local references are very infrequently incorporated into the text, as in the *Legend of Good Women*:

> And whan this book ys maad, yive it the quene
> On my behalf, at Eltham or at Sheene.

$$(496-7)$$

Another poem identifies its location in London:[41]

> Vpon temse fro london myles iij
> jn my chambir riht as j lay slepyng. . . .

(1-2)

For fuller answers the critic must resort to the actual manuscripts and by examination of language and flyleaf scribbles, date and locate their verses. The Findern Anthology, previously noted, provides an excellent example of what careful inspection of the manuscript can reveal.

The answer to the fifth question, why was the poem written, grows out of the nature of the extremely restricted, élitist, class-conscious and literate audience: for diversion. Writing and reading poetry provided a means for leisured ladies and gentlemen to pass the time pleasantly, and ranked on a par with feasting, dancing, playing games, conversing, singing, and flirting. Indeed, criticism of English court poetry is as much sociological as it is literary; its foundation rests on a societal and historical basis.[42]

Given this social situation, the final questions, what does the poem say and how does the poem say it, are more easily solved: Court love poetry is ephemeral, for the contrived situations it deals with, of falling in and out of love, of flirting, or having an affair, are themselves ephemeral. Never in any Middle English court love lyric does a gentleman propose marriage; never in any Middle English court love lyric does a gentlelady lament an unwanted pregnancy.[43] In fact, there is not only little relation to 'real life', but there is a striving to avoid real-life situations and to live in the fantasies of an exclusive privileged class. Not for nothing are many of the longer court poems set as events in a dream world. No churl had access to the high-walled gardens attached to most castles and manor houses or to their spacious halls with the glazed bay windows, and no churl, even after *Le Roman de la Rose*, mingled with the assemblies of lords and ladies at the courts of love, the natural setting for love lyrics. While intimate court scandal (with possible overtones of censure) could be hinted at, as Chaucer did in his *Complaint of Mars*, as a general rule there is no moral seriousness in court love poetry, no critical reflections on manners or society. Social diversion takes precedence over ethics.[44]

The foregoing brief description of court poetry might serve for other periods. What distinguishes the Middle English is its emphasis on the polite society background against which the poems develop and which itself becomes part of their fabric (as the detailed descriptions of palace life in the *Assembly of Ladies* or the formal games in the gardens in the *Flower and the Leaf*).[45] And because the audience was limited to a

close-knit coterie of upper-class families, and the subject matter confined
to affairs of the heart, listeners or readers could reasonably anticipate
inclusion of contemporary social events or relationships familiar to most
of the in-group. In fact, the slight narrative framework of the longer *dits
amoureux* might even be built round the amorous adventures of one's own
friends, like the modern university *roman à clef* (for example, the *War
between the Tates*).

Descriptions of the courtly setting can still be appreciated; the actors
are generally (and perhaps wisely) discreetly masqued by conventions
and allusions. Yet if a student is to 'read each work of wit/With the same
spirit that its author writ', he should have some familiarity with the
circumstances of its composition. Obtaining that familiarity is the major
difficulty in studying the court love poems.

Ideally, the manuscript copyist should have appended an explanatory
rubric specifying the occasion and the people involved. John Shirley in
Trinity College Cambridge MS. 600 did exactly that: for Lydgate's
ceremonial verses for a noble marriage, he wrote:[46]

> And nowe here begynnethe a comendable balade by Lydegate
> Daun Iohan at the reuerence of my Lady of Holand [=Hainault]
> and of my lord of Gloucestre to fore the day of theyre
> maryage in the desyrous tyme of theyre truwe lovying.

While basically a ceremonial piece, the machinery is that of a court love
poem. Lydgate opens its twenty-eight rhyme royal stanzas with the
customary gambit of the god Cupid and 'his moder deere', and the 'cours
eterne of the sterres cleere'. Then he eulogizes the bride: he lists the
catalogue of famous heroines (Esther, Dido, Helen, and the rest) to
which his lady might be compared; he notes Jacqueline's heraldic
colours, black, white, and red (interpreted allegorically as stableness,
soberness, and cleanness[47]) and records her motto, 'Ce bien rayson'.
Then Lydgate makes a similar *descriptio* for the bridegroom, ranking him
with the Nine Worthies, and giving his motto, 'Sanz plus vous belle'.
Without the information previously supplied, the reader could not
understand the concluding Envoy to Jacqueline. It is a hodge-podge of
all the conventional epithets of courtlydom, 'princess of bountee', 'lood-
sterre of al goodelyhede', and so forth, duplicated or paralleled in dozens
of similar poems:

> Pryncesse of bountee, of fredam emparesse,
> The verray loodsterre of al goodelyhede,

> Lowly I prey vn-to youre hyeghe noblesse
> Of my rudeness not to taken heed;
> And where so it be this bille that yee reed,
> Hathe mercy ay on myn ignoraunce,
> Sith I it made, bytwix hope and dreed,
> Of hoole entent yowe for tyl do plesaunce.
>
> (190–7)

In case the rubric were lost, Lydgate introduces Jacqueline's name into the text, enshrined in another morass of descriptive clichés:

> Thoroughe oute the worlde called of wommanheed,
> Truwe ensaumple and welle of al goodenesse,
> Benynge of poorte, roote of goodelyheed,
> Soothefast myrrour of beaute and fayrnesse,
> I mene of holand the goodely fresshe duchesse,
> Called Iaques, whos birth for to termyne,
> Is by descent imperyal of lyne.
>
> (64–76)

Such rubrics and interior references are (save in Lydgate) very, very rare.

The longer poems, of course, offer more scope for introducing members of the court coterie into poetic situations, but even short love lyrics contain a few personal allusions which can identify the lady. For example: Charles d'Orleans about 1440 wrote a roundel to Anne Molins, since 1429 a widow and the then object of the Duke's romantic attentions; her name he spelled out in an acrostic in one of his English poems.[48] In the anonymous *A Goodly Balade to his Lady Margaret*, the initial letters beginning each stanza form an imperfect anagram on Margaret Dame Jacques, either the widow or else the daughter of John Jakes, gentleman, of Essex.[49] With other lyrics, identification is less sure: a balade expressing a lover's devotion concludes with an acrostic to Alison. Could Alison be Alice de la Pole, Duchess of Suffolk and Chaucer's granddaughter?[50]

Other court love lyrics, however, seem to have faded beyond recovery. *To his Soverain Lady*, a love lyric of some sixteen eight-line stanzas, is an apt illustration.[51] It is full of tantalizing gestures. Numerous clues are embedded in its lines, but neither its occasion nor its protagonists can be recreated beyond the fact that it is a Valentine poem to some noble-woman, perhaps French, by a man of equal rank. The *aversios* to 'soverain lady dere' (35) or 'of women chief princesse' (70) could be read figuratively or literally (to indicate royalty). The lady is heraldically identified (16) with the lily (? of Valois) and with the violet, a *flour desiree*, perhaps a French princess named Violante or Yolande. Some lines are borrowed from other poems. What does this signify? The opening line ('I have non English convenient and digne') recalls Chaucer's *Man of Law's Tale* (778); line 21 quotes 'Your eyen two wol slee me sodainly' from Chaucer's *Merciless Beaute*; line 73 recalls the *Nun's Priest's Tale* (3160); line 105 ('Alone I live alone') comes from a popular love song. The lyric incorporates twelve lines in French; two of these (14 and 98) occur in *Birds' Praise of Love* (88: 'Estreynez moy de cuer Ioyous', and 104: 'je ay en vous tut ma ffyaunce'). Skeat submitted 'a pure guess' that it was suggested by Queen Katherine's visit to England in 1415 – Henry V having left his Queen at Dover on 2 February arrived in London on 14 February.[52] Seaton suggested the recipient of the poem (about 1445) was Yolande d'Anjou, elder daughter of King René, whose motto and device she saw in lines 99–101.[53] The lyric is clearly *une poèsie à clef*, but who was the lady?

With most of the short love lyrics, it is at worst frustrating if the name of the author of a love lyric sent to a lady on St Valentine's Day or the name of that lady be unknown – she might have been a Mistress Margaret or a Mistress Joan, and the same 'bill' or epistle could in fact have served both:[54]

> And pray to you, noble sainte Valentine,
> My ladies herte that ye wolde enbrase
> And make her pitee to me more encline
> That I may stonden on her noble grace.

(46–9)

But it is a matter of major importance when ceremonial and public occasions are transferred to the never-never-land of the *dits amoureux*, for without the card the race is lost. In the *Book of the Duchess*, Chaucer mentioned 'goode fair White' (941), 'A long castle with walles white . . . on a ryche hil' (1318–19). Blanche, Lancaster and Richmond are obvious enough and were intended to be obvious, for Chaucer was writing a public poem for the Duke of Lancaster (like Lydgate for the Duke of Gloucester), who, at that uneasy period, might welcome praise of his popular deceased duchess to shore his own political image. If the 'man in blak' had not been established as England's most powerful duke, I question whether critics would so determinedly praise this poem for its alleged psychological insight in comforting him. Lydgate's comparable 'man in blake and white', because he was not a living person, is passed over.

The clarification which Chaucer inserted into the *Book of the Duchess* is unique in English *dits amoureux*. On the other hand, for the amusement of the royal court on a certain St Valentine's Day, Chaucer memorialized in poetry the political negotiations of three suitors for the hand of an English princess. He transmogrified humans into birds and had them plead their case before Venus, thereby brilliantly presenting some of the difficulties brought on by dalliance, love, and even marriage. The *Parliament of Fowls* never had its Shirley to pen rubric or colophon, so it remains ambiguous; after all the decades of Chaucer research, the three princes and the princess remain unknown.[55]

Another Valentine's Day poem is similarly ambiguous and similarly impenetrable. Chaucer's *Complaint of Mars* is a typical specimen of sophisticated court poetry. The chief characters, depicted as mythological divinities (Mars, Venus, Phoebus), should (with a rubric) be identifiable. Their amorous plight is clear: an impetuous lover, interrupted *in flagrante delicto*, sees his mistress flee to a safe haven, and for her peccadillo seeks sympathy from an audience of 'hardy knyghtes of renoun' and 'ladyes that ben trewe and stable'.[56] To one of the seven manuscripts Shirley did indeed append a colophon, but it raises as many problems as it solves.[57] An alternate hypothesis places John Holland as Mars, and casts Elizabeth, John of Gaunt's second daughter, as Venus. In 1380 Elizabeth had been betrothed as a child bride to the Earl of Pembroke; in 1385 she had an illicit liason (the 'conjunction') with Holland. Quickly she secured an annulment from Pembroke, and Holland became her husband. While this interpretation seems tenable, it is still hypothetical.[58]

The other *dits amoureux* are more obscure. *The Isle of Ladies* has even fewer scraps of evidence than the *Parliament of Fowls* or the *Complaint of Mars* to help identify a marriage.[59] After many magical adventures, a beautiful queen, ruling an island of women,[60] marries a noble knight; as a minor mirror image, the poet and his lady are also married. Why was the *Isle of Ladies* written? Why were some particular topics and some particular imagery selected in preference to others? Clearly, some marriage between two noble families is involved. But whose? Speght in 1598 interpreted the allegory as 'a covert report of the marriage of John of Gaunt, the King's son, with Blanche, the daughter of Henry, Duke of

Gloucester.' Herzberg saw the alliance of John of Gaunt with Katherine Swynford; Brandl and Sherzer (who edited the text), the marriage of Henry V with Katherine of France. Skeat thought the poem written about 1450, Seaton about 1435, and Sherzer about 1415.[61] The sole point on which all agree is that the *Isle of Ladies* is an occasional poem for some more or less important occasion.

One final example of a *dit amoureux* redolent with clues of heraldic flowers and colours is Lydgate's *Temple of Glass*, now nearly impossible to decipher.[62] There are three recensions of this poem, and little agreement on the earliest or the latest.[63] The problems concern the variations in the colours of the heroine's dress and the crown bestowed on her by Venus, and the mottos embroidered on her surcoat. For ease of comprehension, the variations may be shown schematically:

Object	Tanner MS. group	Addit. MS. group	Fairfax MS. group
gown	green and white	black, red, white	green and white
crown	green and white branches of hawthorn	white and red roses	white and red roses
Motto 1	De mieulx en mieulx	Humblement magre	De mieulx en mieulx
Motto 2	De mieulx en mieulx	Humblement magre	Humblement magre

In the Additional MS. 16105 group, a modern reader does not need the daisy colours (as in Chaucer's *Legend of Good Women*) to indicate a Lancastrian heroine, for this version gives her name, Margaret, no doubt Queen to the Lancastrian Henry VI. Now what was the purpose of switching colours and mottos? Was Lydgate, emulating Chaucer's re-use of *Purse* as a begging poem originally made for Richard II and later dolled up for Henry IV, revamping his own poem so as to flatter each new patron to whom he presented his work?[64] Most commentators have shied away from interpreting these changes; Norton-Smith found only 'moral significance . . . green for constancy and white for chastity'.[65] MacCracken, linking the motto 'de mieulx en mieulx' to the Pastons, hazarded that the Tanner MS. 'not unlikely . . . was originally written to celebrate the marriage of William Paston and Agnes Berry'.[66] Seaton rejected as 'rather too easy' the proposal that the *Temple of Glass* celebrated the marriage of Henry V (hawthorn) and Katherine of Valois (green and white).[67] Modern critics may take some cold comfort from a later-fifteenth-century reader of Bodley MS. 638, who in the margin at line 847 ('And therwithal Venus . . .') wrote, 'hic vsque nescio quis', and at line 970 ('Princes of iouthe, and flour of gentilesse') commented, 'Who in all godly pity maye [she] be.'[68] How rapidly do personal allusions, so fresh at the time of writing, fade into the Lethe of oblivion. If our seven questions for comprehending a poem can be answered only thus vaguely, then our appreciation of the poem must likewise remain vague. About all a critic can do today is to try to recreate some of the circumstances in which the court love lyrics were composed.[69]

How can the foregoing discussion of Middle English court poetry help us appreciate a typical Middle English court love lyric? As an illustration, let us consider a poem in the middle range, neither outstanding not yet insipid:[70]

Compleynt

Knelyng allon, ryght thus I make my wille,
  as your seruant in euery maner wyse,
To whom I yive myn hert and myn gode wylle
  Euer to be suget to your seruyse,
  Ryght as ye lyst to ordeyn and deuyse,
    I wyl be yours, and that I yow ensure
    Not for to chaunge for erthely creature.

Syth ys it so, my lady and maistresse,
  That I must nede by fortuns ordynaunce
Depart fro yow which is [my] most gladnesse,
  It ys to me the most heuy greuaunce
  That euer yit cam to my remembraunce,
    But euery man ys ordeyne to endure
    The stroke of Fortune and of auenture.

Wherefore my lady, I can say no more,
  But I am yours, with hertys obeyssaunce,
And wyll be forthe, as I haue ben byfore,
  Abydynge styll your reule and ordynaunce
  As fortune wylle, so must I take my chaunce.
    I can no more, but alle my faythfull tryst
    It lythe in yow, demene me as yet lyst.

Examining first the entire manuscript rather than the single poem in isolation, we find this is the fifth of a series of twenty short formal love lyrics in a very typical court collection, Fairfax MS. 16 (to which reference has been made previously). The lyrics may be autobiographical and may form a chronological progression, emphasized by interior references to 5 December, 2 February, 28 February, and 29 April in four of the poems (14, 17, 18, 20), on the vicissitudes of unrequited love.[71] By comparison with manuscripts and holographs of Charles d'Orleans, MacCracken boldly identified the author of these English lyrics as William de la Pole, Duke of Suffolk, who had guarded the Duke of Orleans during his imprisonment in England.[72] Whether or not this suggestion be accepted, this is perhaps the most 'frenchified' series of English court poems extant.[73] The existence of other copies of some of these lyrics implies some limited circulation within court circles.[74]

'Knelyng allon' is a *complaint d'amour* against Fortune for separating two lovers, the topic of the middle stanza. Separation is a very vague reason for complaining; in fact it is difficult to imagine at least one occasion when a poem like this could not have served any pair of lovers. Encircling the middle stanza are two other stanzas which are *saluts d'amour*, since here the separation theme is subordinated to expressions of devotion.

In the first stanza the last will and testament topos is introduced, the lover bequeathing his heart to his mistress. Surgery like this was not uncommon in medieval court poetry. In one lyric, the poet offers his heart to his mistress, since he will 'be syldyn in youre syght'.[75] In another, the poet instructs his heart to go with his lady, while the poet remains 'alone in heuynes . . . as a hertles body'.[76] In one rare poem it is a woman who laments her lover's absence and offers him her heart:[77]

> my hert shall I neuer ffro hym refrayn;
> I gaue hitt hym with-owte constrayn,
> euer to contenwe so.
>
> (18–20)

Another novelty appears in the acrostic (Katerin), which puts 'knelyng allon' into the little group of a dozen or so poems in Middle English with such decoration.[78]

If the seven basic questions were completed for this poem, the lyric would be charted thus:

Who. According to the indications from the manuscript (ownership, contents), the high style of the poem, its tone (not a commoner), a nobleman, possibly (according to MacCracken) William de la Pole, Earl of Suffolk.

To Whom. An unknown lady, identified only as Katherine.

When. The manuscript can be dated before 1450; since the whole series has Chaucerian echoes, after 1400.

Where. Not established (dialect characteristics insufficient.)

Why. Possibly a literary biography of twenty love lyrics, assembled for private circulation among the author's friends, originally perhaps each poem written as an address to an individual as a social game.

What. Typical *complaint d'amour* against Fortune for separating two lovers.

How. Extremely formal high-style, written under strong French influence; a near-strict ballade (lacks repeating rhymes in stanza 3 and lacks envoy); typical court phraseology; acrostic (rare); use of metaphysical 'portable heart' topos.

For verse such as this, not especially distinguished, identifying the genre and placing the poem within its own literary tradition must suffice. 'Knelyng allon' is a fair specimen of most of the three hundred similar court lyrics.

'Sumwhat musyng' is another complaint against Fortune.[79] It looks like a similar poem to 'knelyng allon', with the same conventional phraseology and the same assumptions between poet and audience.

The poem is found in several manuscripts, three of these fragmentary, but all set to music.[80] The complete words and music appear in BL Additional MS. 5465, the 'Fayrfax MS.', compiled about 1500 by the Master of the Chapel Royal; and in BL Additional MS. 31922, the so-called 'Henry VIII MS.', probably commissioned about 1515 by Sir Henry Guildford, Comptroller of the Household. It was evidently very popular in court circles, for no other court lyric exists in so many manuscripts.[81]

> Sumwhat musyng
> and more morenyng
> in remembrynge
>   the vnstedfastness,
> this wordle beyng
> of such welyng
> me contraryyng,
>   what may I gess?
>
>
> I fere doutless
> remedyless
> is now to cess
>   my wofull chaunce,
> for vnkyndness

withouten less
and no redress
   me doth avaunce

with displesaunce
to my grevaunce
and no suraunce
   of remedy;
lo, in this trance,
now in substaunce
such is my daunce,
   willyng to dye.

me thynketh truly
bounden were I
and that gretly
   to be content,
sayng playnly
fortune doth wry
all contrary
   for myn entent.

my lyff was lent
to an entent;
it is ny spent;
   Well-cum, fortune.
yet I ne went
thus to be shent;
but she it ment—
   such is her wone.

Ostensibly, this poem seems akin to the foregoing: a complaint against
Fortune:

fortune doth wry
all contrary
   for my entent

just like Chaucer in *Anelida and Arcite*:

(30–2)

For sorowe and routhe of your unkyndenesse
I wepe, I wake, I faste; al helpeth noght.

(292–3)

Another poet also lamented that he too, 'past all despeyres, was 'remedylesse':[82]

> for me nothyng may comforte nor amende
> Tyl deith come forthe and make of me an ende.
>
> (6–7)

Yet another is 'wyth-owten remedy'.[83] Our poet may have to die – 'such' is my daunce' (23) – just as another poet complained that if he did not see his mistress hastily, 'to the deth hit wil me bryng'.[84] In fact, separation is death: 'Welchome, my deth certeyne'.[85] Fortune is all powerful:

> But she it ment –
> such is her wone.
>
> (39–40)

Many a poet enveighed against Fortune. 'A-lace ffortwne, thou art on-kynd', says one.[86] And another, 'Alas, alas, and Alas, why/hath fortune done so crewelly?'[87] Although the separation theme is not here explicitly mentioned, it can be assumed since in the other court lyrics a condemnation of Fortune is always associated with amorous situations.

If the theme is common and commonplace, the metrical pattern of 'Sumwhat musyng' is assuredly not: it is the English version of a *virelai*, of which only a half dozen specimens exist in Middle English.[88] With specimens so few, it would be unwise to be dogmatic about the form, but apparently the Middle English *virelai* consists of five stanzas, each rhyming *aaabaaab*, with each succeeding stanza interlocked with its foregoing, the *b* rhyme of one becoming the *a* rhyme of the next.[89] Another *virelai*, a pseudo-Chaucerian *Lover's Lament*,[90] is so close in theme and form that it is conceivable it provided a model for 'Sumwhat musyng', as Thomas Percy suggested two centuries ago.[91] The fifth stanza in particular parallels the third stanza of 'Sumwhat musyng', even in its rhyming words:

> But in substaunce
> Noon allegeaunce
> Of my greuaunce
>   Can I nat fynde;
> Ryght so my chaunce
> With displeasaunce
> Doth me auaunce
> And thus an ende
>
> (33–40)

A schema of the seven basic questions about 'Sumwhat musyng' would read as follows:

Who. Not established. Because of its appearance in fashionable manuscripts, very likely by a nobleman.

To whom. Not established. No direct mention of lady. Perhaps directed to a public audience or composed for a *pui.*

When. Late fifteenth century; two manuscripts early sixteenth century.

Where. Not established. Its presence in the 'Henry VIII MS.' implies use at a royal court.

Why. Possibly metrical exercise, a high society *tour de force,* to demonstrate skill in employing unusual metrical form.

What. Typical *complaint d'amour* against Fortune (separation of lovers implied). Because text preserved with music, perhaps more 'public' than most similar poems.

How. High style; very similar expressions in other complaints against Fortune. Rare example in English of *virelai;* perhaps based on another lament in form of *virelai.*

It is a complaint against Fortune all right, but for what reason? If instead of going to the later court manuscripts which set the song to polyphonic music, we look at the earliest manuscript, where the poem appears only in a defective version, quite a different interpretation is revealed.

Cotton MS. Vespasian A. xii contains a late-fifteenth-century chronicle, *Rossi Warwiciensis Historia Regum Angliae,* by a contemporary historian John Rous.[92] Rous gave a first-hand account of the circumstances of composition of this lyric: 'in tempore [1483] incarcerationis apud Pontem-fractum edidit unum Balet in anglicis, ut mihi monstratum est, quod subsequitur sub hic verbis . . .'.

'Sumwhat musyng' now takes on a very tragic hue: the final words of a gentleman, aged forty-one, brother of the Queen of England, writing on 24 June, 1483, a day or two before his execution. The poem is no longer a courtly love lyric denouncing Fortune, but a tragic acceptance of a fate beyond man's control; he never thought to have been executed, his span of life has not been all consumed. Such is Fortune.

The author was Anthony Woodville, Earl Rivers, Lord Scales. Arrested on orders of Richard III, confined in the castle of Sheriff-Hoton in York, and notified of his impending execution, Earl Rivers was allowed to make his will on 23 June, 1483. Suddenly removed to Pontefract the following day, Earl Rivers added a one-sentence codicil of his desire to be buried there, 'before an Image of our most blissed lady'. The original of the will is not extant, but a copy is preserved in the Prerogative Office at Canterbury; Rous apparently saw a copy of the will and the original holograph of the poem.[93]

Paul Murray Kendall, drawing on Rous, made a vivid and moving story of the final days of Lord Rivers in prison:[94]

> He is given spiritual consolation. He is given pen, ink, paper. In a maelstrom of all moods he desperately gathers his thoughts and sets himself to make his will:
>   He earnestly desires that his debts be paid. He prays that sufficient of his goods be allowed to his executors so that bequests to the poor and to the Church will be honored. Struggling to cleanse his soul, he recalls some recent transactions in property in which he may have acted with a high hand and begs that the matter be looked into and justice done . . .
>   He is a man of letters and he has writing materials; he seeks to order his throbbing mind at this terrible moment by the discipline of composition, to crowd upon paper some final reckoning with the world. It takes the form of a little ballad, genuinely pathetic in its accents, but in form a surprisingly typical medieval plaint upon the mutability of life.

With this new information, answers to the seven questions are now completely changed; they are no longer vague and stereotyped. Only the seventh (How) remains unchanged, for the techniques would serve for whatever interpretation:

Who. Anthony Woodville, Lord Rivers, an accomplished and prolific writer and translator.

To whom. His second wife (Mary) and his household.

When. 24 June, 1483.

Where. Pontefract Castle, Yorkshire.

Why. To pursue some familiar cultural activity for distraction on the eve of his execution.[95]

What. A unique death song, personal and intimate. Later, this lyric for whatever reason (perhaps its macabre associations with a distinguished author) became extremely popular as a polyphonic court song.

How. A formal court lyric, with full use of all the court conventions, no whit different from the typical complaint it seems to be in the five music manuscripts

We have now come full circle to our original premise for approaching any piece of literature: a Middle English court poem must be placed in its historical and literary context – under what circumstances was it written. Sometimes, as here, clues within the poem itself will be insufficient to explicate it, and the lyric will remain misunderstood.[96] In such an event, fully to comprehend the work, a reader must go back to the manuscripts in which it is preserved – and not always can even manuscripts help. Without Rous's chronicle describing Earl River's final hours, scholars would have had no inkling that 'Musyng allon' was anything more than a conventional love lyric berating Fortune for separating the poet from his mistress.

While the majority of Middle English court poems seldom rise above the level of occasional verse, nevertheless, if this form can be recycled to convey an intense and personal *cri de coeur*, it must possess a certain resilience. And I think this potential for serious poetry over and above *vers de société* survived beyond the fifteenth century and, by providing models (some copied almost verbatim) fostered the great lyrical production of Wyatt and Surrey and of Spenser.

NOTES

1. For an analysis of court and non-court poetry in Middle English, see Rossell Hope Robbins, 'The Vintner's Son: French Wine in English Bottles', in *Eleanor of Aquitaine: Patron and Politician*, ed. William W. Kibler (Austin: University of Texas Press, 1976), pp. 147–72.
2. For Chaucer starting his career as a French-speaking poet, see Rossell Hope Robbins, 'Geoffroi Chaucier, poète français, Father of English Poetry', *Chaucer Review* 13 (1978), 93–115.
3. See Hugh Maclean, '"Restlesse anguish and unquiet paine": Spenser and the Complaint, 1579–1590', in *The Practical Vision: Studies in English Literature in Honour of Flora Ray*, eds Jane Campbell and James Doyle (Waterloo, Ontario: Wilfred Laurier University Press, 1978), pp. 29–47.
4. Mary Giffin, *Studies on Chaucer and his Audience* (Hull, Québec: Éditions L'Éclair, 1956), pp. 67–88, suggests Chaucer's *Man of Law's Tale* directed to London merchants about 1383 to gain support for invasion of Castile.
5. For Chaucer as esquire see James Root Hulbert, *Chaucer's Official Life* (1912; repr. New York: Phaeton Press, 1970), with supporting documentation in *Chaucer's Life Records*, eds Martin M. Crow and Clair C. Olson (Oxford: Clarendon Press, 1966).
6. George H. Cowling, *Chaucer* (London: Methuen, 1927), p. 74.
7. See Ronald Sutherland, *The Romaunt of the Rose and Le Roman de la Rose* (Berkeley: University of California Press, 1968), p. xxxiv. James Wimsatt, *Chaucer and the French Love Poets* (Chapel Hill: University of North Carolina Press, 1968); *The Marguerite Poetry of Guillaume de Machaut* (Chapel Hill: University of North Carolina Press, 1970); 'Machaut's Lay de Confort and Chaucer's Book of the Duchess', in *Chaucer at Albany*, ed. Rossell Hope Robbins (New York: Burt Franklin, 1975), pp. 11–26; and 'Guillaume de Machaut and Chaucer's *Troilus and Criseyde*', *MAE*, 45 (1976), 277–93; William Calin,

A Poet at the Fountain (Lexington: University Press of Kentucky, 1974), with bibliography, esp. pp. 253–54 (for Chaucer). Haldeen Braddy, *Chaucer and the French Poet Graunson* (Baton Rouge: Louisiana State University Press, 1947), rev. J. A. W. Bennett, *MAE*, 18 (1949), 35–7.

8. Best text in T. A. Jenkins, 'Deschamps' Ballade to Chaucer', *MLN*, 33 (1918), 268–78.

9. CUL MS. Gg. 4. 17, Part 1 b, f. 3r (sixteenth cent.), apparently never reproduced.

10. For description and bibliography see Rossell Hope Robbins, 'The Chaucerian Apocrypha', in *A Manual of the Writings in Middle English 1050–1500*, gen. ed. Albert E. Hartung (New Haven: Connecticut Academy of Arts and Sciences, 1973), 4, 1061–1101, 1285–1306.

11. For relations of lyrics and *dits amoureux* see Rossell Hope Robbins, 'The Structure of the Longer Middle English Court Poems', in *Chaucer Problems and Perspectives, Essays Presented to Paul E. Beichner, C. S. C.*, eds Edward Vasta and Zachary Thundy (Notre Dame: University of Notre Dame Press, 1979).

12. All quotations from *The Complete Works of Geoffrey Chaucer*, ed. F. N. Robinson, 2nd ed. (Boston: Houghton Mifflin, 1957).

13. The *Temple of Glass* is very typical: after introductory catalogue of twenty-one famous tragic lovers, the poem revolves round a series of complaints: lady's complaint (321–78), the knight's complaint (566–93), knight's complaint to Venus (701–847), knight's complaint to lady (970–1039), all followed by appropriate dialogues. *Lydgate's Temple of Glass*, ed. J. Schick, *EETS* es 60 (1891, repr. 1924).

14. For example, a pastourelle in *Supplicacio Amantis*, lines 415–36 (*EETS* es 60, 64); the series of aubes in *Troilus and Criseyde*, III, 1421–42, 1450–70, etc.

15. For description of Fairfax MS. 16 (Bodleian 3896) see references in *Manual*, 4, 1289.

16. *Chance of the Dice*: see Carleton Brown and Rossell Hope Robbins, *The Index of Middle English Verse* (New York: Columbia University Press, 1943), and Rossell Hope Robbins and John L. Cutler, *Supplement to the Index of Middle English Verse* (Lexington: University of Kentucky Press, 1965), No. 803; *Ragman's Roll, Index*, No. 2251.

17. John Norton-Smith, *Geoffrey Chaucer* (London: Routledge & Kegan Paul, 1974), p. 26, fn. 12. Ethel Seaton, *Sir Richard Roos* (London: Hart-Davis, 1961), pp. 83–4, suggested Thomas, Lord Stanley (1405–1459), Comptroller of the Royal Household, who also quartered the arms of Hooton. The heraldic shield (below the picture of Mars and Venus, f. 14v) is reproduced in Chauncey Wood, *Chaucer and the Country of the Stars* (Princeton: Princeton University Press, 1970), Fig. 14.

18. Seaton, *Roos*, pp. 104–5, who tentatively suggested Ralph, Fifth Lord Greystoke (ca. 1414–87); the manuscript later passed to his son John Greystoke (whose name is scribbled on a flyleaf).

19. Rossell Hope Robbins, 'The Findern Anthology', *PMLA*, 69 (1954), 610–42. See also *The Findern Manuscript*, intro. by Richard Beadle and A. E. Owen (London: Scolar Press, 1977). Close analysis in Seaton, *Roos*, pp. 85–92, 175–7, 233–5, 399–402, etc. The Findern MS. contains some non-court material like *Sir Degrevaunt*, Burgh's *Cato Major*, and chronicles of the *Kings of England*. See also *Manual*, 4, 1289.

20. John M. Manly and Edith Rickert, *The Text of the Canterbury Tales* (Chicago:

University of Chicago Press, 1940), 1, 406–14; Seaton, *Roos*, pp. 106–8.

21. *Index* and *Supplement*, No. 3412.

22. *Index* and *Supplement*, No. 851.

23. Part 1, a (early 15th cent.) is not connected with Part 1, b (early 16th cent., see fn. 9), or with Part 2 (13th cent. romances). See Manly and Rickert, *Text*, 1, 170–82; Seaton, *Roos*, pp. 108, 359, 370, 376, 382, 453; *Manual*, 4, 1289.

24. For the Gloucesters, see Seaton, *Roos*, pp. 109, 288; fully developed in Manly and Rickert, *Text*, 1, 181.

25. Manly and Rickert, *Text*, 1, 180: 'From the size of the volume and the elaborate decorations and miniatures, it is clear enough that he [the owner] was a person of wealth and importance'.

26. The notion of English court poetry has been slow to gain currency, despite the work of earlier scholars like MacCracken, Brusendorff, Galway, and notably Seaton. Some recent critics accept it, e.g., Wimsatt (see fn. 7); the excellent chapter, 'Court Poetry', in Derek Pearsall, *Old English and Middle English Poetry* (London: Routledge & Kegan Paul, 1977), pp. 189–221; also Norton-Smith, *Chaucer*, pp. 1–34, 213–25; A. C. Spearing, *Medieval Dream-Poetry* (Cambridge: Cambridge University Press, 1976), pp. 171–218 ('The Chaucerian Tradition'); and a chapter mainly on style in Pamela Gradon, *Form and Style in Early English Literature* (London: Methuen, 1971), pp. 332–81.

27. *Manual*, 4, 1095, where I note that 'Hazlitt quoted nine stanzas to illustrate Chaucer's power of describing nature scenery'.

28. I do not distinguish here between palace and court; *Sir Gawain and the Green Knight* is obviously composed for some provincial court, but not the royal palace (cf. Pearsall, *Poetry*, p. 184; and cf. p. 213 for quasi-royal households); this work is also captivated by games of love: see Christopher Dean, 'The Temptation Scenes in *Sir Gawain and the Green Knight*', *Leeds SE*, 5 (1971), 1–12.

29. To argue that what a medieval poem says to the twentieth-century reader is what matters, not what the poem said to the contemporary fifteenth-century reader, obviates the need for poring over bookes olde, but it also alienates a critic from the Middle Ages, and perhaps excludes him from being considered a medievalist. See Rossell Hope Robins, 'Middle English Misunderstood: Mr. Speirs and the Goblins', *Anglia*, 85 (1967), 170–281; 'A Highly Critical Approach to the Middle English Lyric', *College English*, 30 (1968), 74–5; and review article, 'Medieval English Literature', *Archiv*, 205 (1969), 489–94.

30. I have discussed the pitfalls in criticism to which neglect or ignorance of the manuscripts lead in 'Caveats for Critics', publication pending.

31. For discussion of authorship see *James I of Scotland: The Kingis Quair*, ed. John Norton-Smith (Oxford: Clarendon Press, 1971), pp. xix–xx; *The Kingis Quair of James Stewart*, ed. Matthew P. McDiarmid (London: Heinemann, 1973), pp. 45–50.

32. For works allegedly by William de la Pole, see *Index*, Title Index, p. 781, and *Supplement*, Title Index, p. 548; Richard Beauchamp, *Index* and *Supplement*, No. 1288; Edward Stafford, *Supplement*, Nos. 158.9, 2409.5; Anthony Woodville, *Supplement*, No. 3193.5, and for his other works, *DNB*, 52 (1910), 410–13; Sir Richard Roos, *Index* and *Supplement*, No. 1086, and Seaton, *Roos*; Sir John Clanvowe, most recently edited by V. J. Scattergood, *The Works of Sir John Clanvowe* (Cambridge: Brewer, 1975).

33. *Index*, No. 1288; Henry Noble MacCracken, 'The Earl of Warwick's Virelai', *PMLA*, 22 (1907), 597–607. My transcription.
34. *Index* and *Supplement*, No. 2407; Henry Noble MacCracken, 'An English Friend of Charles of Orléans', *PMLA*, 26 (1911), 161–62. Note Chaucer in *Mars* 263. 'So fareth hit by lovers and by me', perhaps implying some distinction.
35. *Index*, No. 869; *The Minor Poems of John Lydgate*, ed. Henry Noble MacCracken, *EETS* 192 (1934), 380.
36. *Index*, No. 1507 (*Complaint of the Black Knight*), *EETS*, 192, 382, note from BL Addit. MS. 16165, f. 190v.
37. Is there a hint of parody of a courtly love lyric in *Mary Magdalene* in *The Digby Plays*, ed. F. J. Furnivall, *EETS* es 70 (1896; repr. 1967), 70, lines 422–5 (Flesh addressing Lechery):

> now, the lady lechery, yow must don your attendans,
> for yow be flower fayrest of femynyte:
> yow xal go desyyr servyse, and byn at hur attendavns,
> for ye xal sonest enter the beral of bewte.

38. For estimates see, *inter alia*, W. Denton, *England in the Fifteenth Century* (London: Bell, 1888), pp. 127–31; Josiah Cox Russell, 'The Clerical Population of Medieval England', *Traditio*, 2 (1944), 179; and *British Medieval Population* (Albuquerque: University of New Mexico Press, 1948); N. Denholm-Young, *The Country Gentry in the Fourteenth Century* (Oxford: Clarendon Press, 1969), pp. 15–16.
39. For interpretation see Aage Brusendorff, *The Chaucer Tradition* (1925; repr. Oxford: Clarendon Press, 1967), pp. 19–23; Margaret Galway, 'The Troilus Frontispiece', *MLR*, 44 (1949), 161–77; George Williams, 'The *Troilus and Criseyde* Frontispiece Again', *MLR*, 57 (1962), 173–8. P. M. Kean, *Chaucer and the Making of English Poetry* (London: Routledge & Kegan Paul, 1972), qualifies, 'The Poet Reading to his Audience' (frontispiece, vol. 2).
40. *Index*, No. 2595; MacCracken, *PMLA*, 26, 171.
41. *Supplement*, No. 3844.5; J. A. van Dorsten, 'The Leyden "Lydgate Manuscript"', *Scriptorium*, 16 (1960), 318.
42. A few critics have realized the difference between a modern and a medieval approach to literature; the modern treats a poem as art, the medieval as an artifact serving a social function. So Pearsall, *Poetry*, p. 220, stresses the nature of the court poems as society games: 'They need, more than any other poetry, their social context in the courtly "game of love" in order to be appreciated, their relationship to the excitements, snares, and intrigues of court society, the dialogues and games, the covert allusions, the cults and ceremonies of "the olde daunce"'.
43. On the other hand, the popular songs and carols are full of laments; see *Secular Lyrics of the XIVth and XVth Centuries*, ed. Rossell Hope Robbins, 2nd ed. (Oxford: Clarendon Press, 1955), Nos. 21, 23, 24, 25, 26, 27, 28 and 29 (lines 37–40):

> none my wombe began to swelle
> as gret as a belle;
> durst y nat my dame telle
> Wat me betydde this holyday.

44. When Chaucer in his *Retraction* abjured 'many a song and many a leccherous lay', and all his poems of 'worldly vanitees', which 'sounen into synne', he was underlining their a-moral, even immoral, nature, for the aristocratic values they promote have no justification in the needs of any part of Christian society. 'Mercy', 'pity', and 'grace' are code words which drape the goal desired, and it is seldom that a lover spells out his intention as clearly as did Ulysses in *Lydgate's Troy Book*, ed. Henry Bergen, *EETS* es 106 (1910), Part 3, 858. Ulysses dreams of a beautiful lady who asks what he wants, 'and he to hir the platte trouthe tolde'. His speech is the normal response of any courtly lover, repeated in all the court love poems, with the exception of one explicit couplet:

> 'Certis,' quod he, 'my lyues emperesse,
> Wher that ye ben a woman or goddes
> I can not deme nor Iugen half aright,
> I am so dirked and blendid in my sight;
> But I dar wel affermyn in this place,
> My lyf, my deth stant hooly in your grace,
> More of mercy requiryng thanne of right
> To rewe on me, whiche am your owne knyght,
> And of pite and compassioun
> Goodly to sen to myn sauacion:
> For my desire but I may fulfille,
> This silfe nyght to haue of yow my wille,
> To my recure I can no remedie,
> For lak of routhe but I moste dye.
> Now haue I al, a-twexe hope & drede,
> My silf declared to youre wommanhede.'   (2985–3000)

45. Both texts easily accessible, ed. D. A. Pearsall (London: Nelson, 1962).
46. MacCracken, *EETS* 192, 601.
47. Since the personage in this poem has already been named, Lydgate can afford to interpret the heraldic colours allegorically. So Norton-Smith with the *Temple of Glass*; see fn. 65. But if these colours belong (as Lydgate shows here) to a particular person, why were they twice changed after the original attribution in the *Temple of Glass*. White and red are Lancastrian colours, frequently linked to the hawthorn and to the daisy or marguerite; in fact there is a little sub-group of daisy poems (including the *Legend of Good Women*, the *Assembly of Ladies*, and the *Complaynt* appended to the *Temple of Glass*). Mottos are especially difficult to identify without direct help (as here); first, there is no catalogue or listing of mottos used by nobility and gentry, save Mrs Bury Palliser/Fanny Marryat Palliser, *Historic Devices, Badges and War-cries* (London: Sampson Low Son and Marston, 1870); second, one person might use several mottos; and third, one person might assume a motto for one special event. In the *Assembly of Ladies*, each lady and gentleman has a motto, like 'Une sans chaunger', 'onques puis lever', 'Entierement vostre', and so forth. Possibly these mottos are occasional; if Lady Loyalty represents Queen Margaret, her moniker plays on her motto, 'Humble et loial' (see Seaton, *Roos*, p. 196). Collecting and identifying mottos relies mainly on hints in county histories and scattered mention in manuscripts. From the manuscripts in the

BL Royal collection, the following have been culled: 'Elas sy longment' (William, Earl of Pembroke, 1460); 'Josne et joyeulz' (Edward IV); 'Euer feythfull' (William, Earl of Arundel, 1438–1487); 'Loyalte me lye' (Elizabeth, Queen of Henry VII); 'Ma ioye' (Shirley, 1456); 'Me sovent sovant' (cf. 'Souente me souenne', Henry Stafford, Duke of Buckingham); 'Oublier me puis' (Charles the Bold, 1470–80); 'Sans departir' (Richard II); and 'Tout pur le meuz' (possibly Richard II). Sometimes a set of heraldic devices will turn up in a book of hours, like the white eagle, the black antelope, and a tree root of the Duke of Bedford (about 1423), with one of his mottos, 'A vous entier', and the motto of his wife, Anne of Burgundy, 'J'en suis contente' (E. Carleton Williams, *My Lord of Bedford 1389–1435*, London: Longmans Green, 1963, p. 249). Some mottos in 'Standards' in Samuel Bentley, *Excerpta Historica* (London, pr. pr., 1831), pp. 50–63, 163–70, 314–40; and in Jh. de Champeaux, *Devices, cris de guerre, légends – dictons* (Dijon, 1890).

48. *Index*, No. 158; *Charles of Orleans: The English Poems*, ed. R. Steele, *EETS* 215 (1941), 221. Charles had been a widow since 1432. See Seaton, *Roos*, pp. 385, 560 col. ii.

49. *Index* and *Supplement*, No. 2223; *Chaucerian and Other Pieces*, ed. Walter W. Skeat, Supplementary Volume 7 to *Complete Works* (Oxford: Clarendon Press, 1897), pp. 405–7. 'Of course this is a guess which is to easy to deride' (p. lxxi). Rejected by Seaton, *Roos*, pp. 200–1, who suggests Margaret, widow of Lord William Roos. *Manual*, 4, 1076, 1295.

50. *Index* and *Supplement*, No. 2749; Skeat, *Chaucerian Pieces*, pp. 359–60. See fn. 78. *Manual*, 4, 1075–6.

51. *Index* and *Supplement*, No. 1309; Skeat, *Chaucerian Pieces*, pp. 281–4.

52. Skeat, *Chaucerian Pieces*, p. xlviii; *Manual*, 4, 1076–7, 1294.

53. 'Almost certainly this younger Yolande (Violante) is the violet-lily of the English poem' (Seaton, *Roos*, p. 285). I question Rosemary Woolf, *The English Religious Lyric in the Middle Ages* (Oxford: Clarendon Press, 1968), p. 279, that this poem is 'a very supple and delicate handling of secular conventions for religious purposes'.

54. *Index*, No. 2626; *The Complete Works of Geoffrey Chaucer*, ed. Walter W. Skeat, 2nd ed. (Oxford: Clarendon Press, 1900), 4, xxix–xxxi. *Manual*, 4, 1080, 1297. For further valentines see *Index*, Nos. 231, 1309, 1487.

55. For convenient summary of arguments and extensive bibliography see Donald C. Baker, 'The Parliament of Fowls', in *Companion to Chaucer Studies*, ed. Beryl Rowland (Toronto: Oxford University Press, 1968), pp. 355–69.

56. Perhaps the knights and ladies of the Duke of Lancaster's own court. Chaucer often uses the phrase 'ye lovers' to address members of the royal establishments; e.g., *Knight's Tale*, A. 1347, 1531; *Mars*, 1, 5, 290; *TC*, Book 1, 11, 22, 198, 331, 344; Book 2, 1068, 1751; Book 4, 323; *LGW*, 69, 743.

57. For Shirley's annotations in Trinity Coll. Camb. MS. 600, see Robinson, *Chaucer*, p. 856, who summarizes various arguments; also (in full) in Norton-Smith, *Chaucer*, p. 23. See further Seaton, *Roos*, pp. 328–33, who regards Shirley starting a false trail; Norton-Smith, *Chaucer*, pp. 23–34, gives a very ░░░░ ░░░░░░░ ░░ ░░░ ░░░░░░ ░░░░░░░░░░ (░ ░░) ░░ ░░░░ ░░░░ ░░░░ ░░░░░░░░ ░░░ 'the very large Lancastrian household'. For general account of Chaucer's short court poems see Rossell Hope Robbins, 'The Lyrics', in Rowland, *Companion to Chaucer*, pp. 313–31.

58. Even with the second hypothesis, there are problems: an unlucky fisherman who 'baiteth hys angle-hoke with some plesaunce' (238) is Sir William Neville, Lord Fawcomberg; the chamber of Venus, 'depeynted was with white boles grete' (86) appears to indicate his crest.

59. *Index* and *Supplement*, No. 3947; *The Ile of Ladies*, ed. Jane B. Sherzer (Berlin: Mayer & Müller, 1903); Seaton, *Roos*, pp. 140–8 (interprets motto *'al en un'* woven into line 672 as that of Eleanor Cobham). *Manual*, 4, 1096, 1304 (bibliography).

60. Possibly an allusion to an England denuded of its knights off on some foreign expedition?

61. *Manual*, 4, 1097.

62. Ed. J. Schick, *EETS* es 60 (1891, repr. 1924).

63. For a new dating see *John Lydgate: Poems*, ed. John Norton-Smith (Oxford: Clarendon Press, 1966), pp. 176–9, incorporating his earlier 'Lydgate's Changes in the *Temple of Glas*', *MAE*, 27 (1958), 166–72. I have followed the dating proposed by Seaton, *Roos*, pp. 375–83, who added a third to the two recensions of Schick.

64. See Sumner Ferris, 'Chaucer, Richard II, Henry IV, and 13 October', in *Chaucer and Middle English Studies in hounour of Rossell Hope Robbins*, ed. Beryl Rowland (London: Allen & Unwin, 1974), pp. 210–17.

65. Norton-Smith, *Lydgate*, p. 183; but see J. Huizinga, *The Waning of the Middle Ages* (1924; repr. Garden City, N. Y. : Doubleday, 1954), p. 183 (Machaut: 'En lieu de bleu, dame, vous vestez vert'); and Francis Lee Utley, *The Crooked Rib* (Columbus: Ohio State University Press, 1944), Nos. 175 (refrain, 'In stede of blew, thus may ye were al grene'), 194 (refrain, 'When she hath on her hood of grene'. Green is an unusual colour for constancy, but cf. *LGW* (F 242), where Queen Anne is 'corowned with whit, and clothed al in grene'.

66. Henry Noble MacCracken, 'Additional Light on the *Temple of Glass*', *PMLA* 23 (1908), 128–40.

67. Seaton, *Roos*, p. 375.

68. Quoted by Seaton, *Roos*, p. 377.

69. I have tried to do this in my 'Chaucer's "To Rosemounde"', *Studies in the Literary Imagination*, 4, no. 2 (Oct. 1971), 73–81, relying solely on the text, since the manuscript gives no help.

70. *Index* and *Supplement*, No. 1826; MacCracken, *PMLA* 26, 158–59.

71. The poem preceding in the Fairfax MS. 16 is 'The Lover's Mass', *Index* and *Supplement*, No. 4186, printed by Thomas Frederick Simmons, *The Lay Folks Mass Book*, *EETS* 71 (1879; repr. 1968), 390–3; and by Eleanor Prescott Hammond, *English Verse between Chaucer and Surrey* (1927; repr. New York: Octagon Books, 1969), pp. 207–12. *Manual*, 4, 1074, 1294; commentary by Seaton, *Roos*, pp. 291–4. Recently, Norton-Smith, *Chaucer*, p. 20, suggested that the 'Oracyon' and prose 'Epistle' of 'The Lover's Mass' form an autobiographic introduction to the Fairfax lyrics; this view may be possibly reinforced by one of the two descriptions in the contemporary index of contents: 'The solemne service of a lover to his lady, the orision and Epistle in prose with other Balads' (assuming that other ballades are to come, not the lyrics of the 'Lover's Mass'). However, the 'Lover's Mass' closely follows the main part of an ecclesiastical service, and could be quite legitimately considered breaking off after the Epistle (and therefore omitting the Gospel and

Consecration). Whether or not the Epistle is taken as the conclusion of the incomplete 'Lover's Mass' or the introduction to the 'Suffolk' lyrics, it is still legitimate to regard the twenty lyrics as a poetic sequence.

72. MacCracken, *PMLA* 26, 146. Rejected by Hammond, *English Poetry*, p. 198; Seaton, *Roos*, p. 170; and by Steele, *EETS* 215, 220.

73. No other chronological sequence of love poems exists in Middle English, whereas the semi-autobiographical series is well-known in French, e.g., Machaut's *Voir Dit*, Christine de Pizan's *Cent Balades*, and Charles d'Orléans *balades*.

74. For example, *Index*, No. 2182 (item xiv) appears in the later Lambeth MS. 306 as an eight-line variant (*Index*, No. 2247), where it forms the second in a little secular catena of four interconnected love lyrics.

75. *Index* and *Supplement*, No. 1120; Robbins, *Secular Lyrics*, pp. 135–6.

76. *Index* and *Supplement*, No. 922, by Charles d'Orléans; Robbins, *Secular Lyrics*, p. 183.

77. *Index* and *Supplement*, No. 2279; Rossell Hope Robbins, 'The Findern Anthology', *PMLA* 49 (1954), 633–4.

78. The Fairfax MS. 16 has another court poem, *Index*, No. 2479, with an acrostic (Aleson), a kind of Envoy to Clanvowe's *Book of Cupid*. See fn. 32. For other acrostics see Subject and Title Index in *Index*, p. 740, and *Supplement*, p. 526.

79. *Supplement*, No. 3193.5; *Manual*, 4, 1066, 1078, 1296 (list of MSS.).

80. For texts, including fragments, see John Stevens, *Music and Poetry in the Early Tudor Court* (London: Methuen, 1961), pp. 359, 361–2, 423–4, 427. My transcription from BL Addit. MS. 5465, ff. 34r–35r; stanzas 4 and 5 are written on ff. 34v–35r, and repeated again on lower half of f. 35r.

81. Stevens, *Music and Poetry*, p. 219: 'It was perhaps the easy amorous analogy that contributed to the popularity of the poem. . . . They apply, by analogy, to Any Lover.' Another popular song, in three manuscripts, was 'The Kynges Balade', 'Passetyme with good cumpany'. See Stevens, *Music and Poetry*, pp. 344, 388, and 389 (Panmure MS. 11, the third MS., one voice, is not listed in *Supplement*, No. 2737.5).

82. *Index* and *Supplement*, No. 3613; Robbins, *Secular Lyrics*, p. 156; followed by *Supplement*, No. 2277.8 (spoken by woman), Robbins, *PMLA* 69, 638: refrain, 'alas vnkyndeness thus haith my herte slayne'.

83. *Index* and *Supplement*, No. 1331; Robbins, *Secular Lyrics*, p. 158.

84. *Index* and *Supplement*, No. 146; Robbins, *Secular Lyrics*, p. 150, complaint with music.

85. *Index* and *Supplement*, No. 138; Robbins, *Secular Lyrics*, p. 151.

86. *Index* and *Supplement*, No. 2245; Robbins, *Secular Lyrics*, p. 151.

87. *Index* and *Supplement*, No. 139; Robbins, *Secular Lyrics*, p. 156.

88. *Index*, No. 267, noted below; and *Index* and *Supplement*, No. 1288, a *salut d'amour* written by Richard Beauchamp, Earl of Warwick; see fn. 33. Hoccleve wrote several pseudo-virelais; *Index* 3402 (five stanzas, *ababbcbc*, which maintain interlocking rhymes), *Index* 3854, 783, and an envoy to the *De Regimine Principum* (in Huntington MS. only, *Index*, No. 2229, *EETS* es 61), but these have only three stanzas. *Index* and *Supplement*, No. 353, is a oneful only musically.

89. Described by John M. Berdan, *Early Tudor Poetry* (New York: Macmillan, 1920), p. 151, who prints two stanzas of 'Sumwhat musyng'.

90. *Index* and *Supplement*, No. 267; Robbins, *Secular Lyrics*, pp. 162–3; *Manual*, 4, 1078, 1295–6; Seaton, *Roos*, p. 402; for continuation of *virelai* in the sixteenth century see Raymond Southall, *The Courtly Maker* (Oxford: Blackwell, 1964).

91. Thomas Percy, *Reliques of Ancient English Poetry* (London: Bell, 1876), I, 278: 'In imitation of a poem of Chaucer's ... beginning thus: "Alone walkyng".'

92. John Rous, *Rossi Warwiciensis Historia Regum Angliae*, ed. Thomas Hearne (Oxford, 1716, 1745), pp. 213–14; printed (from Ritson's edition) with account from Rous in *Chronicles of the White Rose of York* (London: Bohn, 1845), pp. 208–10; lengthy account with Earl Rivers's will (in English) in Bentley, *Excerpta Historica*, pp. 240–8. Rous is briefly noted in Charles Lethbridge Kingsford, *English Historical Literature in the Fifteenth Century* (1913; repr. New York: Burt Franklin, n.d.), pp. 184–5.

93. For will, see Bentley, *Excerpta Historica*, pp. 247–8, and p. 244, fn. 1.

94. Paul Murray Kendall, *Richard the Third* (1956; repr. New York: Doubleday, 1965), pp. 230–1.

95. *Chronicles of White Rose*, p. 210: 'Like Boethius of old, the Earl Rivers felt the considerations of Philosophy and Learning, even in the hour of an ignominious death, which by their means was deprived of its greatest bitterness.'

96. It was of course a convention that gentlemen write poems while in captivity; typical examples include complaints by Charles d'Orléans and the Earl of Suffolk (who wrote in French); another poem written before the author's execution is *Supplement*, No. 158,. 9, by Edward Stafford, Third Duke of Buckingham. The twenty-two quatrains each end 'remedyles', and the poem begins

Alas to whom shuld I complayne
or shewe my woful hevynes.

Curiously, recalling the use put to Earl Rivers's *virelai*, the first four lines of Stafford's farewell were turned into a lover's complaint (*Supplement*, No. 181.8).

Index

Names and titles

Poetic terms